China's Challenge to Liberal Norms

Catherine Jones

China's Challenge to Liberal Norms

The Durability of International Order

Catherine Jones
University of Warwick
Coventry, UK

ISBN 978-1-137-42760-1   ISBN 978-1-137-42761-8 (eBook)
https://doi.org/10.1057/978-1-137-42761-8

Library of Congress Control Number: 2018934422

© The Editor(s) (if applicable) and The Author(s) 2018
The author(s) has/have asserted their right(s) to be identified as the author(s) of this work in accordance with the Copyright, Designs and Patents Act 1988.
This work is subject to copyright. All rights are solely and exclusively licensed by the Publisher, whether the whole or part of the material is concerned, specifically the rights of translation, reprinting, reuse of illustrations, recitation, broadcasting, reproduction on microfilms or in any other physical way, and transmission or information storage and retrieval, electronic adaptation, computer software, or by similar or dissimilar methodology now known or hereafter developed.
The use of general descriptive names, registered names, trademarks, service marks, etc. in this publication does not imply, even in the absence of a specific statement, that such names are exempt from the relevant protective laws and regulations and therefore free for general use.
The publisher, the authors and the editors are safe to assume that the advice and information in this book are believed to be true and accurate at the date of publication. Neither the publisher nor the authors or the editors give a warranty, express or implied, with respect to the material contained herein or for any errors or omissions that may have been made. The publisher remains neutral with regard to jurisdictional claims in published maps and institutional affiliations.

Cover credit: Thousand Word Images by Dustin Abbott

Printed on acid-free paper

This Palgrave Macmillan imprint is published by the registered company Macmillan Publishers Ltd. part of Springer Nature
The registered company address is: The Campus, 4 Crinan Street, London, N1 9XW, United Kingdom

Acknowledgements

I am acutely aware of the limits of this text and the places where the contents have been edited or curtailed. All the limitations and omissions or inadvertent errors of the contents remain with me. In particular, in the manuscript the deliberate intention was to focus on the relationship of the empirical materials to the conceptual framework. Hence, there are many places where a greater discussion of the literature could have been possible; however, it would have detracted from the central contribution of the work and the argument. I hope that the deficiencies or silences in this work only serve to demonstrate space for more research and contributions in this area.

This project started life in 2009, and since this time, numerous people, places and institutions have enabled the completion of this book. Above all, my thanks go to the Leverhulme Trust who—through the 'Liberal Way of War' programme—supported the research that enabled the initial idea to become reality. Alan Cromartie, as director of the programme, gathered together a group of scholars across a number disciplines, to meet regularly and exchange ideas and arguments. Both Alan and Dominik Zaum made comments and supported the intellectual development of the project. My examiners also provided me with the intellectual stimulation to develop the project further beyond the PhD. I am grateful to them both for all of their thoughts and insights.

At Warwick, this book would not have been possible without the help, support, patience, guidance and continual encouragement of Shaun Breslin and Chris Hughes. The Department of Politics and International

Studies at the University of Warwick, also provided research funding for the fieldwork to extend the fieldwork undertaken and the evidence collected. My colleagues at Warwick have also been exceedingly encouraging of this book and inspiring through their own work.

The team at Palgrave Macmillan have also been incredibly supportive and patient during the evolution of the book. Imogen and Ambra, in particular, have been patient beyond measure as delays continued to appear.

I also must acknowledge the contribution of my interviewees (some of whom cannot be named), their contribution to my understanding and argument has been indispensable. I simply could not have crafted the study without them, all made a tremendous contribution to improving the argument. In addition, Robert Zuber and the team at 'Global Action to Prevent War' gave me a desk and a warm welcome for my research trips to New York. Robert and Global Action also provided me with a UN grounds pass enabling participant observation of the UN Security Council and Committees that have also enhanced my understanding and critical perspective reflected here.

In the UK, the China Postgraduate Network, British International Studies Association, Political Studies Association and many others have enabled me to present my work and challenged my ideas, preconceptions and assumptions. I have also been privileged to attend a range of seminar series on different aspects of China's rise that have both increased my knowledge and inspired me. In particular, those convened by: King's College, London; St Anthony's College, Oxford; and the Oxford University China-Africa Network.

I have also been fortunate in the huge number of academics who have opened their office doors (answered their phones or responded to emails) to me and given up their time to discuss China with me. In particular, Ian Taylor, Deborah Brautigam, Bill Tow, Miwa Hirono, Franklyn Lisk and Hiro Katasumata amongst others have provided assistance beyond the call of duty. All of these people and others I have met and the experiences they have provided have been critical in ensuring that I completed this research. In addition, David Armstrong and Steve Haigh both read chapters and gave informed and insightful comments on them. Throughout my time in Reading and Warwick, I have been privileged to be amongst a dynamic group of academics, who have challenged me to do better and made each day worthwhile.

The help and support of a number of good friends have also made this book possible: they listened to me interminably talk about China; they picked me up and distracted me when I needed it most; provided accommodation to enable research trips and conference attendance; gave me perspective and kept my feet on the ground; and most of all provided opportunities to get away from it all—whether in the rain of Canberra or the sun of the highlands. In particular, Mike Bagwell, Anna James, Claire Bodenham, Adrian Clifton, Claire McAulay, Vicky and Simon Harris, Rachel Smith and Tim Davies, Jenny Martin, Shelley and Gavin Bragg, Christine Leah, Fitri, Will Abraham, Helen McCabe, Dina Rezk, Astrid Nordin, Alex Bellamy, Sarah Teitt, Andre Broome, Lena Rethel, Alexandra Homolar, Louis Swindley, Trudi and Ken Wheat, Fran and Mike Horsfield, Martin Mik, Florian Reiche, Philip Challans, Terry Conway and Rose Palfy, I cannot thank you enough. My thanks go to all of these individuals however, all errors, omissions and any mistakes remain my own responsibility.

Finally, to Tizzy, Philip and my parents, they gave me the space and time to live and breathe. You trusted me and had patience when I was out of contact. Mum and Dad, you truly did give me roots to grow and wings to fly.

Contents

1 Introduction   1

Part I   Conceptual Tools

2 China as a Normative Power?   27

3 Concepts of International Order   43

4 Norms, Order, and Social Change: Laying Out a Toolkit for Normative Change   57

Part II   Re-Interpreting Sovereignty by Contesting Norms: China and the United Nations

5 Concepts of Sovereignty Their Evolution and Status   99

6 China's Engagement with the UN Security Council in Debates on Sovereignty   111

7	China and the Responsibility to Protect	139
8	Conclusion: China and the Norms of Sovereignty	177

Part III Evolution or Revolution in International Aid Practices? China and International Development

9	Liberal Development: The Practice and Assumptions of Aid	185
10	Wider Implications of China's Rise as a Development Partner	223
11	Conclusion: China and the Norms of Development	245
12	Conclusion: China's Challenges to Liberal Norms	253
Bibliography		265
Index		291

Abbreviations

ADB	Asian Development Bank
AFC	Asian Financial Crisis
AfDB	African Development Bank
AFP (A4P)	Agenda for Peace
APEC	Asia-Pacific Economic Community
ARF	Association of Southeast Asian Nations Regional Forum
ASEAN	Association of Southeast Asian Nations
CCP	Chinese Communist Party
CPIA	Country Policy and Institutional Assessment
DCD-DAC	Development Cooperation Directorate
DPRK	Democratic People's Republic of Korea (North Korea)
EAS	East Asia Summit
ECOWAS	Economic Community of West African States
EU	European Union
FDI	Foreign Direct Investment
GA	United Nations General Assembly
GDP	Gross Domestic Product
GNP	Gross National Product
IATI	International Aid Transparency Initiative
ICCPR	International Covenant on Civil and Political Rights
ICISS	International Commission on Intervention and State Sovereignty
IMF	International Monetary Fund
MDGs	Millennium Development Goals
PLA	People's Liberation Army
PPG	Provision of Public Goods
PRC	People's Republic of China

ODA	Official Development Assistance
OECD	Organisation for Economic Cooperation and Development
R2P	Responsibility to Protect
RMB	Renminbi
ROC	Republic of China (Taiwan)
ROK	Republic of Korea
RP	Responsible Protection
RwP	Responsibility while Protecting
SC	United Nations Security Council
SCO	Shanghai Cooperation Organisation
TAC	Treaty of Amity and Cooperation
UDHR	Universal Declaration on Human Rights
UN	United Nations
UNPK	United Nations Peacekeeping
UNPKO	United Nations Peacekeeping Operation
US	United States
USSR	Soviet Union
WB	World Bank
WSOD	World Summit Outcome Document
WTO	World Trade Organisation

List of Figures

Fig. 2.1 Elements of power 30
Fig. 4.1 Norm development 69

CHAPTER 1

Introduction

How and with what effect does China engage within international institutions? At risk of great oversimplification, when considering China's global activities the current literature has coalesced around two major schools of thought which focus on two competing and ostensibly mutually exclusive claims. Either China should be increasingly socialised into compliance with the norms, rules and institutions of international order[1] or that China should challenge international norms in an effort to replace them with institutions better reflecting its own interests, values and its status as a great power.[2]

This central debate leads to a number of more challenging questions about both how and with what effect China engages with the world: Can China change the world? Does China want to change the world? Do 'we' want China to change international order? These questions pervade and imbue the current international relations discourse.

Year on year, a plethora of books, articles and reports express a cacophony of views concerning what this means for the rest of the world. Publications addressing these questions encompass a wide spectrum of potentially plausible scenarios: from the re-emergence of a modernised Chinese World Order to the gradual shaping of China into the norms and practices of the international order created by liberal states.

Nevertheless, the preponderance of these questions, debates and their myriad of answers tend to focus on China's capabilities, capacities and trajectory. Yet, there is—at least—one other side to these questions: What does China's rise reveal about the relationship between rising powers and international order? What mechanisms has the current international order made available for its own mutation? What forms of agency (and therefore what forms of power) are necessary to make use of these mechanisms? What can these questions tell us about the durability of the current international order? As an extension to these works, this book primarily explores the relational aspect of a particular rising power and the current (and dynamic) international order. Hence, whilst many authors have chosen to focus on whether China is exceptional or whether China presents a challenge to international order wholesale, this research explores how China may present challenges to norms through its broadening and deepening engagement *within institutions*. Hence, this book starts from the claim made by Wang Yizhou, that China is engaged in 'creative diplomacy' whereby China is engaged and active within institutions.[3] In particular, this book explores Wang's claim that China can carve out new space in diplomatic relations and forge new patterns of engagement. Wang's work, however, leaves space for other scholars to explore the details of what this 'involvement' looks like; hence, although he indicates the potential and possibility of such an approach, and outlines and number of indicative cases (including Myanmar and Sudan),[4] he doesn't expound how Chinese engagement differs from previous practices or how these processes can create durable changes to global order.[5]

This book enters this debate by suggesting that rather than starting from consideration of whether China is changing international order, we should start by conceptualising how it might be able to do so. It therefore acknowledges that China is rising into a particular and—in many ways—peculiar international order. Unlike previous rising powers, China is confronted with an institutionalised international order—wherein the challenges arise within the institutions, not to their existence.

In order to narrow the scope of this agenda, this book also starts from intuiting that the most likely area for China to seek to challenge international order is around the liberal interpretation of global norms: liberal intervention and international development.

The Research Puzzle and Scope

Based on China's domestic preferences, its own development experience and its stated foreign policy aims, it would not be expected to 'buy-in to' these norms. For example, China's stated defence of state sovereignty suggests that it should oppose international interventions into sovereign states. Furthermore, China's capitalist/communist fusion style economic system and no-strings approach to economic development it would be a reasonable expectation that China should also oppose development approaches that link good governance to economic development.

Yet, despite these expectations, China continues to increase the breadth and depth of its engagement with global institutions that espouse these liberal norms, such as the United Nations (UN), the World Bank (WB) and in its partnership with the Organisation for Economic Cooperation and Development (OECD). These institutions also contribute to a stable international environment that has enabled China's remarkable growth. Hence, despite a preponderance of literature on China's international engagements, we are left with a puzzle and a central research question: *How can China challenge the liberal norms contained within international institutions?*

The approach to responding to this question argues that it is necessary to open the 'black box' of international order and suggest that the current liberal order is liberal in two dimensions. It espouses liberal norms, but it is also liberal in its formal structures. The argument herein is therefore that China can internally challenge the norms within the structures but at the same time abide by the formal structures that both prescribe and proscribe appropriate behaviours that contribute to the continuation of China's rise.

Hence, these areas of the liberal agenda—developments and intervention—form the basis for analysing whether China presents a challenge in these most likely areas. This selection is appropriate for a number of reasons but primarily because China is institutionally invested but also has a stated objection to a liberal interpretation of norms.

Although this may be interpreted by some as starting from a problematic point, that could be seen to assume that China's engagement is having an effect on international order, this is not the case. Rather, the claim is that, because the current international order is both unique and dynamic (see Chapter 3), before it is possible to discern whether there is a challenge, it is necessary to set out what that challenge could look like. Only then is it possible to make any assessment as to whether a challenge is being presented. This does mean that this project has to be constantly aware of the potential of creating a tautological argument.

The research risks of this approach are also mitigated by and indeed made possible by building on the increasing trend within the literature on China that highlight that this 'broadening and deepening' is a reality.

These discussions therefore suggest that it is necessary to consider that although China may increasingly be incorporated within institutions, it will still seek to adapt or modify the actions/behaviours/processes of these institutions so they are increasingly beneficial to China's needs. According to the trend of the literature, although there is a continued discussion of China's involvement in institutions, there is an absence of a link between these discussions and normative change. Hence, there is a dearth of explorations that set out how particular preferences may be enunciated or realised.

Nestling within this trend in the broader literature, the focus here is *how* rather than *whether* China challenges the liberal norms within institutions of the current international order. Importantly, there are also three more specific contributions: first, in understanding how change may occur; second, whether there is evidence of the utilisation of these mechanisms; and third, isolating whether China is the agent producing such changes or challenges. As a result, this discussion contributes to understanding the durability of international order by exploring whether it can persist whilst adapting to change.

The Argument

The central argument presented here is that China is gradually nudging prevalent international norms away from solidarist liberalism, back towards the pluralist interpretations of the early 1990s. In consequence, the outcome of China's challenge results in norms that are 'differently liberal' rather than 'illiberal'. Moreover, China's agency is enhanced when it operates within rather than outside current frameworks and forums. In presenting and enabling this argument, the conceptual framework proposes a range of mechanisms and forms of agency through which powers within institutions may utilise to affect changes to the implementation, practice or interpretation of international norms.

The focus and central contribution are, therefore, that China's challenge to international order exists within international institutions. It is therefore necessary to map out how norms can be challenged and then consider whether China is pursuing any of these pathways. Looking through this lens, and by exploring China's engagement at this level, enables an exploration of the durability of international order and the resilience of particular and specific liberal interpretations of international norms. As such, this volume seeks to explore in more detail and depth the claims of, for example, John Ikenberry, who argues that the liberal order can cope with change, it can adapt and its greatest triumph is its inclusive nature. Here, I argue that China presents, possibly the first, hard case for these claims; as a result, it is necessary to look at how institutions cope with 'adaption', 'change' and 'inclusion'.

One caveat in the argument presented here is that whilst there are 'many China's' in the sense that Chinese foreign policy may not be a joined-up or coherent as it is commonly assumed to be, it is not possible to engage with all the contributors to Chinese foreign policy within the scope of this volume. Rather, this research is logically and logistically focused on actors directly involved with international institutions.

Why Explore China and Normative Change Within Institutions?

China is not the first rising power the world has seen, nor is the academic literature devoid of discussions of power transition. Moreover, this project is not (directly) concerned with whether China is an exceptional power and therefore requires 'special' treatment. But, rather in highlighting that the international order that China is rising into, benefits from, and is a participant in presents challenges and opportunities for rising powers that necessitate developments in the discussions of rising powers, power transition and normative change. Furthermore, because of the institutional structures and norms that characterise international order, discussions of this type also require reflection on the fungibility of both power and agency.

As has been well noted by other scholars, China needs a stable international environment and the public goods provided by the USA to continue its economic growth. Consequently, China's continued engagement with liberal institutions will be necessary to sustain its economic and political rise. Moreover, China will not only have to comply with rules and norms but also help those institutions to function, resulting in its increasing socialisation and acceptance of existing norms and practices, despite their liberal bias.

China's rise then presents a paradox: it is dependent on these liberal institutions and rules, but its rise raises concerns about the continued existence and agenda of these institutions. For example, China's diplomatic weight is presented within the United Nations Security Council (SC), and its economic rise continues to be advanced through its membership in the World Trade Organisation (WTO); yet, it is only the rapid expansion of the economy that makes the military build-up possible.

Consequently, any close observer of Chinese engagement with the contemporary world and its institutions is confronted with a conflicting picture. On the one hand, China is increasingly connected to and involved with the institutions of international order. On the other hand, it is also busy creating parallel institutions that overlap and compete with existing institutions and therefore impinge upon their liberal norms.

This reality presents a puzzle: How is China challenging the liberal elements of international order? In seeking to respond to this question, this project examines the possible tools that may be used to challenge this liberal international order. In this sense, it is a radical departure from the approaches adopted in the current literature. It does this by making the presumption that it is not possible to identify whether China's engagement is producing changes in the current international order, until we understand how those changes may emerge. Once all the possible theoretical options are set out, then it is possible to compare whether any of China's patterns of engagement conform to these tools.

In doing this, I provide a thick narrative of China's engagement with the key elements of international order that make it liberal.[6] In making this argument, it is necessary to respond to a number of related questions:

- Do states challenge the norms of institutions without challenging the existence of those institutions?
- Are challenges to institutions (through both their norms and practices) the result of structural or agential changes (or both)?
- How far and in what ways are great powers' actions constricted?
- Finally, is compliance synonymous with acceptance?

Each of these questions contributes to understanding the mechanisms and the agency of rising states in challenging or changing the existing order. These mechanisms are obscured by the existing grand narratives that currently dominate the debate.

Literature on China and International Order

In this very brief literature review, it is important to note why these previous attempts to make predictions about the rise of China have been unsatisfactory or incomplete and suggest the research forbears for this current study. Of relevance, here are three collections of claims.

The first of these is that Chinese behaviour will be changed through engagement with and socialisation into liberal institutions. The second is that China will become a competitor with the USA in economic, military or technological spheres, and through increasing competition, the risk of conflict will arise, fundamentally changing international order and in particular challenging the relevance of international institutions and their ability to function. The final one is that China is not rising to become a great power and consequently presents no real challenge to international order. As noted above this research is situated in the first of these schools of thought.

Liberal Institutionalists

The first strand of the literature reviewed here suggests China will adapt to global norms and practices. Key proponents of this idea include John Ikenberry,[7] Daniel Deudney,[8] Evan Medeiros,[9] Richard Rosegrance,[10] Alastair Johnston[11] and Quddus Snyder.[12] They comprise a group that Aaron Friedberg has called 'liberal optimists'.[13]

Their claim rests on two arguments: first, that China benefits from the existing international order to such a degree that the trade-off that it would have to accept in forcing a change would not be worthwhile; second, that as China engages more with international institutions and contributes to practices, it is socialised into them. This approach also rests on an underlying ascription of asymmetric agency. Liberal powers have agency to shape and change international norms and practices in liberal ways (broadly defined). However, illiberal powers (despite equalising material capabilities) are subject to both the agency of others and the inertia towards illiberal change in the structures of international order. These approaches are structured around an implicit assumption that modernity is linear and teleological, and that economic development inevitably leads to greater democratisation and liberalisation.[14]

On the one foot, this assumption is supported by theoretical work that focuses on the inertia in international institutions towards change and the particular difficulties in producing change that requires a new 'frame' for action,[15] incurs considerable costs and has outcomes that are uncertain.[16] In supporting these arguments, liberal optimists point to the change in the character of international order, from being a pluralist society of states towards an international society with an agenda to pursue good governance and respect for human rights.[17] As China engages with this 'increasingly liberal' international order, its ties and interdependencies with the USA and institutions also increase[18]; as a result, a socialisation effect can be claimed.[19]

On the other foot, there are numerous problems with these assumptions and the supporting evidence. Firstly, there is validity in the claims that institutional inertia limits the prospects for change, and that these prospects are further limited if there are no other experiences of modernity that challenge the cohesion and dominance of liberal norms and practices. Nonetheless, these narratives obscure or diminish the different pathways to and expressions of modernity in Asia.[20] In addition, they overstate the level of cohesion present within liberal groups of states. As will be explored in Chapter 4, 'liberalism' and its implications and manifestations in international and domestic society remain contested. This then has implications for the ease or difficulty of changing institutions.[21]

There are some key nuances between these authors. Johnston, for example, focuses on the level of China's engagement with international institutions and whether it is tantamount to acceptance of international norms. Even in viewing China as a status quo power, he suggests there is scope in future for China to challenge international institutions from within.[22] Ikenberry and Deudney, however, suggest that through engagement and economic development, China will be changed to become an increasingly democratic and liberal state.[23]

One of the biggest limitations of this approach is that the snapshot of China's engagement within international institutions that these authors provide is limited. Ikenberry and Deudney present an unproblematic picture of the democratisation of China that doesn't reflect on the problems of domestic instability—which could easily turn into international instability—resulting from rapid social and political change in a country of over one billion people.[24] Ikenberry's presentation of the liberal international order becoming 'increasingly liberal' is also problematic given the historical analysis provided, and the claims to the success of this liberal international society fail to take note of the problems of realising the liberal dream domestically let alone internationally.

By far, the best empirical work on China and international institutions is done by Johnston, who provides compelling evidence to support suitably limited claims that suggest trends in China's participation in international institutions. Nonetheless, his approach adopted in *Social States* and *China as a Status Quo power* does not allow for any clear conclusions to be drawn regarding changes taking place within international institutions, their norms and practices. Nor does he indicate the mechanisms through which engagement may lead to change.

Further limitations of the 'liberal optimists' approach, that this research aims to fill, have been highlighted by Stephanie Kleine-Ahlbrandt and Andrew Small, in their assessment of China's changing treatment of pariah states like Myanmar, North Korea or Sudan. They suggest that although China has been a constructive partner and has started to become a 'responsible member' of international society, this has resulted in China presenting a more sophisticated approach to justifying its international actions and as resisting socialisation into international norms.[25] Bergsten et al.[26] go further suggesting that although the USA has tried to make a place for China within the current order that is no longer a workable proposition.[27]

This view is supported by other commentators who suggest that in order for the current international order to continue in some form, the USA must allow China a bigger role in developing and setting international rules, rather than just insisting on it following them.[28] This would require the USA to acknowledge the rise of China and the stake it consequently has in ordering the world. This perspective is not adequately portrayed in the mainstream literature on China's rise, and therefore answers as to how this type of deeper cooperation could be or is achieved are also absent.

In summary, there are many weaknesses with this approach. Firstly, the assumption of a liberal teleology of international order is theoretically problematic. Secondly, some of the evidence presented to support the increasingly liberal line of argument misrepresents or overlooks the problems and challenges that are inherent within liberalism and are particularly pronounced at the international level. The historical analysis in Ikenberry's work in particular is drawn from a reading of the rise of the USA, which assumes that the liberal dream is the only route to modernity and that liberal norms encapsulate the achievement of modernity. By contrast, the methodology used by Johnston sets up an interesting avenue for further research, because it allows for the assessment of the effect of China's engagement with international institutions, norms and practices. The methods he uses—as he recognises—are well suited to setting up this approach but not for further exploration, which then adds a qualification to his conclusion that at present China is a 'status quo power'. Thirdly, as a result of 'seeing' China's actions in international order through this teleological-dominated framework, it obscures such interesting avenues of exploration as the effect China is having within international institutions, and in particular, how China is challenging liberal norms and practices.

China's Rise Producing Conflict with the USA

The second strand of the literature argues that the rise of China will create a new bipolar distribution of power that will pose a threat to US hegemony and the liberal order that rests on it. This position is mostly associated with scholars of the realist school and authors such as Stuart Harris,[29] Nuno Monteiro,[30] Steven Mosher,[31] Hugh White,[32] John Mearsheimer,[33] Robert Kaplan,[34] Christopher Layne,[35] Aaron Friedberg,[36] Colin Gray,[37] Hugh White,[38] Edward Luttwak[39] and Robert Ross.[40] Stuart Harris claims the result of competition between the USA and China could lead to a 'systematically adversarial relationship'[41]; Colin Gray postulates that 'China does not, and will not, accept the position of prominent member of a posse for world order led by the American sheriff'.[42] The arguments and predictions of this group of scholars rest largely on a realist, state-centric and realpolitik understanding of international relations, and they rely heavily on historical analysis to evidence their claims. From this common starting point, these authors offer three reasons for their perception of the likelihood of change: rising great powers tend to be revisionist states; the USA will attempt to reverse a relative decline; and structural changes to the balance of power are necessitating change. Few of these authors suggest that military conflict is likely,[43] yet, they all suggest that the conflict between the USA and China will not be mitigated through international institutions, and as such will radically change the conduct of international relations. Indeed, Friedberg argues 'if current trends continue, we are on track to lose our geopolitical contest with China. Defeat is more likely to come with a whimper than a bang'.[44] These authors can more adequately be discussed by dividing them into two groups: structural theorists and revisionists.

Structural theorists, such as Mearsheimer,[45] argue that conflict is inevitable. Nonetheless, the precise nature or form of conflict will take is unknown and unknowable. However, because of the perception of institutions as being unable and unsuitable for dealing with sizable power changes in the international system, a form of conflict will occur. As a result, institutions will be unable to mitigate or prevent violence or conflict between dominant and rising powers. The focus of these authors has been to make claims about broader theoretical frameworks rather than looking at the specific and unique rise of China. Consequently, they perceive change as systemic rather than specific or unique and assess the challenge from rising powers at a system level rather than at the level of the normative content of international order. Embedded within this approach is an understanding of great powers that focuses on material capabilities. Accordingly, the predictions of these authors stem from a limited conceptualisation of state interests, a system-level understanding of what great powers should do and what capabilities are then required.[46] When viewing China, their analysis rests on a narrow view of China's international behaviour applied to narrowly conceived 'lessons of history'. As a result of the assumptions and the systemic rather than particular approach, these theorists adopt their works are problematic and diametrically opposed to the research agenda undertaken here.

Nonetheless, the 'Revisionists' that form the second sub-strand of the literature on how China challenges international order have a vast amount to contribute as a basis for this research. They argue that China is both a rising and a revisionist power and consequently will seek to change international order.[47] Their works therefore form a bedrock for this study; nonetheless, there is a remaining gap in the scholarship here in tendency not to look at China from a particular theoretical perspective and use it to test broader theoretical predictions. Rather, they take a more nuanced perspective and examine the specific policies that China has pursued and their implications for international order.

Authors of this persuasion include: Rosemary Foot,[48] Ann Kent,[49] Pak Lee, Steve Chan, Lai-Ha Chan,[50] Naazneen Barma, Giacomo Chiozza, Ely Ratner and Steven Weber.[51] It is also an approach that is compatible with the views of some liberal optimists, such as Alistair Johnson, who at the end of *Social States* concludes that it is unclear what form Chinese socialisation is taking and what implications arise from this.[52] Hence, even though plausible, China is not explicitly challenging the status quo, if it is 'mimicking' the behaviour of other great powers, rather than being more extensively socially influenced or persuaded through its compliance, the possibility of China competing with these norms remains.

These authors share the assumption (or reach conclusions) that China's rise will present a marked challenge to the practice of international relations. Furthermore, through their analysis they contribute significantly to the understanding of the practice of Chinese foreign policy.

Nevertheless, they leave an important gap to be explored: *How* does the competition between China and the USA shape international order?[53] Indeed, even in Foot and Walter's *China, the United States and Global Order*,[54] their focus was specifically at the compliance of both the USA and China with existing norms and suggest that change in order may occur where there is clear divergence in compliance and acceptance of particular norms between these two powers, as these are then opened up for contestation.[55] Similarly, a range of works examine different Chinese conceptions of global order, but do not examine the methods that China might be using to achieve it.[56] In contrast, this dissertation examines *how* China's engagement with the institutions of international order might change them.

China Is Not Rising Significantly Enough to Challenge the International Order
The final strand of the literature—briefly reviewed here—is also the smallest. It suggests that although China's power is growing militarily, politically and economically, it is not currently able to challenge international order, and that it is unlikely to be able to do so any time soon. Much of the work in this vein builds on Gerald Segal's seminal 1999 *Foreign Affairs* article,[57] where he highlighted key conditions for being a great power—economic and military superiority, regional hegemony, diplomatic muscle and being a generator of ideas—and showed how they were not met by China at the time. In particular, he stressed that China was not a regional hegemon, a path through which great powers have in the past sought to achieve regional dominance before seeking global dominance.[58] He also sought to stress the limitations of the uneven development in China and the challenges to its internal stability that were far from resolved and were (arguably) growing.

Segal's framework was reassessed five years later in a major edited volume.[59] However, the world has changed since 1999, and as shown in the reassessment (which still presents a sceptical view),[60] the most recent works of Buzan and Foot suggest that their scepticism is declining.[61] In more recent works, the rise of China has also been questioned by Sutter,[62] whilst in the economic field the durability of the Chinese economy has been questioned. The rise of China and the limits of a developing country becoming a great power able to effect change have been explored by Susan Shirk, who highlights the numerous domestic challenges to the continuation of the rule of the CCP and the limits this internal fragility has in the international actions of China.[63] This literature—whilst dwindling in volume—is still providing some nuanced and detailed accounts of the potential position of China in relation to other great powers.[64] Crucially, it also provides a consistent critical approach to the oft-made assumption about durability and continuation of Chinese power.[65]

The literature on China and international order therefore raises interesting questions about the ability of great powers to affect international order; the means by which they may do so; and the methods and standards of evidence required to support any such claims. There is clearly a gap in the literature conceptually in terms of the ways and means that an emerging power may seek to change the normative and structural dimensions of international order, as well as a gap in the methods and evidence so far produced regarding China as a rising power and what its actions suggest about whether it is seeking maintenance, reform or revolution internationally. The next section looks at how this research seeks to fill some of these gaps. Clearly, any discussion of rising powers and the effects of their actions are merely a snapshot of a dynamic and flowing picture.

Approach and Scope of This Research

This book looks at how China can challenge the normative dimension of order; specifically looking at and accounting for China's role as a rising power in framing the understandings of international events through the emergence of new and modified related norms. It looks at the challenges that have emerged and whether China is a cause (or central component) of these challenges.

Drawing on the literature set out above, we can see that a key component of why China is perceived as having the potential to challenge the existing order is because of its rising economic, military and diplomatic power. Furthermore, because China is a non-liberal and non-democratic state but is still a successful developing state it has the potential to present a different conception of what a 'desirable' international order would look like and what rules and norms and practices might make that a reality, but some authors such as Barry Buzan are sceptical as to whether it is actually possible for China to conceive of an international order that is non-liberal.[66] Thus, a central absence in the literature is that it fails to outline *how* China may present a challenge within international institutions and therefore challenge the liberal character of international order. Without understanding how a challenge may occur, it is not possible to set out whether incremental changes may be occurring.

This approach draws on an understanding of international order as social. Hedley Bull proposed that '[b]y order in social life I mean a pattern of human activity that sustains elementary, primary or universal goals of social life'.[67] The definition and content of 'elementary, primary or universal goals' are derived from both material and normative considerations. Elementary goals of international society can be seen as the maintenance of the position of dominance of a particular group of great powers. This aim, however, is not only fulfilled by a continuing preponderance of material power of these states, but is also achieved through the construction of norms that prescribe behaviour and prevent the emergence of peer competitors.

For the current international order, normative aspects are expressed through rules and laws—which are expressly liberal (explored in Chapter 4). These rules and norms are not created independently from each other or in a formless void; rules and norms of international order are created in response to judgements about existing or pre-existing practices, rules and norms and are shaped with some respect to dominant concepts of what international society 'should' be like. These dominant concepts reflect a convergence of perceptions of what is desirable and what 'works' and what does not. These convergent perceptions provide form and direction for the shaping of international rules and norms. Within this order, ideas (and their promotion by states) are central to their ability to effect (or prevent) change through the creation of new (or redefined) norms, rules and laws. Through this method of change, China poses a 'new' type of challenge because it is the only great power within the current international order that has a different ideological basis (see Chapter 4). Therefore, this project is concerned with the underlying norms and values of a liberal international order presented through the policies and practices of core institutions.[68] For example, liberal interpretations of sovereignty norms expressed through practices of liberal interventionism or the Responsibility to Protect.

In adopting this approach, it is intended that this work will fill a gap in the literature (identified above) which looks at China and international order. This research starts from a position that because individual agents are active creators and constitutive elements of the order; they are also capable of challenging it. It then goes on to explore the questions arising from the conclusions of works by Johnston, Foot and Walter in seeking to look at mechanisms for international normative change, drawing conclusions about whether China's interaction with international institutions is challenging their norms and practices. In exploring mechanisms for change within international order, the rise of China forces us to think about the nature of being liberal and liberalism. As will be brought out in the conclusion, China's rise exposes the conflict within international liberal norms.

Appropriately, rather than thinking of the liberal international order as stable and fixed (or teleological), it should be considered to be in a state of flux with common strands of coherence.[69] Institutions play an important role in this process as they provide forums for parties to re-evaluate and reconstruct the norms and values of the order and for their interests to evolve with respect to these ideas over time.[70]

The focus of this project is not on the internal characteristics of China (such as the form of the political regime, the questionable commitment to human rights or its economic success) but is rather concerned with how China interacts with the world at large and the implications that interaction has.[71] However, although it would be wrong to suggest that the internal structure of a state does not impact on its foreign policy decisions,[72] disaggregating and linking all the different domestic voices that contribute to foreign policy is not the central focus herein and would be far beyond the scope of this project.

METHODS AND METHODOLOGY

Exploring how China engages with international order and whether this engagement presents the possibility to produce normative challenges requires a two-stage approach. Firstly, there needs to be an exploration of how normative challenges can happen within international order (the mechanism for this is set out in Chapter 4). Secondly, it needs to be identified if China is the source of any challenge that is seen. Specifically, what possibilities are available to rising powers to act as agents of normative change? This discussion of causation explores how China can be identified as a cause of a challenge to international norms.

In this research, there is a need to identify in what sense challenges in international order can be attributed to China's rise. In order to distil the actual agency attributable to China within the process of normative challenges, an Aristotelian approach (which allows for the separation of different elements of the causal story) is adopted. From this, it is possible to 'see' China's role in the process whilst not neglecting that this role is within a complex map of other factors that have a causal effect. As a result, a different approach to causation and causal inference must be applied. In order to understand *how* China challenges, there is a need to understand the casual processes and mechanisms through which that challenge emerges. This approach is necessary not only because of the adoption of China within international order as an intrinsic case study,[73] but also because of the social dimension of international order (discussed in Chapter 3).

In Milja Kurki's book on international relations and causation, Aristotle's understanding of causation re-enters the debate. Aristotle's approach[74] is summarised as: 'The active power of agents (efficient causes) must always be related to final causes (purposes, intentionality) and, crucially, be contextualised with the constitutive conditioning causal powers of rules and norms (formal causes) and the material conditions (material causes)'.[75] In expanding on this approach, Alexander Wendt describes mechanical (or Humean causation) as limited to efficient causes.[76] He draws a clear contrast between this and the use of Aristotle's four causes; Wendt describes the example of Ulanowicz in the building of a house to demonstrate the difference: 'its efficient cause is the labor of workmen; its material cause is the bricks and mortar of which it is made; its formal cause is the blueprint that gives these materials their eventual form; and its final cause is the purposes of the individuals building it'.[77]

If we take this broader approach to causation in understanding the impact of an actor within a socially constructed order, then we have to consider the interplay between that actor and other 'causes'. It is not sufficient to see one actor, and its actions, as the cause of an outcome, it is necessary to understand the relationship of that actor to 'others' within the international order, which may produce an outcome.[78] Thus, the overall research question of *how* challenges to the practices and ideologies of international order emerge necessitates the creation of processes through which social changes can occur. This approach to causation has an impact on how the conceptual part of this thesis is constructed as well as the 'standards of evidence' required to demonstrate 'causation'.

In Chapter 4, each of these elements of causation is addressed. Efficient and final causes are the elements of agency of a rising power (structural, norm entrepreneurship, ad hoc objection and persistent objection). Material causes are the tools available to that state in actually pursuing a challenge to international norms; the formal causes are the facilitating conditions for challenges.

This approach to causation helps in the identification of China's agency in the process of normative challenges. It aids in the investigation of whether norms are being challenged and whether China is a cause (or more specifically is China the efficient or final cause). In order to apply this approach properly, it necessitates the adoption of a methodology that allows for the presentation of a causal mechanism.

Thus, this approach is tied to the need to adopt a thick narrative which allows for a specific discussion of the mechanisms set out in the conceptual chapters. This narrative approach is based around documentary analysis and draws on approximately two dozen elite interviews and other discussions, which are then related to conceptual sections and then drawn to a conclusion regarding China's challenge to international norms. The interviews adopted a semi-structured or unstructured format[79] and were conducted by phone, on Skype or in person. Where access was available, face-to-face interviews were preferred.[80] In sections that relate to the UN and the UNSC, it has also been possible to pursue a participant observation and use this knowledge to triangulate the other evidence collected.

Structure of the Book

The remainder of the book is set out as follows: Part I sets up the conceptual apparatus for the research. As noted above, because of the unique and risky approach of this research, this section sets up a discussion of Chinese power (Chapter 2), a discussion of international order (Chapter 3) and a final discussion of normative change by states in the context of an international order previously discussed (Chapter 4).

Parts II and III are extensive empirical expositions. Within Part II, Chapters 5 and 6 set out China's engagement with norms of non-intervention and the Responsibility to Protect. These are seen as being emblems of the liberal norms within the institutions of international order. Within these chapters, an argument is made that within these debates China's challenge is presented through its role (in concert with other states) in frustrating the progress of the norm of R2P. In terms of peacekeeping, China's challenge is to the dominant interpretation of sovereignty, couching its position in historical interpretations through which it gains legitimacy.

Part III then goes on to explore China's engagement with forms of development. Chapter 7 sets out how China is presenting a challenge by creating parallel institutions, such as the Forum on China-Africa Cooperation. It also has the potential to reframe the debate within the existing aid organisations away from aid effectiveness to development effectiveness. In addition, its challenge in this arena is related to its appearance as a successfully developing state rather than a specific form of 'agency' that it is using. It is a norm entrepreneur, but by example rather than through explicit self-promotion.

The conclusion sets out *how* China presents an overall challenge. It sets out the instances where China can be seen as a 'spoiler' to the progress of some norms (in Chapter 4, this is described as ad hoc or persistent objection) and instances where its rise is generating new ideas and practices that challenge the existing wisdom and normative architecture (acting as a norm entrepreneur). Following this, there are some tentative conclusions as to where and in what ways China has an impact on the existing liberal international order. It is challenging particular elements within international order rather than presenting a challenge that would strip order of all elements of liberalism

Notes

1. G. John Ikenberry, *After Victory: Institutions, Strategic Restraint, and the Rebuilding of Order after Major Wars* (Princeton University Press: Princeton, 2001); G. John Ikenberry, *Liberal Leviathan: The Origins, Crisis, and Transformation of the American World Order: The Rise, Decline and Renewal* (Princeton University Press: Princeton, 2011); Alastair Iain Johnston, 'Chapter 3: International Structures and Chinese Foreign Policy', in Samuel S. Kim (ed.), *China and the World: Chinese Foreign Policy Faces the New Millennium* (Westview Press: Boulder, 1998); Alistair Iain Johnston, 'Is China a Status Quo Power?', *International Security* (2003), 27(4), pp. 5–56; Alistair Iain Johnston, *Social States: China in International Institutions, 1980–2000* (Princeton University Press: Princeton, 2007); Torbjørn L. Knutsen, *The Rise and Fall of World Orders* (Manchester University Press: Manchester, 1999), pp. 90–91; Henry R. Nau, 'Why 'the Rise and Fall of Great Powers' Was Wrong', *Review of International Studies* (2001), 27(4), pp. 579–592; Ronald L. Tammen and Jacek Kugler, 'Power Transition and China-US Conflicts', *Chinese Journal of International Politics* (2006), 1, pp. 35–55.

2. Barry Buzan, *The United States and the Great Powers: World Politics in the Twenty-First Century* (Polity: Cambridge, 2004); Thomas Donnelly, 'Rising Powers and the Agents of Change', *National Security Outlook* (American Enterprise Institute for Public Policy: Washington, DC, 2006), pp. 1–6; Aaron L. Friedberg, *A Contest for Supremacy: China, America, and the Struggle for Mastery in Asia* (W.W. Norton and Company: New York, 2011); Robert Gilpin, 'The Theory of Hegemonic War', *Journal of Interdisciplinary History* (1998), 18(4), pp. 591–613; Andrew F. Hart and Bruce D. Jones, 'How Do Rising Powers Rise?', *Survival: Global Politics and Strategy* (2010), 52(6), pp. 63–88; Paul M. Kennedy, *The Rise and Fall of the Great Powers: Economic Change and Military Conflict from 1500 to 2000* (Fontana: London, 1989); Woosang Kim, 'Power Transitions and Great Power War from Westphalia to Waterloo', *World Politics* (1992), 45(1), pp. 153–172; Jeffrey W. Legro, 'What China Will Want: The Future Intentions of a Rising Power', *Perspectives on Politics* (2007), 5(3), pp. 515–534; John J. Mearsheimer, *The Tragedy of Great Power Politics* (W.W. Norton New York, 2001), p. 2.
3. Yizhou Wang, *Creative Involvement: New Directions in Chinese Diplomacy* (Routledge: Abingdon, 2017) previously published as: Wang Yizhou, '创造性介入: 中国外交新取向' [Creative Involvement: New Directions in Chinese Diplomacy] (Peking University Press: Beijing, 2011).
4. Yizhou Wang, *Creative Involvement: New Directions in Chinese Diplomacy* (Routledge: Abingdon, 2017), pp. 9–37.
5. Yizhou Wang, *Creative Involvement: New Directions in Chinese Diplomacy* (Routledge: Abingdon, 2017), p. 1.
6. For this book, the key elements of international order are: the rule of law; promotion of human rights (including the protection of individual freedoms); capitalist free market economics; political pluralism; tolerance; a limited role for the state; democracy; and the protection of private property.
7. G. John Ikenberry, 'The Rise of China and the Future of the West: Can the Liberal System Survive?', *Foreign Affairs* (2008), 87(1), pp. 23–37; G. John Ikenberry, 'Liberal Internationalism 3.0: America and the Dilemmas of the Liberal World Order', *Perspectives on Politics* (2009), 7(1), pp. 71–87; G. John Ikenberry and Daniel Deudney, 'The Myth of the Autocratic Revival: Why Liberal Democracy Will Prevail', *Foreign Affairs* (2009), 88, pp. 77–93.
8. Daniel Deudney and G. John Ikenberry, 'The Nature and Sources of Liberal International Order', *Review of International Studies* (1999), 25(2), pp. 179–196.
9. Focuses on the mutual binding of the USA and China to existing institutions and practices will produce stability and continuation. Evan S. Medeiros, 'Strategic Hedging and the Future of Asia-Pacific Stability', *The Washington Quarterly* (2005), 29(1), pp. 145–167.

10. Richard Rosegrance, 'Power and International Relations: The Rise of China and Its Effects', *International Studies Perspectives* (2006), 7, pp. 31–35.
11. Alistair Iain Johnston, 'Is China a Status Quo Power?', *International Security* (2003), 27(4), pp. 5–56 and 49–56.
12. Quddus Z. Synder, 'Integrating Rising Powers: Liberal Systemic Theory and the Mechanism of Competition', *Review of International Studies*, published online 30 November 2011, pp. 1–23.
13. Aaron L. Friedberg, 'The Future of U.S–China Relations: Is Conflict Inevitable?', *International Security* (2005), 30(2), pp. 7–45; included in this group could be those who identify efforts within China to present it as engaged and changing as a response to the 'China Threat Thesis' and therefore the rhetoric of liberal internationalism serves a domestic purpose in China, see, for example, Chih-Yu Shih, 'Breeding a Reluctant Dragon: Can China Rise into Partnership and Away from Antagonism?', *Review of International Studies* (2005), 31(4), pp. 755–774.
14. Ronald Inglehart and Christian Welzel, 'How Development Leads to Democracy: What We Know About Modernisation', *Foreign Affairs* (2009), 88(2), pp. 33–48.
15. Geoffrey M. Hodgson, 'Institutions and Individuals: Interaction and Evolution', *Organisational Studies* (2007), 28(1), pp. 95–116, p. 110.
16. Vinod K. Aggarwal, 'Reconciling Multiple Institutions: Bargaining, Linkages, and Nesting', in Vinod K. Aggarwal (ed.), *Institutional Designs for a Complex World: Bargaining, Linkages, and Nesting* (Cornell University Press: Ithaca, 1998), pp. 1–29; Johannes Lindner, 'Institutional Stability and Change: Two Sides of the Same Coin', *Journal of European Public Policy* (2003), 10(6), pp. 912–935.
17. Ikenberry, 'Liberal Internationalism 3.0', p. 71.
18. Deudney and Ikenberry, 'The Nature and Sources of Liberal International Order'; Medeiros, 'Strategic Hedging and the Future of Asia-Pacific Stability'.
19. Johnston claims that the Chinese elite have already been socialised to the international order and that this will mean that they do not seek to challenge it. Johnston, 'Is China a Status Quo Power?', p. 49.
20. For a good discussion of different modernity's, see Martin Jacques, *When China Rules the World* (Penguin: London, 2012), pp. 117–172.
21. See Chapter 4.
22. Although in previous articles, he has been keen to point out that engagement does not necessarily lead to socialisation and internationalisation of norms Alaistair I. Johnston, 'Treating International Institutions as Social Environments', *International Studies Quarterly* (2001), 45(4), pp. 487–515; Alastair Iain Johnston, *Social States*, pp. 207–212.

23. Ikenberry and Deudney, 'The Myth of the Autocratic Revival', pp. 77–93.
24. Mark Leonard, *What Does China Think?* (Harper Collins: London, 2008), pp. 60–64.
25. Stephanie Kleine-Ahlbrandt and Andrew Small, 'China's New Dictatorship Diplomacy: Is Beijing Parting with Pariahs?', *Foreign Affairs* (2008), 87(1), pp. 38–56, p. 39.
26. Bergsten et al., *China's Rise*, pp. 237–238.
27. Ibid., p. 238.
28. 'Engagement must mean more than simply offering China the opportunity to follow the rules. It requires acknowledging Chinese interests and negotiating solutions that accommodate both American and Chinese objectives' Robert S. Ross, 'Beijing as a Conservative Power', *Foreign Affairs* (1997), 76(2), pp. 33–44, p. 43.
29. Stuart. Harris, 'China's Regional Policies: How Much Hegemony?', *Australian Journal of International Affairs* (2005), 59(4), pp. 482–492.
30. Nuno P. Monteiro, 'Unrest Assured: Why Unipolarity Is Not Peaceful', *International Security* (Winter 2011/12), 36(3), pp. 9–40.
31. Steven Mosher, 'Does the PRC Have a Grand Strategy of Hegemony?', http://www.au.af.mil/au/awc/awcgate/congress/mos021406.pdf, accessed 1 March 2010.
32. Hugh White, 'The Limits to Optimism: Australia and the Rise of China', *Australian Journal of International Affairs* (2005), 59(4), pp. 469–481, p. 476.
33. John J. Mearsheimer, 'China's Unpeaceful Rise', *Current History* (2006), 105(690), pp. 160–162.
34. Robert D. Kaplan, 'The Geography of Chinese Power', *Foreign Affairs* (2010), 89(3).
35. Christopher Layne, 'The Waning of U.S. Hegemony—Myth or Reality? A Review Essay', *International Security* (2009), 34(1), pp. 147–172.
36. Friedberg, 'The Future of U.S–China Relations'; Friedberg, *A Contest for Supremacy*.
37. Colin S. Gray, *Another Bloody Century* (Weindenfeld and Nicolson: London, 2005), pp. 168–211; Colin S. Gray, 'The 21st Century Security Environment and the Future of War', *Parameters*, Winter 2008–2009, pp. 14–26; Colin S. Gray, 'Why Worry? Sino-American Relations and World Order' FCO Update, available http://ukinchina.fco.gov.uk/en/about-us/working-with-china/Foreign_and_Security_Policy/News_Updates/Why_Worry, Updated 13 March 2012, accessed 2 May 2012.
38. Even in this optimistic work, the sceptre of conflict is still very much a possibility. Hugh White, *The China Choice: Why America Should Share Power* (Black: Collingwood, VIC. 2012).
39. Luttwak, *The Rise of China vs. The Logic of Strategy*.

40. Timescale is longer term and his argument is less structural than that of the other authors but clearly sees great potential in the possibility of a clash between with USA and China. Ross, Robert S. 'Beijing as a Conservative Power'; Ross, 'Comparative Deterrence', pp. 13–49.
41. Harris, 'China's Regional Policies', p. 483.
42. Gray, 'The 21st Century Security Environment', p. 20.
43. A few notable exceptions: Gray, 'The 21st Century Security Environment'; Robert Kagan, *The Return of History and the End of Dreams* (Atlantic Books: London, 2009).
44. Aaron L. Friedberg, *A Contest for Supremacy*, p. 6.
45. John J. Mearsheimer, 'Why We Will Soon Miss the Cold War', available http://teachingamericanhistory.org/library/index.asp?documentprint=713, accessed 11 February 2010; Mearsheimer, *The Tragedy of Great Power Politics*; Mearsheimer, 'Why China's Rise Will Not Be Peaceful'.
46. Kaplan, 'The Geography of Chinese Power'; Condolezza Rice, 'Campaign 2000: Promoting the National Interest', *Foreign Affairs* (2000), 79(1), pp. 45–63.
47. For example, Rosemary Foot, *The Practice of Power: US Relations with China Since 1949* (Clarendon: Oxford, 1995), pp. 264–265.
48. For example, Rosemary Foot, 'The Responsibility to Protect (R2P) and its Evolution: Beijing's Influence on Norm Creation in Humanitarian Areas', *St Anthony's International Review* (2011), 6(2), pp. 47–66.
49. Ann E. Kent, *Beyond Compliance: China, International Organizations, and Global Security* (Stanford University Press: Stanford, 2009).
50. Pak K. Lee, Gerald Chan and Lai-Ha Chan, 'China in Darfur: Rule-Makers or Rule-Taker', *Review of International Studies* (2011), 38(2), pp. 423–444.
51. Naazneen Barma, Giacomo Chiozza, Ely Ratner, and Steven Weber, 'A World Without the West? Empirical Patterns and Theoretical Implications', *Chinese Journal of International Politics* (2009), 2(4), pp. 525–544.
52. Johnston, *Social States*, p. 207–12.
53. Rosemary Foot and Andrew Walter, *China, the United States and Global Order* (Cambridge University Press: New York, 2011), pp. 298–300.
54. Ibid.
55. Ibid., pp. 1–30.
56. Daniel A. Bell, *China's New Confucianism: Politics and Everyday Life in a Changing Society* (Princeton University Press: Princeton, 2010), pp. 20–28; Luke Glanville, 'Retaining the Mandate of Heaven: Sovereign Accountability in Ancient China', *Millennium—Journal of International Studies* (2010), 39(2), pp. 323–343; William Callahan, 'China's Dreams of the Future', *China Seminar Series* (Oxford: St Anthony's College: University of Oxford, 2011).

57. Gerald Segal, 'Does China Matter?', *Foreign Affairs* (1999), 78, pp. 24–36.
58. Barry Buzan, 'Conclusion: How and to Whom Does China Matter?' in Barry Buzan and Rosemary Foot (eds.), *Does China Matter? A Reassessment: Essays in Memory of Gerald Segal* (Routledge: Abingdon, 2004), pp. 143–164, p. 145.
59. Ibid.
60. The conclusion suggests that there is room for doubt based on both China's relations with its neighbours and the experience of Japan that China may not become a great power, even though the USA increasingly shapes its foreign policy around perceptions of threat from China. Ibid., pp. 143–164.
61. Barry Buzan, 'China in International Society: Is 'Peaceful Rise' Possible?', *Chinese Journal of International Politics* (2010), 3(1), pp. 5–36; Barry Buzan, 'The Inaugural Kenneth Waltz Lecture A World Order Without Superpowers: Decentred Globalism', in *International Relations* (2011), 25(3), pp. 3–25; Rosemary Foot, 'China and the United States: Between Cold and Warm Peace', *Survival* (2009), 51(6), pp. 123–146.
62. Robert G. Sutter, 'China's Rise in Asia—Promises, Prospects and Implications for the United States' (Occasional Paper Series: Asian Centre for Security Studies, 2005).
63. Susan Shirk, *China: Fragile Superpower* (Oxford University Press: Oxford, 2007).
64. Michael Beckley, 'China's Century? Why America's Edge Will Endure', *International Security* (Winter 2011/12), 36(3), pp. 41–78; Zha Daojiong, 'Comment: Can China Rise?', *Review of International Studies* (2005), 31(4), pp. 775–785; Bijian Zheng, 'China's 'Peaceful Rise' To Great-Power Status', available http://www.irchina.org/en/news/view.asp?id=397, accessed 25 November 2009.
65. See, for example, Xuetong Yan, 'The Rise of China and Its Power Status', *Chinese Journal of International Politics* (2006), 1(1), pp. 5–33.
66. Barry Buzan and Amitav Acharya (eds), *Non-Western International Relations Theory: Perspectives on and Beyond Asia* (Routledge: Oxford, 2010), p. 2 and 37.
67. Hedley Bull, *The Anarchical Society: A Study of Order in World Politics* (Columbia University Press: New York, 2002), p. 4.
68. Hurrell, 'Hegemony, Liberalism and Global Order'; Friedrich Kratochwil and John Gerard Ruggie, 'International Organization: A State of the Art on an Art of the State', *International Organization* (1986), 40(4), pp. 753–775.
69. John Gray, *Two Faces of Liberalism* (Polity Press: Cambridge, 2000), pp. 105–106.

70. 'Institutions are important in helping to explain how new norms emerge and are diffused across the international system, and how state interests change and evolve', Hurrell, 'Hegemony, Liberalism and Global Order', p. 6.
71. However, as will be noted in Chapter 6 one of the problems in understanding China as an emerging development partner or even recognising what it is doing in terms of development in developing countries is the diversity of actors and the complexity of their engagement with each other within China. A similar point is made with respect to the making of Chinese foreign policy in Campbell et al., *China and Conflict-affected States*, p. 7.
72. Robert D. Putnam, 'Diplomacy and Domestic Politics: The Logic of Two-Level Games', *International Organization* (1988), 42(3), pp. 427–460.
73. Richard E. Stake, *The Art of Case Study Research* (Sage: Thousand Oaks, California, 1995), pp. 1–14.
74. Aristotle, *Metaphysics*, Books 4–6 (Clarendon Press: Oxford, 1993).
75. Milja Kurki, *Causation in International Relations: Reclaiming Causal Analysis* (Cambridge University Press: Cambridge, 2008), pp. 296–297.
76. Wendt, 'Why the World State is Inevitable', p. 495.
77. Ibid.
78. Jane Elliott, *Using Narrative in Social Research: Qualitative and Quantitative Approaches* (Sage: London, 2005), p. 111.
79. Because of the nature of the information being sought, it was determined that semi-structured or unstructured interviews were likely to be most useful, as the data that was required was not going to be used to directly compare one individual's responses with another but rather to gain their impressions, or understandings of particular situations, as such semi- or unstructured interviews were most likely to yield these results. Sandra Halperin and Oliver Heath, *Political Research: Methods and Practical Skills* (Oxford University Press: Oxford, 2012), pp. 258–276.
80. Given the potential for there to be less data from phone interviews as well as the relatively few opportunities to address any power differences for a younger researcher (such as handshakes, exchange of cards, etc.). However, some of the phone interviews were follow-ups on previous meetings (when an interview was not practical). William S. Harvey, 'Strategies for Conducting Elite Interviews', *Qualitative Research* (2011), 11, pp. 432–441, p. 439.

PART I

Conceptual Tools

CHAPTER 2

China as a Normative Power?

There have been many discussions of how to characterise the nature of China's power: rising power, global power, great power, regional power or as having soft power. Indeed, think of an adjective and it has probably been used as a prefix to describe the kind of power China may be in the past (or next) two decades. However, despite this abundance of power-related thinking, there has been little about the connections between what China might want to change, the context in which that change could happen, and whether China has the necessary attributes to achieve this. The closest the literature has come is in the discussions of China as a great power, because these discussions centre on the link between whether China has a plan and the means to implement it.

This chapter seeks to achieve one small objective. That is to simply establish how it is possible to get from the abstract concept of power, to being able to outline the particularity of the current context in which China may use its power and then indicate whether China has the tools to (at least theoretically) be able to use mechanisms for normative change. The overall argument is that structural and positional changes to China's international status are necessary but not sufficient in order to demonstrate normative challenges to international order.

To address this main objective, this chapter advances a definition of power within international order. It makes the claim that because power is both relational and contextual what makes a state powerful changes as the context changes. As we shall see in Chapter 4, the context within which China's power exists is social. Consequently, the basis of China's status as a great power must be both normative and material (outlined below).

What Is Power?

In its most basic definition, power can be conceived of as the ability for person (or entity) A to get person B to do something they would not otherwise desire (or be inclined) to do.[1] The implication of this simple definition is that power is relational. This relationship—and the social context in which it takes place—dictates what capabilities are important in making an actor 'powerful'.[2]

This definition suggests three things about power: firstly that it is a relationship between two (or more) actors; secondly, 'power' does not have any specific substantive content, and it does not specify what methods or capabilities count as 'power'; and finally, it suggests that what A wants B to do exists within a social context,[3] which can have an impact on the kind of capabilities that contribute to an entity's 'power'. As Steven Lukes indicates, the ability to shape the context in which A and B interact shapes the interests and preferences of B. Consequently, A may not need to influence B's actions directly if A has successfully managed to shape B's interests by shaping the context in which they are formed.[4]

'Power', then, is concerned with more than just material capabilities; it is made manifest through different relational situations. Michael Barnett and Raymond Duvall separate out four dimensions of power: compulsory, institutional, structural and productive.[5] Productive and structural dimensions of power relate to each other and refer to the determination of a social context; these elements of power are 'not controlled by specific actors, but are only effected through the meaningful practices of actors'.[6] This book, then, is concerned with institutional and compulsory power; power related to actors' ability to 'shape the circumstances or actions of another' and an 'actors' control of others in indirect ways'.[7]

This shaping occurs in both the material and the normative dimensions of power. In the material dimensions of power, this shaping can clearly be seen—for example, the acquisition of nuclear weapons has shaped other states' perception of what comprises a militarily dominant state. In the ability to shape the normative dimension of power, authority, and leadership become central concerns. Authority can be created through (e.g.) the perceived possession of knowledge, experience or success[8]; these attributes add credibility to claims made by an actor with respect to the norms they sponsor.[9] However, authority is not just the possession of these tools but the acceptance of their meaning by other actors—other actors have to agree that a particular actor has relevant knowledge and experience in order to be in the best position to determine the most effective norms. This acceptance or consent to the authority and leadership of an actor then gives the norms that actor sponsors a greater chance of development.[10] The absence of authority would lead to an actor's ability to exert influence being dependant on their material capabilities. As will be discussed later, this consent may arise from a small group within international society or from the whole society. Where this identification comes from has an impact on the extent of authority and the actors' 'power'. Authority—in respect to this discussion—has two essential components: legitimacy (discussed below and in Chapter 4) and knowledge.

Legitimacy results from an actor being seen to be acting within the rules or norms arrived at by a group.[11] It is, therefore, related to the ability of an actor to shape the context of their social interactions. As a result, the ability to shape the rules by which actors must abide (if they are to be seen as legitimate) is an important aspect of power.

Talcott Parsons notes there is special element of power which is 'the binding of its [the systems] units, individual and collective, to necessary commitments'.[12] The ability of an actor to perform this function—to bind others to a particular goal or aim through specific commitments—is related not only (indeed possibly not often) to their ability to coerce through the use of their material resources, but also to the perception of the authority of this actor by other actors. A key element in this perception is the perception of legitimacy of the actor: if an actor is seen to be abiding by and subjugating themselves to the same rules, they increase their legitimacy and authority in shaping those rules.

A further aspect of the dynamics of this relationship and the construction of the context in which power is 'operationalized' are the relativities of material and normative power.[13] Just because a state or an actor is powerful in one context does not imply they are powerful in all contexts. Consequently, what 'things' make an actor powerful in one context may vary between contexts.[14] For example, having the use of four armoured divisions may be 'powerful' in a military theatre, but its power is less significant in an international diplomatic arena in discussions of development. Thus, this chapter has to address both normative and material power capabilities. This description of power can be demonstrated in Fig. 2.1.

Before moving on to how this discussion of power relates to great powers in international order, there is a need to linger a moment on the expression of power. One reason for the focus on material capabilities in the literature on power in IR is that they can easily be 'seen' to be in operation and their effects are relatively easy to measure. 'Soft' forms of power[15] are more difficult to quantify and 'see' at work. Therefore, they are more difficult to grapple with in a useful way. Thus, any claims made about the 'soft' power capacities of a state are less tangible and more elusive. Nevertheless, if power is seen as A getting B to do something, through either coercion or attraction, then these capabilities are central and essential to any discussion of power. Whilst essential, they need to be treated with caution and rely on a better understanding of intended outcomes of an interaction rather than *any* outcome of an interaction.[16]

As a result, any discussion of what makes a great power needs to incorporate both material and relational aspects of power. The more fungible an actor's power resources, the more situations their capabilities can be used in. This relates to how powerful they are. Actors may be able to increase their relative power by gaining a better understanding of their situation—tailoring their resources to fit this understanding.[17]

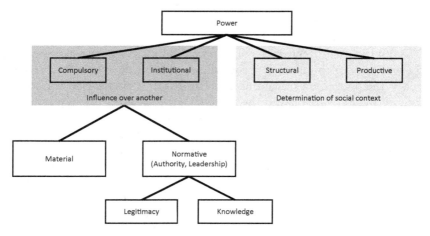

Fig. 2.1 Elements of power

Accordingly, the knowledge an actor has is important in being able to determine their relative power.[18] On a related issue, knowledge has an intimate relationship to authority: the more knowledgeable an actor is, the greater their potential to be seen as an authority, and consequently, their relative power increases.[19]

WHAT MAKES A NORMATIVE POWER?

How does this general understanding of 'power' relate to the concept of a great power? A basic definition of a great power is a state that is capable of projecting power and influence on at a global level. However, what makes a state a great power is contested. Across different theories, the 'content' of what it means to be a great power varies: from a focus on material capabilities[20] to acknowledgements of the importance of less tangible attributes such as social status, recognition and context.[21] Whilst the realist position and focus on capabilities is clearly an essential ingredient to enable the projection of power (and China's capabilities in this regard are discussed in depth later in this chapter), within the social context of international order (discussed in Chapter 3) recognition, legitimacy, authority and credibility[22] are also essential attributes for great powers. Whilst a Realist—capability focussed—account of great powers would suggest that great powers are functionally and formally equal, in reality there are great inequalities between great powers.[23] In part, these inequalities are derived from varying capabilities, but they are also a reflection of how states relate to and recognise each other as having a particular status[24] and as a result have differential special rights and responsibilities.[25] Consequently, a capability-based definition is inadequate in capturing the relational dynamics between actors and explaining the differentiation between great powers.[26]

In looking at great powers as socially, as well as capability constituted, the social context in which interactions take place becomes vitally important.[27] The current international order is a social space; there are formal, semi-formal and informal groupings in which states interact in a social manner.[28] There are also formal, semi-formal and informal patterns of recognition of states within these different forums, resulting in a range of places and pathways for states to be recognised as great powers.[29]

Recognition can be separated out in different ways: formal/semi-formal/informal, and/or vertical/horizontal. Formal recognition can be through the occupation of institutional positions with extraneous responsibilities; semi-formal recognition and informal recognition come through groupings where powers are seen as essential for the effectiveness of outcomes but either their role in that grouping or the grouping itself is informal. Alternatively, recognition may be divided between (moral/horizontal)[30] *authority* and (structural hierarchical/vertical)[31] *influence*; great powers are expected to have international influence; however, influence may be derived from moral authority or structural (coercive) power resources. For example, in looking back at the discussion in Chapter 1, the structures of the Cold War order—acceptance of spheres of influence, permanent seat in the Security Council—ensured that the US and USSR had influence over a region and over the globe.[32] Structural influence is distinct from but related to authority. The USSR may have had influence across the globe, but its authority was more limited; nonetheless, it was recognised as a great power. Authority implies acceptance and can help to explain stability in international order despite changes in power capability distribution.[33] Similarly, a state with authority may have 'power' where it has no structural influence.

How a state is recognised and the means by which that recognition is made explicit is contingent on the context. The social dimension of the current international order allows for (and may call for) formal/semi-formal/informal and horizontal/vertical recognition[34]; whereas during the Cold War due to the different context of great power interaction, means of explicit recognition were more limited. As will be explored further in Chapters 3 and 4, legitimacy is important to the ability of a great power to produce change (or challenge); legitimacy is also the elephant in the room (in so far as other authors don't engage with this concept) in this discussion of recognition.

The most obvious expression of recognition is through formal acknowledgement within international institutions. In these forums, recognition may take the form of the fulfilment of certain positions within existing institutions (e.g. the Permanent 5 in the UNSC); the creation of new institutions that fill a perceived gap in either the economic or security architecture; or supporting or enabling the functioning and development of existing frameworks. Informal recognition may take the form of the perceived 'need' for a particular state to be involved in international agreements for them to be effective (this may also be semi-formal if form of a state's involvement takes place within an institutional setting).

In looking back to the discussion of power above, the distinction between normative (authoritative) power and material (coercive) power was made. Both elements are essential to a state being powerful. However, in terms of recognition, they may not be acknowledged in the same contexts. In determining great power status, the extent of material capabilities must have a global reach, but it may only have recognition of normative power within a constrained social grouping. An example helps to clarify here: the USSR during the Cold War had recognition as a great power because of its material capabilities, but it only had recognition as a normative great power over a given 'sphere of influence' (as indicated in Chapter 1). Its authority to shape the rules of its relationships with other powers and their relationships with each other only extended as far as the 'consenting' group of satellite states. Within that consenting group of states all are stakeholders—they all have functions and duties to perform for the whole to function, and responsible stakeholders recognise and fulfil their functions. By contrast, because the current international order is not structurally and geographically divided into recognised 'spheres of influence', China must develop a normative great power status on a global scale. The following section discusses China as a great power looking at the material and social capabilities that indicate whether China can be recognised as a great power.

Recognising China as a Normative and Great Power?

The ability for China to create a challenge within international order is dependent not only on China's material power but also on its position within international order. It needs to be recognised by other powers not only in the right to be heard but a right to be asked its opinion. For China, recognition is not merely a matter of honour and respect but also mitigates fears of China as a threat.[35] As shall be shown in looking at the levels of recognition that China has achieved in various states and organisations around the world, China appears most threatening to states that do not accommodate and adjust to China's growing importance.

Recognition can reflect a preponderance of material capabilities producing an undeniable shift in the balance of power, and/or it can recognise normative influence. Recognition of whether China has become influential as a normative power will form one of the themes of discussion throughout the rest of this work. The focus here will be on the formal and informal mechanisms that demonstrate a changing status that then makes it possible (and useful) to discuss whether China is capable of influencing others and challenging international order.

Within a social, normative and international order, the recognition of a state as a global great power is essential. This recognition can be formal or informal, and it can recognise either/both coercive and/or normative power. This section briefly outlines how China is recognised along each of these dimensions. The focus is on the recognition of the projection of potential coercive power, with the recognition of China as a normative power then forming a key element in the remainder of this work. Recognition of China's status can be seen to take place within the formal structures of international institutions—such as the UN, regional and international organisations, and negotiations—as well as in the shifting bilateral relationships between China and other states.

Since 1971, China's role within the Security Council (SC) has changed. As China's position and capabilities relative to other SC members have altered, the roles and functions China fulfils have changed, reflecting the recognition of China as a great power. China has been more assertive in Council discussions and has become more sophisticated in its interactions with debates in the Council rather than depending on the use of its veto.[36] Throughout China's time on the SC its approach, understanding of diplomacy and how to use the tools of institutions to their benefit has evolved. This has resulted in the increasing sophistication of the Chinese UN delegations and their ability to use the bias of the UN against action.[37] China's engagement with the SC is indicative of how much China's approach to institutions has changed and how it has used its increased knowledge and experience of these institutions to pursue its own agenda.

In other international organisations, China's changing status has also been recognised, an example being the WTO. Accession took place in 2001 with a view that China should have conformed to all rules by 2008,[38] but China by 2012 it was still in violation of many of the terms and agreements for its accession[39] and has been successful in stalling the Doha round of negotiations.[40] The ability of a single state (apart from the USA) to be able to have such significant challenge to the proceedings of the WTO and escape violating procedures in this way is unprecedented. Similarly, China's proportion of the voting share at the World Bank has also increased to reflect its new position in the world economy.[41] Furthermore, in the Busan discussions on aid effectiveness, China's contribution was seen as essential for future developments to the architecture of development (see Chapter 9). In looking at regional organisations, the creation of the Shanghai Cooperation Organisation

(SCO) and the extension of the Association of South East Asian Nations (ASEAN) dialogues to include China are further evidence of the region's acknowledgment that it is important to ask and take note of China's views.

In terms of multilateral agreements, China is increasingly being 'invited to the table' and becoming an essential part of successful negotiations. The reported role of China in the Copenhagen climate change accords[42] is a further indicator of the power that other actors are ascribing to China and its emerging status. China has viewed itself as a great power since the 15th Party congress (1997),[43] but, as stated above, in order to achieve great power status, it is important for it to have legitimacy and the recognition of other actors.[44] The Copenhagen climate conference and the subsequent media debates regarding China's actions—fuelled by government press releases—suggest that other great powers are beginning to accept China's growing significance within this club.[45] The condemnation of China at the conference and the demonstration of China's ability to persuade other states (in particular other emerging powers)[46] suggest that China has enough power to sway other actors—if it can be blamed that blame must be credible based on the actions and resources at China's disposal.[47]

China has also increased its diplomatic reach with the use of both informal and new organisations. China's involvement in the six party talks concerning North Korea's nuclear developments has been instrumental in bringing North Korea to the table.[48] Even in the reportage of the 2013 North Korean aggression, the importance of China to negotiations and international responses has been well noted.[49] Furthermore as the North Korean crisis has evolved in from 2016 to 2018, China's role as a crucial (and conflicted) player has been noted.[50] This increased influence is also reflected in China's involvement in attempts to deal with Iran's nuclear ambitions.[51]

In addition to institutional recognition, other states can also demonstrate appreciation of a new (or shifting) balance of power, and a new status of another power in a number of different ways, i.e. by increased monitoring of activities (increased attention paid to policy statements and comments); invitations to negotiations or invitations of opinions/ consultations; extension of formal relationships (such as new or extended free trade agreements); and speech acts that confer status (naming of a state as a great power). An important dimension of this recognition is that it may be positive (China as a useful and constructive power) or negative (China as a threat), and it may also be intentional (to promote the fulfilment of certain roles and responsibilities) or unintentional (the careful monitoring of military developments to seek to stymie the emergence of China as a great power). In other discussions of China as a great power, separating out these types of recognition and their correlating practices may be vitally important. Here, however, it is necessary only to note that other states (through their actions) recognise China as a great power. This discussion focuses on recognition of China as a great power by other powerful states or groups of states (the USA, Japan and the EU).

The increased monitoring of China's rise (and responses to that monitoring) is amply demonstrated by the attention that is paid to China by the governments in the USA, Japan, across the Southeast Asian region, and as well as by other regional bodies. In the USA, this increased monitoring and attention are shown with the advent of annual congressional reports to Congress[52] and mounting concerns over the lack of transparency in the PLA military (in both the defence budget and in the development of the military).[53] The monitoring of China's economic and military performance is also evident in other powers; for example, in the 2009 Japanese military white paper on Japan's Security Environment, China is given an entire section (equal to the space devoted to the USA).[54]

Invitations to international groupings as an observer or new participant are noted above, and these also extend to the bilateral sphere; for example, the increasing number of bilateral meetings between China and the USA (highlighted in particular in the US presidential elections)[55]; the invitations to the EU; and centrality of China's inclusion in consultations on dealing with the financial crisis.[56] China has also become the subject of an increasing number of formal bilateral agreements; in particular it has become involved in a number of free trade agreements and enjoys 'most favoured nation' status with the USA. In the UK, China has also been subject to new preferential trading deals.[57]

Increasingly, China's new status is made evident in the speeches and actions of world leaders and the press coverage that accompanies them. 2012 saw the start of a new China section in *The Economist*[58]; leadership scandals in China have become front page news across the globe[59]; and Chinese military developments have been central in policy decisions in both Japan and the USA.[60]

To conclude this chapter, China can be classed as a great power based on its increasing economic dominance, placing it at as the second largest economy in the world. It can be seen as a great power in terms of its increasing military strength and its development of a blue-water navy as well as having the largest land army in the world able to evolve its tools and training because of the increasing budget assigned to it from the central government. Furthermore, China has been recognised as a great power by its neighbours within the ASEAN community, through informal groupings both within the region and globally, and through its increasing involvement through international institutions. All of them not only recognise that China should have a voice in international order, but also that China should be consulted about changes to that order. This chapter continues to outline how China is opposed to some of the ideological bases of that order (because of its domestic regime) and why that may be significant in understanding China's engagement. At this point, the 'hard' bases of China's power are left and the 'status' of China within the social networks of international order is pursued through the remainder of this work.

NOTES

1. Robert A. Dahl, 'The Concept of Power', *Behavioral Science* (1957), 2(3), pp. 201–215 and 202–203; also, David A. Baldwin, 'Power Analysis and World Politics: New Trends Versus Old Tendencies', *World Politics* (1979), 31(2), pp. 161–194 and 162–163.
2. A number of discussions on Power highlight this relational aspect. See Michael Barnett and Raymond Duvall, 'Power in International Relations', *International Organization* (2005), 59(1), pp. 39–75; Steven Lukes, *Power: A Radical View* (Palgrave Macmillan: London, 2005); Talcott Parsons, *Structure and Process in Modern Societies* (Free Press of Glencoe: Illinois, 1960); Martin A. Smith, *Power in the Changing Global Order* (Polity: Cambridge, 2012).
3. The 'context' is discussed in more depth in Chapter 3.
4. Lukes, *Power A Radical View*, p. 37.
5. Barnett and Duvall, 'Power in International Relations', pp. 49–57.
6. Ibid., p. 55.
7. Ibid., p. 49.
8. Michael A. Hogg, 'A Social Identity Theory of Leadership', *Personality and Social Psychology Review* (2001), 5(3), pp. 184–200, p. 189; Xuetong Yan, 'International Leadership and Norm Evolution', *Journal of Chinese International Relations* (2011), 4(3), pp. 233–264, p. 241.

9. Simon Reich, *Global Norms, American Sponsorship and the Emerging Patterns of World Politics* (Palgrave Macmillan: Basingstoke, 2010), pp. 32–68.
10. Ian Clark, *Hegemonny in International Society* (Oxford University Press: Oxford, 2011), pp. 19–23.
11. See David Beetham, *The Legitimation of Power* (Palgrave Macmillan: London, 1991); John Dowling and Jeffrey Pfeffer, 'Organizational Legitimacy: Social Values and Organizational Behavior', *The Pacific Sociological Review* (1975), 18(1), pp. 122–136; Ian Hurd, 'Legitimacy and Authority in International Politics', *International Organization* (1999), 53(2), pp. 379–408, p. 381; Parsons, *Structure and Process in Modern Societies*, p. 175.
12. Parsons, *Structure and Process*, p. 205.
13. Smith, *Power in the Changing Global Order*, pp. 8 and 11.
14. For further discussion of this point see Catherine Jones, 'Understanding Multiple and Competing Roles: China's Roles in International Order', unpublished paper, presented at ACPS Kings College London, June 2011.
15. Joseph S. Nye, *Soft Power: The Means to Success in World Politics* (Public Affairs: New York, 2004).
16. This then relates back to the reason for selecting a casual descriptive approach to methodology in this book and the need to apply an Aristotelian four dimensional approach to causation.
17. This is what Baldwin describes as understanding the game. Baldwin, 'Power Analysis and World Politics', p. 164.
18. Ernst B. Haas, *When Knowledge Is Power: Three Models of Change in International Organizations* (University of California Press: Berkeley, 1990).
19. Ibid., p. 21.
20. Dominant within the classical and Neo-Realist schools see Barnett and Duvall, 'Power in International Relations', p. 40.
21. These are key features of the English School approach as well as some constructivist accounts see Hedley Bull, *The Anarchical Society: A Study of Order in World Politics* (Columbia University Press: New York, 2002), pp. 194–222; Barry Buzan, *The United States and the Great Powers: World Politics in the Twenty-First Century* (Polity: Cambridge, 2004); Ian Clark, *Hegemonny in International Society* (Oxford University Press: Oxford, 2011), pp. 44–49.
22. Dahl, 'The Concept of Power', p. 203.
23. Jack Donnelly, 'Sovereign Inequalities and Hierarchy in Anarchy: American Power and International Society', *European Journal of International Relations* (2006), 12(2), pp. 139–170.

24. Recognition of a state and its sovereignty is dependent on 'another state's judgement and will' G.W.F. Hegel, *Hegel's Philosophy of Right*, trans. T.M. Knox (Oxford University Press: London, 1952), p. 212, para. 331.
25. Dahl, 'The Concept of Power', p. 203; K.J. Holsti, 'The Concept of Power in the Study of International Relations', *Background* (1964), 7(4), pp. 179–194, p. 181.
26. The foundation of the state's system is a state recognition by other states J. Samuel Barkin and Bruce Cronin, 'The State and the Nation: Changing Norms and the Rules of Sovereignty in International Relations', *International Organization* (1994), 48(1), pp. 107–130, p. 110; Andrew Hurrell, 'Hegemony, Liberalism and Global Order: What Space for Would-Be Great Powers?', *International Affairs* (2006), 82(1), pp. 1–19, p. 4.
27. Dahl, 'The Concept of Power', p. 204.
28. A.I. Johnston, 'Treating International Institutions as Social Environments', *International Studies Quarterly* (2001), 45(4), pp. 487–515.
29. Jack Donnelly, 'Sovereign Inequalities and Hierarchy in Anarchy: American Power and International Society', *European Journal of International Relations* (2006), 12(2), pp. 139–170 and 152–153.
30. Ibid., pp. 152–153.
31. Ibid.
32. Also noted by Ringmar, that USSR struggled to gain recognition from liberal states, Erik Ringmar, 'The Recognition Game: Soviet Russia Against the West', *Cooperation and Conflict* (2002), 37(2), pp. 115–136.
33. Paul W. Schroeder, 'The 19th-Century International System: Changes in the Structure', *World Politics* (1986), 39(1), pp. 1–26.
34. Donnelly, 'Sovereign Inequalities and Hierarchy in Anarchy', pp. 144–153.
35. Yong Deng, *China's Struggle for Status: The Realignment of International Relations* (Cambridge University Press: Cambridge, 2008), p. 21.
36. See Chapter 5, also, Allen Carlson, 'Protecting Sovereignty, Accepting Intervention: The Dilemma of Chinese Foreign Relations in the 1990's', *China Policy Series* (National Committee on US-China Relations: New York, 2002); Allen Carlson, *Unifying China, Integrating with the World: Securing Chinese Sovereignty in the Reform Era* (Stanford University Press: Stanford, CA, 2005); Ann E. Kent, *Beyond Compliance: China, International Organizations, and Global Security* (Stanford University Press: Stanford, 2009); Stephanie Kleine-Ahlbrandt and Andrew Small, 'China's New Dictatorship Diplomacy: Is Beijing Parting with Pariahs?', *Foreign Affairs* (2008), 87(1), pp. 38–56.
37. James Traub, 'The World According to China', *New York Times*, published 3 September 2006.

38. Cooper, 'World Economy Past and Future 1950–2030'.
39. National Intelligence Council, 'Global Trends 2025: A Transformed World', available www.dni.gov/nic/NIC_2015_project.html, accessed 22 January 2018.
40. C. Fred Bergsten, Charles Freedman, Nicholas Lardy, and Derek J. Mitchell, *China's Rise: Challenges and Opportunities* (Peterson Institute for International Economics: Washington DC, 2008), pp. 15–16.
41. World Bank, 'World Bank Reforms Voting Power, Gets $86 Billion Boost' (updated 25 April 2010). http://web.worldbank.org/WBSITE/EXTERNAL/NEWS/0,,contentMDK:22556045~menuPK:34463~pagePK:34370~piPK:34424~theSitePK:4607,00.html, accessed 18 May 2010.
42. Mark Lynas, 'How Do I Know China Wrecked the Copenhagen Deal? I Was in the Room'; Network, 'Britain Blames China for Copenhagen 'Farce'', *The Guardian*, 22 December 2009 (Environment Section).
43. According to Shih, China claimed in the 15th Party congress that views itself as a Great Power. Chih-Yu Shih, 'Breeding a Reluctant Dragon: Can China Rise into Partnership and Away from Antagonism?', *Review of International Studies* (2005), 31(4), pp. 755–774.
44. Hurrell, 'Hegemony, Liberalism and Global Order'.
45. E. Felker, 'U.S., China Deadlock in Copenhagen: Obama to Arrive as Expectations Sink Even Further', *The Washington Times*, 17 December 2009, sec. Politics; M Lynas, 'How Do I Know China Wrecked the Copenhagen Deal? I Was in the Room', *The Guardian*, 22 December 2009, sec. Environment; ABC Network, 'Britain Blames China for Copenhagen 'Farce'' (updated 22 December 2009). http://www.abc.net.au/news/stories/2009/12/22/2778031.htm, accessed 8 March 2010.
46. See for example the Statement made on behalf of the G77 countries, Ibrahim Mirghani Ibrahim, 'Statement on Behalf of the Group of 77 and China by H.E. Ambassador Dr. Ibrahim Mirghani Ibrahim, Head of the Delegation of the Republic of Sudan, at the Closing Plenary of the Session of the Resumed Ninth Session of the Ad Hoc Working Group Under the Kyoto Protocol', issued 6 November 2009, available http://www.g77.org/statement/getstatement.php?id=091106b, accessed 29 July, 2011; Qin Gang 'China says Communication with other developing countries at Copenhagen summit transparent', 20 December 2009, available http://www.china-embassy.org/eng/xw/t646954.htm, accessed 3 August 2011.
47. See Catherine Jones, 'Understanding Multiple and Competing Roles: China's Roles in International Order', unpublished paper, presented at ACPS Kings College London, June 2011; also, Catherine Jones, 'Understanding Multiple and Competing Role: China's Roles in International Order', Special Issue. *Pacific Focus* (2013), 28(2), pp. 190–217.

48. Robert Ross, 'Comparative Deterrence: The Taiwan Strait and the Korean Penninsula', in Johnston Alastair Iain and R.S. Ross (eds), *New Directions in the Study of China's Foreign Policy* (Stanford University Press: Stanford, 2006), pp. 13–49.
49. Leo Lewis and David Taylor, 'China Joins Obama as World Condemns North Korea's New Uranium Bomb Test', *The Times*, 13 February 2013; Bronwen Maddox, 'To Keep Pyongyang in Check, Call on Beijing', *The Times*, 13 February 2013; see also Catherine Jones, 'The Party's Over for the Use of Sanctions? China and the Authorisation of the Use of Sanctions at the UN', unpublished paper, presented at the PSA Annual Conference, April 2013.
50. See for example: Catherine Jones, 'Chinese Interests, Actors and the Implementation of Sanctions against North Korea' (ASAN Open Forum, November/December 2015), available http://www.theasanforum.org/chinas-interests-actors-and-the-implementation-of-sanctions-against-north-korea/ (published online 24 September 2015).
51. Adam Ward, 'Closing Argument: Beijing Calling', *Survival* (2009), 51(6), pp. 249–252.
52. United States-China Economic and Security Review Commission, available http://www.uscc.gov/, accessed 6 June 2012.
53. US Department of Defence, 'Annual Report to Congress: Military and Security Developments Involving the People's Republic of China 2010, available https://www.defense.gov/Portals/1/Documents/pubs/2010_CMPR_Final.pdf, accessed 22 January 2018; US Department of Defence, Annual Report to Congress: Military and Security Developments involving the People's Republic of China 2017, available https://www.defense.gov/Portals/1/Documents/pubs/2017_China_Military_Power_Report.PDF, last accessed 22 January 2018, p. 42.
54. See Japanese Ministry of Defence, *Defence of Japan White Paper* 2009, available http://www.mod.go.jp/e/publ/w_paper/2009.html, accessed 6 June 2012; Ministry of Defence, *Defence of Japan White Paper 2010*, available http://www.mod.go.jp/e/publ/w_paper/2010.html, accessed 6 June 2012; Ministry of Defence, *Defence of Japan White Paper 2011*, available http://www.mod.go.jp/e/publ/w_paper/2011.html, accessed 6 June 2012.
55. Rachel Will, 'US-China Today: The China Card: China in the 2012 U.S. Presidential Race', US-China Institute, available http://www.uschina.usc.edu/w_usci/showarticle.aspx?articleID=17946&AspxAutoDetectCookieSupport=1, accessed 6 June 2012.
56. See for example, The Financial Times, 'China Shapes the World: Analysis', *Financial Times*, 18 January 2011; New York Times, 'Paulson Praises China's Cooperation in Easing Financial Crisis', *New York Times,* Published

22 October 2010 online http://www.nytimes.com/2008/10/22/business/worldbusiness/22iht-22paulson.17155092.html, accessed 23 May 2011; China Daily 'WEF Head Praises China's Role in Talking Financial Crisis', in *China Daily*, 14 September 2009, available http://www2.chinadaily.com.cn/business/2010-09/14/content_11299961.htm, accessed 23 May 2011.
57. George Parker, 'China Signs £1.4bn in UK Trade Deals', *Financial Times*, 27 June 2011, available http://www.ft.com/cms/s/0/254b7294-a0b0-11e0-b14e-00144feabdc0.html#axzz1x1jyraUs, accessed 6 June 2012.
58. Launched in *The Economist*, 27 January 2012, available http://www.economist.com/blogs/analects/2012/01/our-new-china-section, accessed 6 June 2012.
59. See, for example, the extensive coverage of the Bo Xilai incident, in *The Guardian* 'Bo Xilai', available http://www.guardian.co.uk/world/bo-xilai, accessed 6 June 2012.
60. Alexander Frean, 'Don't Mess with Us, Obama Warns China as He Shakes Up the Military', *The Times*, 6 January 2012; Kathrin Hille, 'China Launches First Aircraft Carrier', *The Financial Times*, 11 August 2011; Demetri Sevastopulo and Kathrin Hille, 'China Defends Naval Actions', *The Financial Times*, 6 June 2011.

CHAPTER 3

Concepts of International Order

As noted in Chapter 1, the argument in this book is contingent on opening up the black box of international order. Accordingly, this chapter focuses on the inter-subjective construction of order.[1] It makes a crucial claim that how we understand international order affects how we might 'see' change to that order—fundamentally it makes a claim that within international order different constitutive elements may be challenged—it is possible to change the character of order without changing its structures. This approach enables a key claim of this research, that the rise China as a great power is manifestly different because it is within a socially constructed order. This means that, contrary to traditional expectations of great powers, in order to affect global change it is essential for China to be seen as a constructively engaged and responsible stakeholder rather than an objectionable outsider.

A fundamental claim of this chapter is that the current structure of international order—the presence of international law and institutions—and the teleology of international order are liberal. But, the mechanisms for change to this teleology within the liberal structure of order are constructivist. As such, liberalism helps to describe the current international order, it is constructivism that provides us with the mechanisms for its change. Indeed, a lacuna in the liberal literature is that scholars tend to suggest that change within institutions is possible[2]—but they don't specify the mechanisms and processes through which that change may come about, nor do they suggest how we might recognise whether a change is or has taken place. Indeed, their only suggestion in this area is to argue that any change is likely to be incremental.

This chapter—as briefly as possible—seeks to achieve two aims: first is to outline the concept of order, examining how order is created and second is to explore socialisation as a tool for maintaining the structures of order—albeit not proscribing the 'character' of that order.

WHAT IS ORDER?

International order is an ambiguous concept, where usage varies across different authors. This variance has implications for what it means for our understanding of international activities and how orders may change.

In the world at large, 'order' is a contextual term. An order in a restaurant is different from an order of the placement of books in a library (one hopes). The understanding of the difference between the usages of the same term does not lead to confusion because of the relationship to the context. However, international order is more problematic as 'order' describes the context. Thus, there is a need to unpick what makes the international context an 'order': because the term describes the context rather than being defined by the context.

In everyday use, 'order' may have three distinct definitions. First, order may be a sequencing of discrete items—such as an alphabetical order. The aim is to apply a structure to a set. What is important is the general structure is observed and replicable. The structuring or the relationship between units generates expectations and predictability. Just as there is an expectation that books in a library are arranged in alphabetical 'order'.

Second, order may also be a sequencing of things aimed at producing a particular end; for example, the laying of stones across a river to form a bridge. Thus, the structure and the aim are of equal importance. As a result of the structuring of units in relationship to each other, there is an expectation of predictability. At the same time, this sequencing has an aim that it is structured towards fulfilling. Thus, an order can be purposive.

Third, order may also be a sequencing of objects or entities aimed at producing a particular end through both formal structures and a particular 'frame of mind'.[3] That is, units in order are in a formal relationship to each other that produces a particular end. Through this formal engagement, relatively stable expectations of the behaviours of others can be developed; behaviours that are not constrained by the formal structure, but constrained by behavioural 'normative' considerations.

These descriptions of order are all composed of different dimensions: sequence, teleology and normative. These three versions of order have different manifestations internationally. What international order is, and in what sense it describes the context in which international relations take place, depend on which of the above formulae of order is adopted.

For this book, the sequencing, the telos and the normative dimensions of order are open to contestation, as will be discussed. China's rise has the potential to operate in both the sequencing and the normative dimensions. Through changes in the sequencing and normative dimensions, it is possible to achieve change within the teleological dimension of order. Through changing power relationships and institutional vicissitudes (the sequencing of international order), it is possible to challenge the telos of that order.

The shifting relative position of actors is important, and verily China's changing position within the current order is a necessary precondition for the claim that China has the potential to produce normative change. Having discussed China's power status in Chapter 2, it is taken as a reality enabling the forthcoming discussion of how China may produce normative—not just structural—changes in order. As a result, it is the connection between a changing structural reality and normative agency that is central here: what this changing power sequence means for China to present a challenge to the 'liberal' character of international order within international institutions.

How Is Order Created?

As noted by Hedley Bull, order within a group means: '… that their basic relationship is not purely haphazard but contains some discernible **principle** … a pattern that leads to a particular result, an arrangement of social life such that **promotes certain goals or values**'[4] (emphasis added). Similar definitions of order can be found in the works of Stanley Hoffmann,[5] Andrew Hurrell,[6] Ian Clark,[7] and in David Armstrong et al.[8] This normative dimension of order (that arises from the social interaction of states)—as well as the sequencing dimension—contributes to the creation and maintenance of a particular order.

This normative dimension complements rather than negates the discussion of China's changing position in international order by contextualising the ability to use changing power relations. What counts as power, what it means to be powerful and what goals power can achieve are contextual issues. In international order, this context derives (in part) from rules and institutions that express and come to reinforce a particular normative dimension of order. This section looks at how normative dimensions of order—the inter-subjective norms and rules—are created and maintained. In exploring this, it engages with the role power plays through the lens of the role of institutions, socialisation and legitimacy.

Power

Material capabilities remain important even though, when looking at the social construction of order, their role is largely obscured. As noted previously, how material capabilities can be used, to what effect and with what outcomes are limited by the social relations between actors; the stability of the order that power distributions produce is dependent not only on the maintenance of that power distribution but also on the resilience of institutions to sudden change and 'quality of socialisation'[9] of all actors in a particular normative order. It is not, then, just the consistency of a distribution of power that is important but also how satisfied existing and emerging powers are with the benefits they gain from that existing order.[10] However, identifying a changing power distribution and satisfaction or dissatisfaction is inadequate to investigate rising powers and normative order. But, because liberal scholars have considered institutional change to be incremental or (to a degree) a natural evolution, it is not seen or related to the agency of states. Hence, changes to this order have been seen as synonymous with the triumph of liberal values and norms—but this may only be the case because of an absence in our ability to identify and track these incremental changes.

International order may be consensually created or coercively constructed. If it is consensually created, then the great powers (and any dominant powers) share interests and have mutually compatible goals; as a result, a dominant power can construct an order (around these commonly conceived ideas and interests) with the acquiescence and assistance of the other great and major powers. However, it is also possible that material power is important in shaping and generating the acquiescence and acceptance of some great and major powers. In the creation of a normative order the ability to provide 'public goods'[11] and stability are important for both the development of shared goals and shaping the interests of actors that engage with institutions and practices of international order. Through the provision of public goods (PPG) and the bringing together of actors, it is then possible to shape the interests of other actors through interaction.

In the process of the shaping of actors' interests and goals through the PPG and the interaction of states within international institutions, the function and type of power resources necessary to maintain this normative order may change over time.[12] Material capabilities may be more important in bringing actors together for the creation of an order; however, the development of legitimacy becomes more important over time (particularly if the relative position of the dominant power diminishes). The process of developing shared objectives derives (in part) from common interests but also from shared normative goals.

If this process of shaping actors' interests is successful, a group of great powers[13] are likely to be satisfied, even when subordinate to a dominant nation directing and marshalling international order. They are therefore unlikely to challenge the existing order even as the relative power of the dominant state declines and as the relative distribution of power between all states shifts. Normative changes in such a context are less likely.[14] Nevertheless, if rising powers are less satisfied or unsatisfied, challenge to the existing order is more likely and—in the advent of shifting power positions—becomes possible. How successful dominant states are in shaping others' interests and goals, relates to their ability to successfully utilise their power advantages. One of the most significant ways this can be done is through the creation and maintenance of institutions.

Institutions

According to John Ikenberry, the restraint exhibited by the USA and its willingness to bind itself are key elements explaining the durability of US dominance in the post-1945 world.[15] One tool for the maintenance of an international order is the creation of institutions: both formal physical bureaucratic institutions and normative regimes. Both are created through common ideas and norms, they require norms to give them direction and purpose. Their creation is one of the public goods provided by a dominant state (or states), and how these institutions and regimes are constructed relates to both the material power capabilities of a dominant state and its willingness to bind itself to particular normative framework. The transferability of a states' power is also essential in institution building—a state needs to have material capabilities (and means of enforcement) but must also be able to translate that power into claims for legitimacy and authority.

Institutions provide a frame and forum for collective action inspired by norms.[16] Alastair Johnston outlines this part of the relationship between norms and international institutions thus: '[w]hat gives them [institutions] causal power are the interpretations or meanings given to them. These interpretations are functions of ontologically separate normative lenses through which actors/agents observe these material facts'.[17] Therefore, institutions enmesh actors into a particular bureaucratic, informal or intergovernmental, structure[18] and provide a particular method of interpreting material 'facts'. In addition, they '… *relativize* rights and obligations to status in the social system, and to the structure of the situation in which persons of a given status are placed, and they define and legitimate *sanctions*, i.e., the types of consequences of the action of an individual'.[19] Institutions, therefore, take the generality of norms and specify them to create firm realities within which actors can engage effectively with each other. Thus, norms shape the reality through which states construct interests. The translation of abstract norms into these types of reality creates complications: for example, which norms should be prioritised? Because of this, institutions are also 'coalitions of coalitions',[20] groups of states with common goals and interests which form a subgroup within an institution. The dominance of these different populations (through the combination of their power resources) can have an effect on the interpretation adopted by the whole institution. In this way, different or competing interests or norms may be masked by the dominance of a particular coalition, obscuring underlying fragmentations in interpretation. This idea of a fragmented whole becomes important when looking at tools for normative challenge in Chapter 4.

In the construction of a particular reality through which all states interact, institutions and the normative regimes that guide them are mutually binding for all states.[21] In order for the dominant state to maintain both its power advantage and the stability of an international order conducive to the maintenance of that power advantage, the dominant state requires legitimacy—it needs to shape the others' interests but also their evaluation of a dominant state as a leader.[22] The maintenance of cooperation and order requires a rationale, as well as functional capability. Common norms give order directionality (a rationale), and norms give institutions activities (functionality).

Institutions, as well as being mechanisms of maintenance, are also forums for challenging orders. 'Institutions may be where state officials are exposed to new norms…; they may act as channels or conduits through which norms are transmitted…; or they may reinforce domestic changes that have already begun to take place…'[23] According to Thomas Risse, within a social grouping where a 'logic of appropriateness' determines actors' actions, the decision about which norms or rules are followed is subject to debate requiring actors to 'argue'.[24] Institutions provide the forum for such argument and a situation whereby new norms may become dominant and old norms may be overridden. According to Ole Jacob Sending, institutions exist to provide an arena in which the 'meaning' of norms can be decided and changed.[25] Thus, an important function of institutions is not just to reflect the norms that created them, but also to act as a vessel through which new norms can emerge and be diffused. Institutions provide a vital forum in which states acting as norm entrepreneurs can initiate and spread new norms, or start the process of reinterpreting existing norms.

There are important limitations on the ability to use institutional forums to establish new norms. States acting within institutions (and seeking change) must have legitimacy and authority (discussed in the next chapter). In gaining legitimacy and authority, they must previously have been seen to be abiding by the rules of that institution.[26] Challenge is possible, but the latitude for challenging within institutions is limited.

The latitude for challenging is also limited by institutional 'stickiness' and institutional inertia, both of which contribute to an institution's role as a maintainer rather than changer of international order. Institutions limit change through the adoption of certain roles and obligations that are hard to change,[27] through providing an institutional memory which creates reference points for actors to set standards of behaviour of what is appropriate or otherwise in certain situations based on previous experience.[28] By providing a history of decisions and actions, institutions can be seen to give frames for actors' engagements within institutions, as well as delimitating what behaviour is appropriate.[29] Institutions are both an explicit expression of normative regimes and a means to maintain those normative frameworks.

The Role and Limits of Socialisation for Maintaining Order

Within the literature, socialisation has been cited as being a key factor in shaping actors' identities to conform to particular ideas about order. As actors come into contact with each other, they learn about each other's interpretations of events and norms. Through interaction within institutions (both formal and informal) and the learning process, they may adapt each other's conceptual frames.[30] This allows for a convergence on a set of common ideas and understandings. If a new actor then joins an established social group, there will still be a degree of adaptation and learning on both sides; nonetheless, there will be a greater expectation that the newcomer will undergo a greater degree of adaptation to the norms and practices of the group. In international order, the degree of socialisation is therefore an important element in understanding change; it forms a part of the dynamic between the agent and the structure, and sets out the scope of agents to produce change within an existing organisation.

According to Alexander Wendt:

> ...from a constructivist perspective the mark of a fully internalised culture is that actors identify with it, have made it the generalised Other, part of their understanding of self. This identification, this sense of being part of the group or 'we', is a social or collective identity that gives actors an interest in the preservation of their culture ... collective interests mean that actors make the welfare of the group an end in itself, which will in turn help them overcome the collective action problems that beset egoists. When their culture is threatened well-socialised actors will tend instinctively to defend it. Actors are still rational, but the unit on the basis of which they calculate utility and rational action is the group.[31]

Therefore, to Wendt, a vital element of socialisation is the extent to which the group is a reference point for the action they take (whether this is in terms of defending a group or preserving a group's values or culture). This definition is complemented by the process of social learning whereby (according to Jeffrey Checkel) 'agent interests and identities are shaped through interaction'[32]; they learn to adjust or abandon their own interests or identities in favour of those values, norms and interests that are to the benefit of the group. Institutions with dense or thick interactions between actors are particularly important in creating a fertile environment for social learning, and so producing higher levels of socialisation.

Yet, '[n]o value system is ever perfectly internalized and institutionalized, but its status is uneven in different personalities and subcollectivities of the society'.[33] It is difficult to measure the extent to which such changes arise from socialisation or from other factors such as self-interest or rationalism.[34] Even though, as Johnston puts it, 'actors who enter into a social interaction rarely emerge the same', it remains unclear how much of that change is the result of socialisation.[35] Additionally, difficulties in measurement and the attribution of causation are caused by variation in the level of socialisation between actors and between issues. Moreover, despite the importance of socialisation to constructivist theories, it is also under-theorised in international relations.[36] This under-theorising has led to assumptions that socialisation is automatic once actors have begun to interact within formal and regulated institutions,[37] and that compliance with laws, rules or norms is indicative of internalisation of those norms.[38]

Socialisation, therefore, may help to create a dominance of particular ideas by forming barriers to acceptance to other ideas in international organisations; by bringing actors together in particular forms of interaction; and by having powerful actors control the dialogue and debate among different actors. These things all help to create a single view of what international order is. However, the dominance of socialisation theories within the literature may mask the other dynamics at play in international interaction. States may interact and seem to 'buy in' to the dominant understanding of order. States may act out of self-interest,[39] a need to engage,[40] or as a method to change the dominant understanding of order. The power of such groups may arise from the dominance of a particular group with authority and a majority, or the socialisation of other actors to a particular interpretation.[41] As such, the appearance of convergence of ideas on international order may in fact mask divergent understandings of their interactions. These differences may only be revealed when a new situation or a new event discloses the private understandings of all parties.

In the body of literature about international order, the major alternative to an actor being socialised to norms and conventions of order is for actors to become persistent objectors.[42] This idea is derived from international law, and there are several key elements that an actor is required to fulfil if it is to be classified as a persistent objector: consistent objection, from the first discussion of a new norm, without abstaining from the discussion at any point. According to Lau: '…if a state persistently objects to the development of a customary international law, it cannot be held to that law when the custom ripens'.[43] Therefore, a state may be within the social group of states but may be outside of some conventions or norms of the group as a whole.

An important element of this idea is '…that international legal order lacks a hierarchically superior sovereign authorized to prescribe rules for the subjects of order. In the absence of such a sovereign, law must result from the concurrent wills of states …'[44] The starting point for this idea is an equality between states; all states' interpretations have equal weighting; and that all states consent to be treated equally according to international law. This places emphasis on the creation of an international customary law to which a state must consistently object,[45] meaning that it must have objected when the rule was only a norm and must have continued to voice an objection once it became a law.[46]

This idea suggests a position revisionist states could adopt, whilst being within the social structures of international order. A state may adapt and be socialised to most of the tenets of international order, whilst also rejecting and objecting to the elements that they see as contrary to their interests. At most, it achieves stasis but the standards for qualification to persistent objector status are high and little is actually gained by achieving this status.[47]

The Construction of Order and the Limitation of Change

The mechanisms of maintenance of a particular order also form mechanisms for change—institutions provide a forum for 'arguing' and producing change; unequal socialisation opens the door for the adoption of alternative normative regimes to emerge; changing power dynamics may inspire change or inspire consolidation. However, within current international order, the abilities for a state to challenge that order from within are limited. For an actor to gain the necessary power tools within an existing order—legitimacy, authority and capacity—it is necessary to bind themselves in some way to a particular understanding and a particular mode of action. In looking at China in this context, it is clear that whilst it was on the margins of the formation of the current international order, since 1978 it has sought to engage and adapt itself to the current order.[48] But, limited room for change is not 'no room for change'. Within the current order, there is scope for engagement to occur without an acceptance of the underlying principles. So when a state seeks to make changes to that order, it reveals its opposition to those principles or a different understanding or interpretation of them.[49] The ability and agency available to states (like China) will be discussed in the next chapter.

CONCLUSION

International order is constructed by different actors—in particular, states—who are brought together by common interests and goals. Consequently, order is maintained and changed by social interactions of states. In these interactions, interests, ideas and goals play an important role in constructing and maintaining a particular order.

A further implication of the social construction of order is that it is necessary for actors to be brought together by agreement on a range of common issues, and common understandings of how to achieve common aims; there is the potential to see the international order as liberal. Through these 'commons', actors create institutions. These institutions have created bureaucracies, laws and patterns of behaviour that are now important in regulating the activities of members of these institutions.[50] But within these institutions diversity and contradictions remain.[51] Although actors agree on a limited range of issues that inspired the creation of the institution, they remain diverse in their own domestic make-up, and their reactions to new events and their interests and priorities. Thus, the liberal order contains many contradictions over the type of liberalism that should be pursued. The next chapter looks at how order can be challenged through challenges to liberal norms.

NOTES

1. Steve Smith, 'Is the Truth Out There? Eight Questions About International Order', in John A. Hall and T.V. Paul (eds), *International Order and the Future of World Politics* (Cambridge University Press: Cambridge, 1999), p. 103.
2. Robert Gilpin, *War and Change in World Politics* (Cambridge University Press: Cambridge, 1982), p. 45; John Gerard Ruggie, *Constructing the World Polity: Essays on International Institutionalization* (Routledge: London, 1998), p. 84.
3. David Armstrong, *Revolution and World Order: The Revolutionary State in International Society* (Clarendon Press: Oxford, 1993), p. 6.
4. Ibid., pp. 3–4.
5. Stanley Hoffmann, *Janus and Minerva: Essays in the Theory and Practice of International Politics* (Westview Press: Boulder, 1987), p. 85.
6. Andrew Hurrell, 'Order and Justice in International Relations: What Is at Stake?', in Rosemary Foot, John Lewis Gaddis, and Andrew Hurrell (eds), *Order and Justice in International Relations* (Oxford University Press: Oxford, 2003), p. 25; Andrew Hurrell, *On Global Order: Power, Values, and the Constitution of International Society* (Oxford University Press: Oxford, 2007), p. 2.
7. Clark sees the post-Cold War order as being regulative with a purpose of allowing democratic states to flourish. Ian Clark, *The Post-Cold War Order: the Spoils of Peace* (Oxford University Press: Oxford, 2001), pp. 227–228.

8. David Armstrong, Lorna Lloyd, and John Redmond, *International Organisation in World Politics* (Palgrave: Houndmills, 2004), pp. 85–117.
9. Nicole Alecu de Flers and Patrick Muller, 'Applying the Concept of Europeanization to the Study of Foreign Policy: Dimensions and Mechanisms', paper prepared for the GARNET Conference 2010, available https://www.ies.be/files/Muller-B3.pdf, accessed 22 January 2018, p. 5.
10. A.F.K. Organski, *World Politics* (Alfred A. Knopf: New York, 1968), pp. 363–375.
11. Chris Brown, 'Do Great Powers Have Great Responsibilities? Great Powers and Moral Agency', *Global Society* (2004), 18(1), pp. 5–19, p. 11.
12. Clark, Ian, *Hegemony in International Society* (Oxford University Press: Oxford, 2011), p. 19.
13. Organski, *World Politics*, pp. 363–375.
14. Ibid.
15. G. John Ikenberry, *After Victory: Institutions, Strategic Restraint, and the Rebuilding of Order after Major Wars* (Princeton University Press: Princeton, 2001).
16. Parsons describes the distinction between norms and institutions as 'Values are modes of normative orientation of action in a social system which define the main directions of action without reference to the specific goals or more detailed situations or structures … Institutions are still generalized and "regulate" action at more differentiated and particularized levels'. Talcott Parsons, *Structure and Process in Modern Societies* (Free Press of Glencoe: Illinois, 1960), p. 171.
17. Alastair Iain Johnston, 'Chapter 3: International Structures and Chinese Foreign Policy', in Samuel S. Kim (ed.), *China and the World: Chinese Foreign Policy Faces the New Millennium* (Westview Press: Boulder, 1998), pp. 68–69.
18. Andrew P. Cortell and James W. Davis, Jr., 'How Do International Institutions Matter? The Domestic Impact of International Rules and Norms', *International Studies Quarterly* (1996), 40(4), pp. 451–478, p. 452.
19. Parsons, *Structure and Process in Modern Societies*, p. 177.
20. Ernst B. Haas, *When Knowledge Is Power: Three Models of Change in International Organizations* (University of California Press: Berkeley, 1990), p. 18.
21. Geoffrey M. Hodgson, 'Institutions and Individuals: Interaction and Evolution', p. 110; Lindner, 'Institutional Stability and Change', pp. 916–919.
22. Clark, *Hegemony in International Society*, p. 17.
23. Andrew Hurrell, 'Power, Institutions, and the Production of Inequality', in M. Barnett and R. Duvall (eds), *Power in Global Governance* (Cambridge University Press: Cambridge, 2004), p. 42.

24. Thomas Risse, '"Let's Argue!": Communicative Action in World Politics', *International Organization* (2000), 54(1), pp. 1–39, p. 6.
25. Ole Jacob Sending, 'Constitution, Choice and Change: Problems with the 'Logic of Appropriateness' and Its Use in Constructivist Theory', *European Journal of International Relations* (2002), 8(4), pp. 443–470, p. 452.
26. Martha Finnemore, 'Norms, Culture, and World Politics: Insights from Sociology's Institutionalism', *International Organization* (1996), 50(2) pp. 325–347, p. 329.
27. J.G. March and J.P. Olsen, 'The Logic of Appropriateness'. http://www.arena.uio.no/publications/papers/wp04_9.pdf, Working Paper WP 04/09; Ole Jacob Sending, 'Constitution, Choice and Change: Problems with the 'Logic of Appropriateness' and Its Use in Constructivist Theory', *European Journal of International Relations* (2002), 8(4), pp. 443–470, p. 449.
28. March and Olsen, 'The Logic of Appropriateness', p. 4.
29. Ole Jacob Sending, 'Constitution, Choice and Change: Problems with the 'Logic of Appropriateness' and Its Use in Constructivist Theory', *European Journal of International Relations* (2002), 8(4), pp. 443–470, p. 455.
30. This can be shown through role adaptation see Catherine Jones 'Understanding Multiple and Competing Roles: China's Roles in International Order' unpublished paper, presented at ACPS Kings College London, June 2011.
31. Alexander Wendt, *A Social Theory of International Politics* (Cambridge University Press: Cambridge, 1999), p. 337.
32. Jeffrey T. Checkel, 'Why Comply? Social Learning and European Identity Change', *International Organization* (2001), 55(3), pp. 553–588, p. 558.
33. Parsons, *Structure and Process in Modern Societies*, p. 173.
34. Gary Goertz and Paul F. Diehl, 'Toward a Theory of International Norms: Some Conceptual and Measurement Issues', *The Journal of Conflict Resolution* (1992), 36(4), pp. 634–664.
35. Alistair Iain Johnston, 'Treating International Institutions as Social Environments', *International Studies Quarterly* (2001), 45(4), pp. 487–515, p. 448.
36. Ibid., p. 489.
37. Ibid., p. 492.
38. Ibid., p. 493.
39. Goertz and Diehl, 'Toward a Theory of International Norms', pp. 639–642.
40. Martha Finnemore, 'Fights About Rules: The Role of Efficacy and Power in Changing Multilateralism', *Review of International Studies* (2005), 31(Supplement S1), pp. 187–206, p. 194.

41. Haas, *When Knowledge Is Power*, p. 13.
42. Kahn, 'American Hegemony and the International Law'; H. Lau, 'Rethinking the Persistent Objector Doctrine in International Human Rights Law', *Chicago Journal of International Law* (2005–2006), 6(1), pp. 495–510; T.L. Stein, 'The Approach of the Different Drummer: The Principle of the Persistent Objector in International Law', *Harvard International Law Journal* (1985), 26(2), pp. 457–482; Jonathan I. Charney, 'Universal International Law', *The American Journal of International Law* (1993), 87(4), pp. 529–551; Kahn, 'American Hegemony and the International Law'.
43. Lau, 'Rethinking the Persistent Objector Doctrine in International Human Rights Law', p. 495; also Kahn, 'American Hegemony and the International Law'; Stein, 'The Approach of the Different Drummer'.
44. Stein, 'The Approach of the Different Drummer', p. 459; Kahn, 'American Hegemony and the International Law: Speaking Law to Power', p. 1; Lau, 'Rethinking the Persistent Objector Doctrine in International Human Rights Law', p. 499.
45. Jonathan I. Charney, 'Universal International Law', *The American Journal of International Law* (1993), 87(4), pp. 529–551, p. 539.
46. Lau, 'Rethinking the Persistent Objector Doctrine in International Human Rights Law', pp. 497–498.
47. Charney, 'Universal International Law', p. 539.
48. '…what is important here is the degree to which Brazil, Russia, India and China all lie either outside or on the margins of, this formation'. Andrew Hurrell, 'Hegemony, Liberalism and Global Order: What Space for Would-Be Great Powers?', *International Affairs* (2006), 82(1), pp. 1–19, p. 3.
49. As Economy and Segal point out 'even after 30 years of engagement the United States and China still disagree on how the world should work', p. 15 and in trying to forge closer cooperation on issues it highlights their 'mismatched interests, values and capabilities', p. 15, Elizabeth C. Economy and A. Segal, 'The G-2 Mirage: Why the US and China Are Not Ready to Upgrade Ties', *Foreign Affairs* (2009), (14), pp. 14–23.
50. Kahn, 'American Hegemony and the International Law', p. 2.
51. C.M. Chinkin, 'The Challenge of Soft Law; Development and Change in International Law', *International and Comparative Law Quarterly* (1989), (38), pp. 850–866, p. 855.

CHAPTER 4

Norms, Order, and Social Change: Laying Out a Toolkit for Normative Change

In Chapter 1, this book set out the methodological approach being used. It made the claim that a Humean approach to causation was not appropriate; rather when looking to understand China's role in challenging the liberal elements of international order, it is necessary to adopt an Aristotelian approach that sets out the four different elements of causation. This chapter then links these causes to the conceptual framework being adopted. Specifically, it links a cause to a mechanism of challenge and in so doing allows this book to situate China's challenge to liberal norms within the complexity of the situation. This complex situation arises from the conclusion of the last chapter; that international order is socially constructed through the social interactions of states, norms, rules and practices.

This framework makes specific claims about how norms can change and about how states can challenge international order by challenging norms. As noted previously, this project is concerned with the *mechanisms* and *processes* through which China can be seen to challenge the norms that characterise international order. Consequently, it is not necessary to set out measures for whether norms have changed or not. But rather, it is necessary to set out the following: the processes through which norms can be changed; what roles states can play in that process; what tools states may utilise in being agents of change; and what factors may make it easier or harder for states to present a challenge. As a result, through the application of this conceptual approach in the empirical chapters, it may be possible to make claims about specific instances where China's challenge has had an impact, but this is not necessary for

© The Author(s) 2018
C. Jones, *China's Challenge to Liberal Norms*,
https://doi.org/10.1057/978-1-137-42761-8_4

this work to achieve its research objectives. It is important to note that these causal inferences are possible only in so far as they can be justified in line with the causal descriptive methodology adopted.

This chapter first sets out the role institutions can play in normative change. This is important because it demonstrates the relationship between the structures of international order and the ability to produce normative change from within these structures. As will be noted later in the chapter, two of the tools that states can use to bring about normative change are to change the 'populations' (or groupings of states) within institutions or to create new institutions. These changes enable challenges to the norms that characterise international order, but they are not in themselves the focus of the book—insofar as institutional change is considered in the empirical chapters, it is as a precondition for (or tools of) normative challenges. Having outlined the role of institutions and the relationship between the structure of order and the normative dimensions of order, this chapter then goes on to discuss norms, looking at the characteristics of norms and how they may be changed. In this, it looks specifically at the role of interpretation in changing norms. Subsequently, it explores how a state may affect norms, by identifying three mechanisms that a state can use: norm entrepreneurship[1]; persistent objection[2]; and ad hoc objection.[3]

Second, the chapter looks at how states can use different tools to express their agency: how can states amplify their position on particular norms to present a more cohesive challenge? It identifies four main tools that states can use: reinterpretation; new issues; new populations; and new institutions. As noted above, these tools bring together both structural and normative elements in producing a challenge to international order; these structural and normative dimensions are complementary to each other rather than competing with each other. Third, it discusses what situations can make normative change more or less likely. This links back to the methodology to isolate China's challenge to the norms of international order (the efficient and final causes) from the elements of international order that are being challenged by other factors in the international relations (the material and formal) of states.

The Role of Institutions in Normative Change

Within a socially constructed international order, institutions have a multifaceted role. First, they help create stability and regularity for state interaction. Second, they act as conduits for the transfer of common interests and norms into practices and behaviours. Third, they create a memory and patterns for future interactions and decisions, contributing to the creation of a schema through which new events are understood, thus stabilising the international environment.[4] Institutions then act as a bridge between the structural and normative elements of international order. This division was indicated previously in the difference between an international order based around the formal structures and one that focuses on the production of a particular 'frame of mind'.[5] As noted in Chapter 3, and in the aims in Chapter 1, this book is concerned with challenge to the norms of international order. It is interested in whether it is possible to change the 'frame of mind' about a particular order without fundamentally changing the structure of that order.[6]

In this endeavour, institutions play an important role. They act as places where normative change takes place. For these normative changes to occur, it may be necessary for new members to be added into the institution (this is noted in the creation of new populations and new institutions). Indeed, in order for China to have a role in challenging the norms of international development, a prerequisite of normative change is that China is engaged with OECD. This then forms a part of China's challenge, but it also enables China to challenge the norms within the institution rather than just presenting a challenge from outside.

Through interactions within institutions, other states (with initially divergent preferences and interests) are socialised to the preferences of dominant and great powers. As a result, shifting rules of membership or rules about behaviour alters the character of international order, yet although these types of changes are plausibly possible they are difficult to achieve without destroying institutions. However, as institutions provide means of stability, they also provide means and geography for normative challenge.

As the norms constituting and regulating international order are socially constructed, they are also open to challenge through social processes. Institutions, because of their role as multilateral 'collective action decision makers',[7] bring states together promoting negotiation, discussion and action, to create commonly held practices and interpretations. Consequently, institutions have a central role in challenging norms. As noted at the end of Chapter 3, the liberal elements of international order are openly contested within a liberal framework: not all contestation is illiberal.

This chapter goes on to explore how norms change. It begins with a discussion of the character of norms and their defining features, and then outlines variations between them.

THE CHARACTER OF NORMS

In order to understand international normative change, it is necessary to understand the characteristics of norms. In particular, it is important in understanding how norms fit together and create the liberal characteristics of international order. It is claimed, in this section, that it is easier to change interstitial norms (norms that link bigger norms) than it is to change meta-norms. Nonetheless, changing how we understand interstitial norms can have an effect on how we understand meta-norms, and as a result how we characterise international order.

Before expanding further on the role that norms can play in creating changes to international order, what norms are needs a brief reflection. Norms are socially constructed facts[8] that are inter-subjective,[9] vary in strength[10] and come together to form a system of regulations about both membership of and state behaviour within international order.[11] The following discussion expands on each of these elements, particularly focusing on the role norms play in constituting and changing international order.

Norms Are Socially Constructed 'Facts'[12]

As noted in the previous chapter, international order is the result of both a positional relationship between actors and a purposive and normatively organised relationship. This normative dimension is constructed through the social interaction of states; states voluntarily interact in order to promote particular interests and goals. The interaction between states creates norms. Through this social interaction and interpretation, norms are specified and given form[13]; as a result, it is through reinterpretation (in a social space) that norms are challenged and changed.

This interaction makes states the agents of change. This agency may be intentional and purposive or it may be unintentional and ad hoc. The amount of agency varies between states; this variation may arise from changes in the positional/hierarchical relationship between states within an international order, or from changing perceptions of a state's moral/recognised legitimacy,[14] or from external shocks to the norms and practices of international order. These elements facilitating normative change are discussed later.

Norms Are Inter-Subjective

Martha Finnemore defines norms as: '…shared expectations about appropriate behaviour held by a community of actors. Unlike ideas which may be held privately, norms are shared and social; they are not just subjective they are *inter*-subjective'.[15] This inter-subjective quality produces stability because shared understandings are more difficult to modify; change or challenge requires changing all members' understandings. Moreover, in the shared nature of norms they gain a degree of autonomy from the interests of the 'sponsoring' state/s.[16] This process of interaction between states allows for modification of norms which results in a changed shared understanding. Consequently, this construction of norms fosters compliance and promotes durability based on positive constraints (socialisation to appropriate behaviours and perceptions of legitimacy) rather than negative constraints (coercion).[17]

This inter-subjectivity gives norms some independence from the interests and the beliefs of states and a degree of stability,[18] as it is the collective interpretation of a web of interconnected norms that has to change.[19] This then presents a constraint on the scope of change (or challenge) that is possible and also the ability of individual agents to change them.

Norms Are Contextual

Norms shape the context in which actors interact with each other; at the same time, context shapes actors' interpretation of norms.[20] Shared expectations and shared understandings between actors about what is appropriate guide actors' thinking as well as behaviour. This contextual feature of norms has three implications for normative change (and also links back to the importance of power as contextual in Chapter 2). First, changing material realities (changing the structures that give norms their content and specificity) can lead to reinterpretations of a particular norm.[21] Second, context shapes, and is shaped by, perceptions of legitimate behaviour. As a result, norm violators must be able to justify their violation within the 'acceptable' parameters of the norm.[22] Third, in delimiting the context of an understanding of a norm, there is also a shaping of the 'realm of the possible' for actors. As such, norms offer limits to what an actor perceives as a possible course of action, and they define pathways open to actors.[23] Norms and systems of norms provide interpretive frames through which actors understand and interpret actions, conditioning every actor's perception of the possible. As discussed previously, the contestations of contemporary liberal international order arise from within as well as outside liberalism. The face of liberalism expressed through norms has created a limited arena for contest. The embeddedness of liberalism and the frame in which norms are situated creates a limited environment within which to conceive 'new' norms.

In addition to who and how many states accept a norm, Vaughan Lowe identifies a difference between 'primary' (or meta-norms) and interstitial or modifying norms.[24] According to Lowe, interstitial norms 'operate at the interstices between primary norms… they do not themselves have a normative force of the traditional kind but instead operate by modifying the normative effect of other primary norms'.[25] These types of norms are, therefore, important in determining which primary norms should be applied and how they should be applied; they form a part of the determination of context. This is a limit not only to the formulation of interstitial norms (the links between meta-norms) but also to the imaginary of how meta-norms can be interpreted (discussed in detail later).

Norms also have a vitally important relationship to institutions and hence the stability of the particular form of liberal international order. Norms limit the extent of change through fostering positive compliance by a majority of states. This limits[26] and contributes to the construction of a schema that limits the range of perceived choices available to states[27] (that defines what states may legitimately do and prescribe their goals).[28] This produces patterns of behaviour through socialisation, education and integration.[29] This then contributes to the stability and predictability provided by institutions because of the linkages that norms necessitate.[30] Meta-norms and interstitial norms create a complex web of interrelated understandings that construct and frame the context in which interactions take place.[31] Consequently, changes (or challenges) to individual practices (that may be possible within a non-normatively regulated institution) become more difficult. Changing this complex norm web necessitates changing patterns of behaviour rather than individual behaviours; this makes social interactions more predictable and resistant to change. Having shaped actors' behaviour and produced some stability by doing so, norms help to shape the institutions that this regularity and stability make space for. By bringing diverse groups of actors together and by highlighting common aims and agendas, norms can help to shape institutions with common enterprises, such as the UN, WTO, EU and

IMF.[32] In this way, norms enable societies to move from one type of order to another, from merely sequencing and producing patterns of behaviour towards producing regular stable patterns of behaviour with an agenda and purpose.[33]

The Strength of International Norms

Norms are not all of equal importance nor are they uniformly accepted: they do not have equal strength.[34] Their strength changes across at least two dimensions: degree of acceptance (level of internalisation) and their relative importance (salience). These dimensions of norms have a significant impact on the ease and conditions for challenges.

The degree of internalisation is discussed in Finnemore and Sikkink in their article '*International norm dynamics and political change*'[35] with respect to their outline of the life cycle of norms. In this article, 'norm entrepreneurs' lead to the production and cultivation of 'norm leaders', who then socialise more actors until finally sufficient numbers of actors have adopted the norm and it 'cascades' to become an identified norm of international order.[36]

Finnemore and Sikkink's norm life cycle[37]:

According to this life cycle, the level of internalisation of a norm and consequently the level of acceptance of a norm increase over time.[38] The level of acceptance can be seen as: not yet accepted, partially accepted or fully accepted. Along this scale, they can, however, move forward and backward; at points of contestation, norms can be more or less accepted and 'one of the most important features of norms is that the standing of a norm can change in a surprisingly short time'.[39] Therefore, it is important to notice that norms do not exist in a linear form towards a particular end, but that the dynamic realm of norm formation means that they may not progress with clear directionality or linearity.[40] This is necessitated by the demand that new norms 'fit' with the social values and actions of a group to whom they apply.[41]

There are three elements that help to judge the degree of internalisation and therefore contribute to understanding positive (non-coercive) compliance: how many states have internalised the norm, which states have internalised the norms, and what type of norm it is. According to the Finnermore and Sikkink's norm life cycle, for a norm to come into being it needs the support of 1/3 of all states.[42] However, who those states are is also important.[43] Great powers are recognised as being: legitimate; having authority; and having command of greater knowledge and experiences. As such, they have increased potential to guide the emergence of norms. In the Security Council, on issues of peace and security, the Permanent Five members (or P5) will always be among the 'critical states', yet in the OECD the group of 'critical states' are Western Liberal Democracies.

The degree to which norms are internalised can be seen across two dimensions of behaviour. Firstly, the reason for compliance with norms indicates a level of internationalisation. Positive behavioural choices display norms complied with by choice; negative behaviours are shown where compliance is achieved through coercion. Norms that are complied with through coercion are more easily changed than those whose compliance is based on positive behavioural choices. Secondly, internalisation of norms also needs to acknowledge that the power of the states that internalise norms has an effect on broader compliance and internalisation: norms that are complied with by all the P5 are more internationally internalised than norms that are complied with by only three of the P5 (this is important when looking at the challenge to sovereignty norms). Similarly, where norms are internalised by 1/3 of states, but all of them are small states and have not been internalised by great powers, these norms are lower in the internalisation hierarchy.

Along with existing on a scale of acceptance, norms also exist within a scale of importance; norms can be privileged over each other. The position that a norm occupies on this scale is affected by: the relative importance of a norm against other norms (the salience of norms); the coherence with coexisting norms; and the role of norms within a particular schema. All of these three dimensions are related to each other; if a norm is highly salient, it is more likely to act as a reference point around which other norms cohere, and it is likely to be directly related to a particular schema—it is more likely to be a meta-norm that determines international order. As can be seen with the attempts to get 'Responsibility to Protect' adopted as a norm, it challenges the position of a particular interpretation of the norm of sovereignty at the pinnacle of international norms.[44] Norms that are further along this scale are more difficult to challenge. Therefore, in seeking to change norms, they must be first understood not only in terms of their development along the life cycle, but also in terms of their position in the scale of norms.

Within this scale, there is an important distinction between interstitial and primary or meta-norms. Meta-norms are more likely to be further along the norm scale as they are linked directly with the determination of the context and content of international order and as a reference point for interstitial norms to cohere around. The presence of these norms on the one hand makes interpretations of norms more stable, but on the other hand, they open a possible pathway for states to shape the application of norms and by doing so have an impact on the character of international order. It is because of their earlier position on this norm scale that it is easier to challenge interstitial norms, than it is to challenge primary norms. However, Lowe suggests that these norms may not be created or authored in the same way as other international norms.[45] The role for individual states to act as agents in the production of these norms is less clear than for other norms. This is because '[a] much wider range of concepts and social pressures come to shape these interstitial norms than is normally the case in international law'.[46] The production (or the reinterpretation) of interstitial norms enables an actor to gradually shape the debates that take place in international institutions, and by doing so gradually shape the links between 'primary' norms, which in turn gradually shapes and changes the application of those primary norms.

In understanding a particular norm in this way, it is easier to conceive of the type of challenge that is needed to change it. For example, whether reference to other norms is possible, or whether it is necessary to couch a challenge with reference to issues of coherence.

How Can Normative Change Be Measured?

From the above discussion, it is clear that understanding whether norms have changed is not a simple binary operation, although it may be desirable to try and do so to enable quantitative researchers to ascribe a number of 1 or 0 in order to identify change. However, it is obvious from the discussion above (regarding the character of norms) that normative change can take place in many dimensions: the strength of the norms (changes relate to their level of acceptance or how hard or soft they are); the context in which they are given understanding or meaning (change results from a particular understanding becoming irrelevant or meaningless in a new context); the inter-subjective understanding of a norm (i.e., the norm of 'non-intervention' may still exist, but how it is understood has changed); or the social construction of the norm. Clearly, each of these is important and related. They complicate the issue as to whether normative change is able to be measured. There have been attempts to understand normative change and whether it is possible to identify when norms change, but most commonly this is done through understanding the emergence of norms and setting a standard of when they have become accepted rather than whether norms have changed.[47]

This is an unwelcome complication to this research project; however, the approach here is that in understanding the process through which it is possible for norms to change, we can better understand whether a norm has been challenged. The adoption of an approach that seeks to identify a *challenge* rather than a *change* through the use of specific tools, forms of agency in a particular context, thus allows for a qualitative approach to be used. As such, by setting out a thick narrative of the engagement with a norm, and how that engagement relates to the ideal and theoretical possibilities for normative change to occur, it is possible to suggest the potential that a change has occured.

Following this logic and if there is sufficient evidence in this causal narrative, it may then be possible to determine whether there is the possibility of a change resulting. That is, there is causal inference in making this last step. However, the leap of faith is reduced, or overcome, through the use of documentary analysis to identify whether there has been a change over time and whether that change is consistent with the presentation of the challenge that have been determined. As noted in Chapter 1, the use of causal description[48] then allows for the identification of the position of the norm within the norm life cycle of Finnemore and Sikkink. Consequently, the causal descriptive method allows the best chance to identify any normative change across all of these dimensions. The next section then sets out how norms chance and how this model can be used to identify the agency of China in challenging norms.

How Do Norms Change?

Most of the literature focuses on processes of normative change—not whether norms have changed but how they have changed. This book looks at how China challenges rather than whether a challenge has had an impact.

In Finnemore and Skikkink's norm life cycle, how a norm moves along the cycle is not fully elucidated. Nevertheless, it is clear that an increasing number of states must come to recognise the existence of a norm for it to move along the cycle. How then can the movement of norms along the life cycle—either forwards or backwards—progress? This discussion highlights the role of interpretation as one of the key drivers, assisted through four distinct tools: new issues, reframing, new populations and new institutions. In aiming to use these tools, state actors may choose to act as norm entrepreneurs or objectors. The tools discussed below then amplify their position and give their interpretation of a norm the greatest chance of being accepted by the necessary 1/3 of states (as determined by Finnemore and Sikkink).[49]

The Role of Interpretation

The norm life cycle is important in reflecting on normative change, but it also needs a method to drive the norm from one stage to another. The claim here is that interpretation acts as a driver.

In a social arena which places importance on legitimacy and legal reference points, the norm life cycle fits well with ideas of the interpretation of laws and norms. This is important as norms only make sense within a context: they are interpreted by a group of actors, within a framework, and applied to specific situations. Thus, the norm may change or adapt or be challenged depending on the interpretation applied to it. Applying the work of Dworkin,[50] Fish[51] and Johnstone[52] proposes the following process for normative change:

Pre-Interpretive stage ➡ Interpretive Stage ➡ Post Interpretive stage

In each of these stages, there is an increased acceptance and an increased coherence of a collection of norms, '... the post-interpretive stage, is not so much the conventions of an interpretive community but rather the coherent set of principles that reside in the "political structure and legal doctrine of the community" as a whole'.[53] As Dworkin puts it '[i]nterpretation folds back into the practice, altering its shape, and the new shape encourages further reinterpretation, so the practice changes dramatically, though each step in the progress is interpretive of what the last achieved'.[54] Therefore, as certain interpretations are perceived to be the 'best' interpretations of rules or practices, they become more regulative than suggestive; an element in the process is the degree of institutionalisation (whether norms are 'soft' or 'hard'—whether they are norms based on obligation or on legalisation). Some norms, through a change, in interpretation may 'need' to become harder (more institutionalised and regulative) in nature. For example, new interpretations of norms in order to ensure compliance may require clear legal frameworks; certainly, any new norms about the centrality of the rule of law require more rules and laws (the interpretation of the content of the norms can determine the degree of institutionalisation).[55]

Thus, norms of action or practice build upon what has gone before, and therefore, the process of norm creation and the discourse surrounding their creation help determine and constitute the final interpretation of the norm between groups of actors. Looking at this understanding of how norms evolve, it is clear to see how Ikenberry et al.[56] perceive the progress of liberal international order towards even greater liberalism. However, it is important to note that these reinterpretations may reaffirm or negate previous understandings, an issue that will be explored towards the end of this chapter (Fig. 4.1).

The diagram on the next page depicts the flows that norms can take; it brings together the life cycle of Finnemore and Skikkink with the driving force of interpretation. It indicates that norms may flow towards acceptance (down the page) or may be frustrated and thus move back up the life cycle (up the page). Moreover, in their movement towards greater or lesser acceptance, they may also move from side to side—towards a softer or harder usage.

What Role Is There for States in Driving Normative Change?

Having set out what norms are and their particular characteristics, and identified states' different interpretations as a central mechanism for bringing about new and changed norms, this section looks at how states can act in order to produce changes in the interpretation of international norms. It looks specifically at what actions a single state may take within international order. The following discussion looks at the tools that a state may use to bring about a challenge. In this sense, it looks at the agent of change, and the subsequent section looks at what tools they have to pursue their challenge. In looking back to the discussion of causation in Chapter 1, these two elements can be seen as the efficient cause and the final cause (the agent) and the material cause (the mechanism). In the final part on normative change, the formal causes (the context of change) are discussed as the facilitating conditions for a challenge.

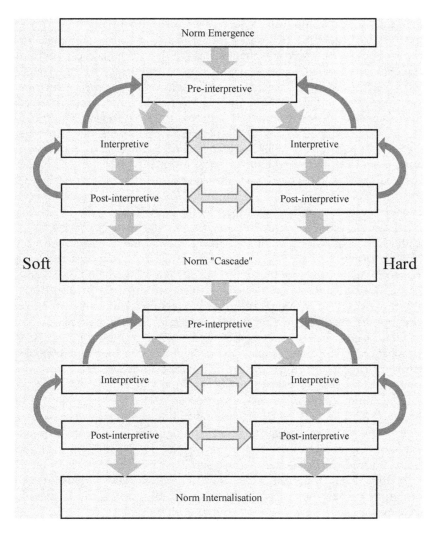

Fig. 4.1 Norm development

Broadly speaking, there are three main actor-driven forces that affect the evolution of norms: norm entrepreneurship, ad hoc objection and persistent objection. Norm entrepreneurs actively promote new norms or the application of existing norms to new situations. Persistent objectors are states that continuously object to the creation of norms and their progress to becoming customary international law. As such, these different types of actor-driven change have different outcomes; the aims of norm entrepreneurs are in the creation of norms, whereas persistent objectors seek to prevent norms. Therefore, the type of outcome required by an actor will shape the type of agency-driven tools they can use to achieve it. For example, if a state wishes to prevent a particular decision becoming a norm that will affect their behaviour, the most appropriate pathway is to become a persistent objector. By contrast, if an actor seeks to change the direction of international law and/or order, they may choose to actively seek the creation of new norms by being a norm entrepreneur.

A persistent objector is exempted from compliance with an international law if it meets the definition of '... a state [that] objects to the establishment of a norm while it is becoming law and persistently objects to it up to present, ...'.[57] This therefore sets a high standard for being able to be exempted from an international law. This definition requires that a state initially and continuously objects to a particular norm in all circumstances.[58] It is not therefore a method for challenge that can be used opportunistically but must be consistent, and for that reason, the benefits of persistent objection are often outweighed by the benefits of compliance.[59] Moreover, some norms are themselves exempt from the persistent objector argument; laws or norms that are deemed to be 'jus cogens'[60]; '*Jus cogens* are a vague subset of norms deemed by the international community to be so important that absolutely no derogation from them will be tolerated'.[61] Therefore, the ability for a state to use the persistent objector rule as a means to challenge international order is limited and may only be useful over a period of time, whilst also applying other means to produce a challenge.

Another avenue for states to use international law to frustrate the formation of new norms is to put discussions (particularly within the Security Council) on an ad hoc footing, whereby decisions are 'exceptional' rather than precedent forming.[62] As such, they prevent the evolution of international law in a normal way and thwart the consolidation of norms.[63] However, like the persistent objector method, this is not a long-term plan for moulding the norms of international order, but it does potentially provide states with a means to 'pause' progress of certain norms along the life cycle.

The other actor-oriented means of challenge is norm entrepreneurship. A norm entrepreneur is a state, group or individual that actively promotes a specific interpretation of a norm. They can do this through a number of methods (outlined below), but they must seek to gather together supporters in increasing numbers, and offer a viable alternative to a norm that already exists or a solution to a new issue or problem. A central issue with norm entrepreneurship is capacity. As state not only needs the internal capacity to formulate a new idea, but also needs the diplomatic capacity and connections to persuade and convince other states.

These three actor-centred forces act to either stop or propel the progress of norms, and it is possible that both objectors and norm entrepreneurs can be active around the same norm at the same time. Similarly, a single actor may be both an objector and entrepreneur for different norms at different times, seeking to get their interpretation of international order accepted by other actors. In fact, some of the most effective norm entrepreneurs may also be persistent objectors, because in objecting to an emerging norm they create 'space' to debate that norm and thus create an opportunity to champion their own position.

Agents may have considerable latitude and ability to act within the current system in order to challenge norms. However, the limitations of action within the current order must also be highlighted, as it has an impact on the tools available. As noted above, the current network of state engagements is social and governed by law; therefore, states are compelled to structure their actions for change within a discursive and legal frame.[64] Actors, therefore, seek to internalise norms and laws both horizontally among the state representatives (groups of diplomats and state leaders) and vertically through their own societies and populations.[65] Within this legal framework, this is achieved largely through the discussion and interpretation of laws, through the power of arguments.[66] Consequently, any attempt to challenge these internalised norms and laws must firstly discredit or delegitimise a current interpretation, or create a perception that it was interpreted on the basis of a bad argument, and that a new interpretation is founded on a better argument.[67]

The result of this is that, although there is considerable scope for agents to either push or halt norms to challenge the dominant perception of international order, their attempts to do so must make reference to the order itself. That is, agents must recognise appropriate and legitimate paths of action to challenge, which are dictated or directed by some elements of order; hence, in order for a state to use their power within a legal order, they must accept limits on how they can use that power legitimately.[68] Namely, if a state wishes to use power within a social order, they must accept that war as a means for change is illegitimate. Similarly, if they wish to produce change from outside an order, attempts to change rules that they are not bound by are not a legitimate option. In the current order, these pathways are through discussion and debate, within recognised forums between actors with authority to speak and be heard. In recognising the role of these forums, we can now turn our discussion to the tools agents can use to get their interpretation accepted by the necessary 1/3 of states.

Tools for Challenging International Norms (Identifying Material Causes)

This section presents the tools that can aid the process of interpretation or reinterpretation of international inter-subjective norms. In the subsequent parts, situations and conditions that facilitate these tools will also be discussed. Each element of these discussions explicates how each tool is presented if used for objection or entrepreneurship. Whether these possible mechanisms are seen to be used by China will be discovered in the empirical chapters. The conclusion will then evaluate which tools and forms of agency can be attributed to China.

Reframing Existing Debates

Persistent objection, ad hoc objection and norm entrepreneurship can all be used to challenge international norms through the reframing of debates, although the actual shape of that reframing will be different with the different forms of state agency.

'The construction of cognitive frames is an essential component of norm entrepreneurs' political strategies, since when they are successful the new frames resonate with broader public understandings and are adopted as new ways of talking about and understanding issues'.[69] Norms limit the range of acceptable responses to different situations. 'The realm of *conceivable* behaviour in a given social structure is normatively determined and it is not as wide as the realm of behaviour that is physically possible'.[70] For this reason, norm entrepreneurs derive huge benefits when creating new norms from being able to frame new ideas in the context of existing norms, because these norms already have legitimacy and resonance among the social group. An ability to draw on existing norms or demonstrate the limitations of existing norms can therefore be utilised by entrepreneurs. Furthermore, by seeking to adapt existing norms through discourse, norm entrepreneurs are actively seeking to change the 'cognitive roadmap that facilitates the interpretation of norms'.[71] This type of normative challenge allows for changes to the meaning, or understanding, or practice of existing norms without explicit contestation. This idea is what Dworkin calls the 'interpretive attitude',[72] whereby over time a supposedly common understanding has developed, but because of a new situation, competing understandings become evident.

A key question for this mechanism is therefore where these debates take place. What is the significance of the status of the place of discussion? If an entrepreneur is seeking to reframe a norm and get it accepted by a social grouping, what is the method of compliance or understanding attached to the norm? Understanding why states comply with an existing norm helps in understanding whether it is likely to be easily changed; as well as how a state may gain compliance from others for the new interpretation.

From the discussion above, there appear to be three possibilities for compliance: coercion (negative constraints), appeal to the self-interest of actors, or to be seen as a legitimate understanding of a norm (positive constraints).[73]

In looking at a new norm from the perspective of compliance, it is clear that coercion without authority is likely to produce resentment as well as high costs to the entrepreneur. Appealing to self-interest is a key to gaining voluntary compliance by other actors; if other actors can see the benefits and reduced costs of new norms, their compliance and acceptance of new norms is more likely. Norm entrepreneurs thus need the ability to reframe an existing norm in a way that satisfies the self-interest of either a greater number of actors or a different group of actors that have not had their self-interest satisfied by the current understanding of the norm.

In order to use legitimacy effectively as a tool, it is important for norm entrepreneurs to engage in a process of delegitimising existing norms by creating an 'actual or potential disparity between the two value systems'.[74] That is, they must change the perceptions of actors to see contradictions between the existing norm and the social context which it references, and encourage them to withdraw their consent to, and compliance with, that norm. It is important that legitimacy may also be a facilitating condition (outside the agency of states) as well as an actively used tool of states.

One potential method of doing this is to use legitimate institutions as a reference point for legitimate action—as using already established institutions gives the debate of norms a semblance of legitimacy. Institutions that are seen as legitimate forums for debate give entrepreneurs a platform and an audience for their ideas.[75]

A further method to promote new norms is to be able to relate them back to previous understandings or meanings of the current norms and outline how the current norms are actually invalid because of a lack of congruence to the original idea. This can be achieved in two ways: first, 'ambitious innovators may well cloak their efforts for change in appeals to restore traditions'[76]; second, 'political challengers may mobilize by deploying familiar models of social organization in unfamiliar ways'.[77]

Thus, in order to use reframing as a tool, a norm entrepreneur must clearly set out an alternative. In achieving this, there should be a clear chain of evidence displayed across three different forms of evidence. First, the documents of international institutions should contain indications that a particular state has proposed a reinterpretation. Second, there should be evidence from elite interviews that a state attempted to persuade others to comply with a reinterpretation. Third, there should be evidence of the emergence of a new norm within the state that proposed it. As a result, there should be an abundance of evidence demonstrating a state's role.

Reinterpretation can also be a tool of a persistent objector or an ad hoc objector. However, it is most likely that 'persistent objector' or 'ad hoc objectors' are used to stymie the progress of a new interpretation by other states. Thus, it would be expected that as a potential new norm emerges a state acting as a persistent objector would consistently object to the new norm or the new interpretation of the norm from the first attempted use. It is much more likely, however, that ad hoc objection to a particular interpretation of a norm is likely to be shown. This is when an attempt is made to use a norm, for example in the case of liberal interventionism to allow for coercive intervention rather than peacekeeping with consent—a state objects to the particular application of the norm, rather than objecting to the norm itself. As a result, because a norm cannot generate a pattern of consistent use, or cannot be applied consistently over a period of time, it has to be reconsidered in order to attempt to gain greater support and therefore use. In looking back to the section on norms internalisation and acceptance, this is where it is important for norms to be supported by all of the P5.

In cases of persistent objection, the evidence should be shown in the documents of international institutions that a state has objected to a particular norm ever since the norm's emergence. It should also be supported by elite interviews that suggest 'it is common knowledge that state X objects to norm A'; there should be a taken-for-granted quality to this objection.

In the case of ad hoc objection, there should also be objection only after a norm has achieved some acceptance by the state concerned. In addition, the evidence available may vary from case to case. There must be an uncertainty before decisions are made as to what the position of state X is, and there would also be an apparent inconsistency in the behaviour of state X around a particular issue. Thus, ad hoc objector's contribution to a challenge to international norms is difficult to prove. However, it is possible to identify whether there is inconsistency in the position of the state. Accordingly, it ought to be possible to collect together a few different instances and compare the justifications for the actions of state X. In addition, it should be evident in the debates, discussions and elite interviews, whether there have been consistent attempts to persuade state X of a particular interpretation of a norm, or whether there have been attempts to achieve the compliance of state X through some adaptation of a norm.

It is important to note that ad hoc objection and persistent objection may be means to ensure an older interpretation of a norm prevails—or continues to be applied. This may then bear some resemblance to norm entrepreneurship. Or it may be a precursor to norm entrepreneurship (it may be necessary to prevent an emerging dominant interpretation of norm in order to make entrepreneurship more likely to succeed).

New Issues

New issues can be seen as a useful tool for norm entrepreneurship. This is because new issues create a new context (or sub-context) in which norms may develop. New issues bring new problems, present new types of information and present the possibilities for actors to think outside the schema. Norms 'make uniform behavioural claims upon dissimilar actors'.[78] New situations give dissimilar actors the opportunity to apply different understandings or interpretations to the same situational or material facts—presenting an opportunity for the development of new norms. In the process of this development and the need (noted earlier) for congruence between norms, it is possible for '…a given set of roles and norms to become obsolete. This sets up "disharmonies and disturbances"'.[79] These disharmonies and disturbances either allow for reintegration of actors into a slightly modified selection of norms or allow for 'norm entrepreneurs' to emerge. These entrepreneurs then have a greater chance of creating and getting new norms adopted. Included in this method of creating change also has to be new common knowledge, because '[t]he creation of new common knowledge alters socially agreed facts about the character … and the consequent motivations of the bargaining parties'.[80] Thus, new knowledge and information can have a similar role to new issues in changing norms.

New issues, therefore, provide the possibilities for new norms to emerge or to reframe/evaluate/reinterpret existing norms; however, they also offer the possibility for current norms to be adapted rather than changed.[81] In terms of success, it is possible that norm entrepreneurs can be most successful in using new issues to create new norms, as this does not necessarily necessitate competition with existing norms but rather offers a level playing field between 'new' norms.[82] Therefore, this is potentially the path of least resistance for new norms as other options will not be further along the scale of acceptance, nor will they be positioned higher in the hierarchy of norms. However, the obvious limitation on the use of this method for creating new norms is that there are not new issues emerging every day, every month or every year. Furthermore, new issues can rarely be predicted or accurately controlled[83] by actors within the order. Whilst this may be the most desirable tool for a state seeking to be a norm entrepreneur in terms of probability of achieving an advantageous outcome, it is not a tool that can be easily controlled or predicted.

In terms of evidence, new issues are likely to be at the centre of a contest between norm entrepreneurs. The important element in identifying the causation of a particular norm entrepreneur is a clear identification of the heritage of the idea. Thus, it is important to identify debates within countries, when they originated, and where possible the interactions between norm entrepreneurs utilising the same new issue.

Although potentially most useful as a tool for a norm entrepreneur, new issues may also be a useful tool for the persistent objector, in attempting to prevent a changing context and the emergence of a new norm. Thus, an objector may use a new issue to reassert a particular context or understanding—by tying a new issue to existing practices or understandings. Or they may seek to prevent the emergence of a particular contextual understanding—they may persistently object to the norm or to the understanding of issues as 'new'. New issues present a clear opportunity for the persistent objector. In this case, it is necessary to trace the objection of a state from the invocation of a 'new' issue. This objection must be consistent. This may provide the simplest identification of the agency of China as a final or efficient cause of a challenge to norms; since as a P5 power, and a rising power, China is in a unique position to fulfil the role of a persistent objector. However, it should be recalled that persistent objectors status may be easy to identify, but it is difficult for a state to achieve.

New Populations
As noted in the discussion of norms (above), in order to reach the tipping point, norms need both the support of the P5 powers and the acceptance of 1/3 of all states. 'Populations' of states, particularly large populations of states that achieve the quota of 1/3 of states, may be essential in a norm entrepreneur being successful or in an objector successfully stymieing a norm's progress.

Norms exist at all levels of societies. Societies are already organised through the use of norms and are therefore more likely to accept new norms so long as they do not conflict with the norms they already hold.[84] These populations may also be seen as 'interpretive communities',[85] where common interpretations of laws and norms are held by a particular group. As noted earlier, institutions are 'coalitions of coalitions',[86] and therefore, exploiting the differences between these coalitions can produce clear communities within institutions.[87] By creating a new 'community', it is therefore possible to give a new or different interpretation of a norm's legitimacy by being able to appeal to the consensus of a body greater than the state.

The size of the population or the social group is important in the creation of new norms. As already noted, norms can be used to bring actors with similar agendas or common goals or values together. Therefore, in seeking to get norms accepted, it makes sense to start within a small group who hold similar values, either to the entrepreneur or to the norm. New norms therefore need to 'fit' and be consistent with other existing norms in the social group.[88] By starting with smaller groups with higher correlation between the types of actors, it increases the chance that the new norm will 'fit' and be adopted. Being able to demonstrate an effective role for a new norm within this smaller grouping gives it greater credibility in being accepted by a larger group: it already has a point of reference for legitimacy, a reference point for achieving self-interested aims, and has tools for coercion to achieve compliance.[89] This idea draws on the work of Amitav Acharya[90] who looked at the top-down approach to norm diffusion; his study looked at how norms from the international level can be transferred to institutions at a regional (or sub-global) level. The idea here is that this flow of norms is bidirectional and that norms accepted at a regional level stand a greater chance of being adopted at the international level for the same reasons.

Populations can be used to amplify the agency of both objectors (persistent or ad hoc) and entrepreneurs. In both cases, the aims are the same: to link the position of the state to a group of like-minded states within an existing institution. However, in entrepreneurship it would be expected that the entrepreneur deliberately and with a cognisant mind tries to persuade other states of their position and preferences. Thus, it should be obvious in the documents and interviews that a particular state attempted to gain support from other states.

In objection, it is less important for a state to try and persuade other states—this may be the case—but it is not essential. The benefit to an objector is that by adopting a position that is similar to other states their objection is perceived to be more legitimate. Furthermore, their objection is amplified by the connection to other states. However, this adds a complication to identifying the agency of a particular state in objecting and whether it was that particular state that was essential in challenging the norm or whether it was other states. The agency of a particular state can then potentially be identified with elite interviews, in addition to documentary evidence that they have objected. The question then arises as to the position of the state in question and requires a fuller discussion of the other states' involvement. There is a need to assess what the nature of the challenge of the group is, where objection seemed to start, and what power a state needs to have to present a challenge that can endure. In the case studies, this approach is used in Part III on development and in the discussion of the Responsibility to Protect. In neither case is it claimed that China has persuaded other states, but that China is important in the expression of a challenge achieving 'critical mass' that carries weight and significance internationally. Thus, it is for this reason that a thick narrative approach was adopted in the methodology, as this method allows for the most appropriate way to identify the actors and the interactions that produce the presentation of a challenge to international order.

New Institutions
This is related to 'populations', but it takes the idea one stage further by formalising the creation of a specific group of states; this makes a particular group of states preferred norms more internationally competitive whilst they are seeking to gain greater international acceptance.[91] Yet, new institutions are clearly a tool used by norm entrepreneurs. In trying to get new norms adopted states can look for the least hostile environment for them to grow and evolve. If regional institutions already have a high density of normative practices, whilst the population of states may be comparatively low, the population of competing norms is still high,[92] and therefore, the chance of a norm being adopted remains low. One solution to this problem is therefore to create new institutions, whereby a small group of like-minded states come together based around a small group of these new norms, giving the new norms (or new interpretations of norms) institutional form and coherence. As such, these smaller groupings offer a testing ground for new norms or new interpretations. These states then need to make their new institution appealing to other states so that they want to be part of its membership and thus spread the pool of compliance to other states. Similarly, if an institutional form (or the norms expressed within it) is perceived to be 'successful', they may be 'mimicked' by other institutions.[93] This mimicking creates a reputation for the institutions but also the sponsoring actor. By growing as an institution and deriving legitimacy from the recognition of the importance of this institution by other states, the new norms associated with it also gain legitimacy. Thus, they become a part of the 'norm pool'[94] in international relations.

In order to create a new institution, there must be a perceived need for a new institution; by creating a new institution that has a significant overlap with existing institutions, an actor may have created its own competition for the spread of that interpretation of norms.[95] The aim of the entrepreneur must be to seek a route for acceptance of new norms through the path of least resistance. Therefore, new institutions may seek to use new issue areas (outlined above), or create new collections of actors focused on specific tasks, or utilise a new approach in multilateralism.

In summation, changing populations of norms and new institutions can produce smaller testing grounds for new norms, give actors a voice, develop reputations, increase soft power and, most importantly, give a new norm the legitimacy provided by the acceptance of other international actors. All of these things, therefore, increase the chances of acceptance within the broader international arena.

New institutions are mostly used as tools by norm entrepreneurs. A norm entrepreneur could seek to get new norms accepted by a small group of like-minded states and then spread the norm to other states.

Facilitating Normative Change (Identifying Formal Causes)

A vital element in understanding a normative challenge is in understanding the context. Indeed, in the discussion of causation and in actually looking to provide a causal description to explain challenges, one element of causation is the need to explore the context of interactions.[96]

In identifying the causes of a challenge to existing or emerging norms, there is a need to separate out any other factors that may be the cause of a challenge or may facilitate a challenge. In the causal descriptive method being used in this project, it is therefore necessary to highlight how the context may be a contributing cause to any challenge. The causal description is incomplete without the formal cause.

In addition to using the tools of challenges and forms of state agency, there are four main elements that can facilitate normative change: changing balance of power within international order (changing the descriptive relative positions of states); external shocks that delegitimise norms; failure of existing norms; and changing perceptions of legitimacy and legitimate action. This section discusses how each of these changes to the context in which norms exist can facilitate changes to those norms.

Legitimacy and Legitimate Action

Legitimacy and legitimate action can be seen as tools of reinterpretation (as noted above). However, they can also be contextually (rather than actor) driven. As a result, legitimacy and legitimate action must also be considered in their role in facilitating normative challenges.

Legitimacy can be seen as the exercise of power within accepted rules and norms.[97] If a state's action is seen as legitimate, actors can reduce costs incurred in the exercise of their power to achieve certain ends. Clearly, an ability to change the rules and norms that guide state's behaviour and make actions legitimate enhances a state's power by allowing that state greater freedom of action.[98] By increasing its hard power, legitimacy and freedom of action, a state can solidify its position as a great power in the world and shape international order. Furthermore, according to Hurrell, '[c]ontrol over the membership norms of international society and the capacity to delegitimize certain sorts of players through the deployment of these norms represents a very important category of power'.[99] Therefore, the ability to manipulate norms and legitimacy contributes to a state's relative power.

Thomas Franck terms legitimacy as 'the capacity of a rule to pull those to whom it is addressed toward consensual compliance'.[100] Taking this definition together with Parsons' definition of the 'appraisal of action in terms of shared or common values in the context of involvement of the action in the social system',[101] legitimacy simply defined is that actions conform to or make reference to rules and practices agreed by the group within which action takes place, or is affected by the action. Legitimacy then is a central part of the story of recognition and authority, and the ability to shape the context in which others exist—and thus shaping the normative world of international order.

Legitimacy is dependent on acceptance by actors within a group; for an act to be seen as legitimate, actors must first recognise certain rules that an action abides by as legitimate and then recognise specific actions in relation to those rules as legitimate. This process works through a social process of a collective understanding of rules and applying a common meaning to those rules. Legitimation is therefore a continuous process,[102] and norms and rules can change from being legitimate to being non-legitimate, based on the interpretation of a norm that is socially held within a group. If the interpretation of a norm changes within a group, then this reinterpretation may necessitate the reappraisal of actions or practices as legitimate or illegitimate with reference to the new interpretation. As a result, practices and actions may change from being legitimate to being illegitimate or vice versa. For example, the norm of empire, and subjugating different cultures, was delegitimised by the norm of self-determination, and correspondingly the political offices and activities related to imperial expansion became illegitimate but also irrelevant.

This, therefore, presents a method of changing norms within the social construction of international order. By challenging what states consider to be legitimate, it is possible to change the interests of other states. This is because, '[c]onceptions of legitimacy are formed ... through interaction with other states in international society, and they shape the interests and identities of the states'.[103] Therefore, by seeking to change the status of a norm as being legitimate and by changing the collective understanding of the group they thereby delegitimise an existing norm and legitimise a new norm. Seeking to produce a stable order based around norms that are seen to be legitimate has two major benefits for the architect: first, it reduces the costs of compliance; second, it makes the order more likely to endure beyond the decline of the architect.[104]

Legitimacy and the need for legitimating a state's action can enable or disable a state's ability to act. As noted above, norms are contextual, socially constructed and inter-subjective. As a result, challenging norms requires an actor to act within the scope of others' interpretation of those norms; as such, an actor must bind themselves—to a degree—to act within both the processes and institutions or an international order, as well as bind themselves to the acceptance of the power of norms. Consequently, this limits the degree of change an actor can produce; however, a successful state/actor may also be empowered by such binding.

Changing Balance of Power
Norms derive meaning and application from specification within a given context. The current context is characterised by asymmetric equality. That is, that states are recognised as equal in their sovereignty. However, within the institutions of order, the ability to produce changes to the patterns of behaviour, actions and norms, is located in a small group of states: the great powers. In order to change the norms of international order, despite the theoretical possibility that it could be achieved by a collection of small and relatively weak states, in reality power still matters. Changes to the balance of power that underpins the current order and maintains some interpretations of the norms of that order open space for a great power to create disequilibrium (necessary for change according to Gilpin)[105] within the order and utilise this space to produce normative change.

Changing the Balance of Power Between Individual States

The most obvious changes to the balance of power in international order are the emergence of new great powers. New powers may rise into an existing order and externally challenge that order (through conflict), and this is the most obvious way international orders change as a result of a changing balance of power.[106] As highlighted in Chapter 2, it is because of China's changing status in relation to other powers that it is possible for China to provoke changes to international order. However, 'challenge' does not have to occur through violence and war even if a rising power is a 'dissatisfied' power.[107]

The challenge of rising powers to international order is a central theme of this book, and therefore, all of the mechanisms in this chapter may be affected by them; however, there are two notable elements that should be considered here. Firstly, rising powers change the membership of international order; secondly, they change the knowledge of 'what is possible'.

In changing the membership of international order, rising powers change the context and the population that discusses and contests norms. Rising powers' ability to shape which states support norms is vital. Finnemore and Sikkink note that it is necessary for a norm to gain the support of 1/3 of all states for it to 'cascade'.[108] Recalling that some states are more important to this process than others, changing relative power balances changes who matters for a norm to cascade (or be prevented from cascading) and the nature of the challenge a norm faces.

The nature of the challenge to a norm's existence, according to Ian Davison, is a significant part of a norm's creation and maintenance. Norms thrive or perish with respect to challenges or opportunities, 'once the challenge has been met, the new values that proved successful tend to decay unless there is a continuing challenge'.[109] In terms of the current international order, the impact of challenges on norms is becoming evident. The changing balance of power since the end of the Cold War has led to the perception of the cascade of liberal norms, as they have already achieved the required number of states to produce a norm cascade and therefore count as international norms.[110] However, in reality, these norms have not achieved enough support to be considered international norms. Instead, they may be characterised as being caught in the delicate stage between the tipping point and the cascade; it may be the case that the absence of contest actually acts to prevent cascade rather than encouraging it.[111] During this phase of the norm's life cycle, it is open to challenge and it is particularly vulnerable to scrutiny (this is what Checkel calls 'policy windows').[112] In the current order, the most significant challenge to these norms is coming from the rising China[113]: its fervent belief in the protection of the sovereignty of states and its alternative development model.[114]

Changing the balance of power also changes the knowledge and experiences around which collectively held understandings are formed: new experiences can prompt re-evaluation of these collectively held understandings and their derivative norms.[115] Within the construction of liberal international order, there is a dominance of experiences and thinking from western rationalism; China—as noted in previous chapters—brings different knowledge and experiences into the collective realm and thus may be seen to prompt reinterpretations of norms and thus change the normative content of international order. One significant feature of changing norms is the need for there to be difference between the internal characteristics, ideology, experiences or capabilities of states.[116] If states merely copy the behaviours of others, then no new norms will emerge except through the mutation that occurs when the next generation misunderstand what has gone before. Nevertheless, states that are fundamentally different from others have the opportunity to create new norms.[117]

Changing Balance of Power Between Regions

In Chapter 3, one of the dynamics of the current order that was outlined was a change in the 'core' of states who determine action in international affairs; shifting balances of power between regions have the potential to affect which groups of states form the 'core' in determining the interpretation of international norms. This 'core', or 'the inner circle'[118] as Johnstone calls it, 'consists of all the individuals directly or indirectly responsible for the formulation, negotiation, conclusion, implementation and application of a particular legal norm'.[119] During the Cold War and in the 1990s, western states had the benefit of a preponderance of power and thus were able to set out a particular 'logic of appropriateness'[120]: which constructed a liberal international order.

Yet, the distinction between the core and periphery—because they too are social constructs—is not fixed. Thus, one facilitating condition for normative change may be a shifting balance of power away from the western core towards an Asian core; that is then able to reinterpret international norms.

In utilising this facilitating condition, there are some necessary characteristics; according to Goetz and Diehl, using groups or utilising the potential shifting balance of power happens 'from the bottom up. Often small groups are the initial supporters; these norms then spread to other groups and then to society as a whole'.[121] As such, this facilitating condition goes hand in hand with the mechanisms of creating new populations and new institutions. To be effective, it needs to operate on two levels, one of which is structural (positional)—breaking up an existing 'core'; the other agential and normative—bringing together new actors to create an alternative.

This tool for facilitating normative change is especially important if the balance of power is shifting in favour of Asian states. It is crucially important as a facilitating factor if China attempts to use a population including Asian states in presenting a challenge to international order.

External Shocks
External shocks to a normative order also facilitate change. These external factors can either challenge a single element of international order or challenge the legitimacy of individual actors or institutions. For example, the standard of civilisation and the norm of empire were challenged in the wake of World War II, resulting in the emergence of a new normative frame of self-determination. Or the financial crisis can be seen as an external shock to the legitimacy of the USA as a guardian of the international financial system; similarly, the Asian Financial Crisis challenged the legitimacy of the International Monetary Fund and the World Bank. These external shocks are not within a state's control; nevertheless, they shape the context in which states interact with each other, and as such function to legitimise and delegitimise different approaches or actions.

Failure of Previous Norms
One of the best opportunities for new norms to be adopted is when previous norms have failed or proved inadequate.[121] According to Florini, this failure must be to the extent that: 'clear failure of the behavioral norms of the previous "generation" to the extent that the previous way of doing things becomes virtually impossible'.[123] Barkin and Cronin suggest that such failure is most clearly demonstrated at the conclusion of wars because new constitutions for international order emerge as a consequence of the failure of the norms of the previous order.[124]

This is necessary because the war was a symbol of the failure of previous norms to cope with new situations; conflict emerged because existing structures could not deal with adequately (or could nor draw on the existing norms) to promote unity between actors.

In looking at commonly held knowledge or interpretations of events, Culpepper sees the process of institutional change as being 'usefully divided into three distinct stages: crisis, experimentation, and consolidation'.[125] In this staging, he helpfully links the relationship between the failure of an existing norm and the arrival of new information or issues that force a reappraisal of existing practices or the relevance of existing norms. As such, we can see that demonstrating the failure of existing norms can be an enormous benefit in producing new norms. It can also be a significant barrier to the creation of norms. Nonetheless, because the hurdle for demonstrating the failure of a norm is so high, presenting and convincing others of the failure is difficult. Moreover, as already noted, there is a limit to the degree of control that an agent can have over the process. Furthermore, as Culpepper also notes, even in the aftermath of a 'crisis', it is difficult to persuade other actors to move from a stable situation to the experimental stage.[126] However, new events that happen to correlate to and confirm a norm entrepreneur's views will enhance the power of persuasion of the entrepreneur.[127]

Analysing China's Challenge to International Order

This discussion of normative change then allows for a meaningful exploration of China's engagement with international norms, and in particular its engagement with liberal international norms. China's rise changes the context in which norms are understood: it changes the material structure, the knowledge of the actors involved in normative debates, it changes the populations and the actors involved. China's rise is occurring at a time when other factors facilitating normative change are also present, for example: the declining perceived legitimacy of the USA; the external shock of the financial crisis; and the corresponding delegitimisation of the 'knowledge' associated with liberal economics.

China, having been on the outside of the construction of international order in 1945 and largely absent from significant discussions and engagement in the early 1990s, has the ability to challenge the knowledge and the experiences from which liberal norms emerged and through this China can present a challenge to them. In particular, this is possible because of China's different road to modernity.[128] Even Russia—although it was a revolutionary and communist power and therefore had a clear agenda to change the international order—still played by the same rule book as its adversaries and within the frameworks created in the West. Even a brief cursory glance at China's history demonstrates the newness of concepts such as sovereignty and rule of law.[129] As such, there is—ostensibly—the potential for China to be positioned to facilitate normative challenge.

The remaining question is that of whether China can be a norm entrepreneur or persistent (or ad hoc) objector. China's engagement and its ability to act as an agent will form a central element of the discussion of the coming chapters. How China applies the tools, or how its rise facilitates changes in international order, will also be highlighted.

The empirical analysis of this book goes on to explore China's international engagement to see if it can be seen as using any of these tools; because of the central role of institutions in providing a forum, rules and a history of interpretation, the focus of this project will be on China's interaction within institutions (both those that it has created and those that it participates in). There will also be a focus on the tools which allow the greatest role for agency. The focus on actor-driven processes allows for a clear determination of whether international order is challenging by happenstance or deliberative action by China. If China cannot clearly be seen to use these tools to create challenges, it generates grave doubt that China has any sort of revisionist tendencies towards liberal order. This process of challenge is not short term; it can take many years and may utilise a mixture of some or all of these mechanisms. Application of a single mechanism may produce change in a specific area but will not be successful in achieving changes to the normative structure of an order.[130]

Conclusion

This chapter is crucial in the presentation of the argument about how China challenges norms and international order. It has established what norms are and how norms link together. In doing this, it separated out the importance of interstitial and 'meta'-norms. It indicates that it is possible for a state to challenge international order by challenging interstitial norms, which then prompts a re-evaluation of the interpretation of meta-norms which characterise international order. These interstitial norms can be challenged either through a state acting as an entrepreneur or as an objector. States can become more effective entrepreneurs or objectors by using one or a selection of tools. These tools then give some specific outlines as to what evidence would be expected in each case if a state was acting as an entrepreneur or an objector through the use of these tools. Thus, these tools provide some key indicators for what should be looked for in the empirical chapters in seeking to identify how China challenges liberal norms of international order.

Finally, this chapter sets out conditions that facilitate the emergence of a challenge to international norms. The aim to these conditions is not to complicate the framework of this research, but rather to indicate that reality is complicated. As noted in the Methodology, it is necessary to identify the role that context plays in causation. As a result, this helps to separate out what liberal norms are challenged by China, and what conditions facilitate the challenge to liberal norms, thus reducing the degree of agency necessary for any state to exhibit in order for a challenge to be seen. Thus, understanding facilitating conditions helps to identify where China is the cause.

Thus, this discussion forms a bridge between the methodology and the previous exegesis of international order, and the empirical parts. This chapter sets out what evidence would be expected to be seen if China was the cause of a challenge to international order by using any of these tools as either an objector or an entrepreneur. The next two parts of the book explore China within the Security Council, looking at whether China challenges the interpretation of sovereignty through debates on the authorisation of peacekeeping missions and the Responsibility to Protect.

Notes

1. Norm entrepreneurs—advocate new norms or new interpretations of norms.
2. Persistent Objectors—states that object to a particular interpretation of a norm from its emergence.
3. Ad hoc Objectors—states that object to the application of a norm on an ad hoc basis preventing the emergence of a pattern of applications of the norm and therefore the emergence of precedents for the use of the norm.
4. The construction of these schemas not only presents patterns of behaviour to be followed in the future but also limits the ability to perceive different choices. Elisabeth S. Clemens and James M. Cook, 'Politics and Institutionalism: Explaining Durability and Change', *Annual Review of Sociology* (1999), 25, pp. 441–466, p. 458.

5. See Chapter 3.
6. The book, is not therefore, centrally concerned with institutional change. For detailed expositions of institutional change see: Adrienne Heritier, 'Theories of Institutional Change', in Adrienne Heritier (eds), *Explaining Institutional Change in Europe* (Oxford University Press: Oxford, 2007), pp. 6–67; James Mahoney and Kathleen Thelen (eds), *Explaining Institutional Change: Ambiguity, Agency and Power* (Cambridge University Press: Cambridge, 2009).
7. Ramesh Thakur (2011), The United Nations in Global Governance: Rebalancing Multilateralism for Current and Future Challenges' paper presented at UN General Assembly 65th Session Thematic Debate on the United Nations and Global Governance, available http://www.un.org/en/ga/president/65/initiatives/GlobalGovernance/Thakur_GA_Thematic_Debate_on_UN_in_GG.pdf, accessed 19 July 2012.
8. Robert Axelrod, 'An Evolutionary Approach to Norms', *The American Political Science Review* (1986), 80(4), pp. 1095–1111, p. 1097.
9. Martha Finnemore, *National Interests in International Society* (Cornell University Press: Ithaca, 1996), p. 22.
10. Gary Goertz and Paul F. Diehl, 'Toward a Theory of International Norms: Some Conceptual and Measurement Issues', *The Journal of Conflict Resolution* (1992), 36(4), pp. 634–664; Axelrod, 'An Evolutionary Approach to Norms', p. 1097.
11. Sheri Berman, 'Ideas, Norms, and Culture in Political Analysis', *Comparative Politics* (2001), 33(2), pp. 231–250, p. 233; Ann Florini, 'The Evolution of International Norms', *International Studies Quarterly* (1996), 40(3), pp. 363–389, p. 366.
12. Axelrod, 'An Evolutionary Approach to Norms', p. 1097.
13. Vaughan P. Shannon, 'Norms Are What States Make of Them: The Political Psychology of Norm Violation', *International Studies Quarterly* (2000), 44(2), pp. 293–316, p. 295.
14. This relates back to the recognition of states by others in Chapter 3.
15. Martha Finnemore, *National Interests in International Society* (Cornell University Press: Ithaca, 1996), p. 22.
16. Simon Reich, *Global Norms, American Sponsorship and the Emerging Patterns of World Politics* (Palgrave Macmillan: Basingstoke, 2010), p. 15.
17. Clemens and Cook, 'Politics and Institutionalism', p. 445.
18. Kate O'Neill, Jörg Balsiger, and Stacy D. Van Deveer, 'Actors, Norms, and Impact: Recent International Influence of the Agent-Structure Debate', *Annual Review of Political Science* (2004), 7, pp. 149–175, p. 160.
19. J. Samuel Barkin and Bruce Cronin, 'The State and the Nation: Changing Norms and the Rules of Sovereignty in International Relations', *International Organization* (1994), 48(1), pp. 107–130, p. 128.

20. Berman, 'Ideas, Norms, and Culture in Political Analysis', p. 233; Shannon, 'Norms Are What States Make of Them', p. 294.
21. Berman, 'Ideas, Norms, and Culture', p. 235.
22. Shannon, 'Norms Are What States Make of Them', p. 302.
23. Antje Weiner, 'Contested Compliance: Interventions on the Normative Structure of World Politics', *European Journal of International Relations* (2004), 10(2), pp. 189–234, p. 190.
24. Vaughan Lowe, 'Chapter 10: The Politics of Law-Making: Are the Methods and Character of Norm Evolution Changing?', in Michael Byers (ed.), *The Role of Law in International Politics: Essays in International Relations and International Law* (Oxford University Press: Oxford, 2000), pp. 207–227, p. 212.
25. Ibid., pp. 212–13.
26. "The stability of a system of sovereign states rests on the adherence by most of the states to a set of rules and common practices" Barkin and Cronin, 'The State and the Nation', p. 128.
27. Martha Finnemore, 'Norms, Culture, and World Politics: Insights from Sociology's Institutionalism', *International Organization* (1996), 50(2), pp. 325–347, p. 326.
28. Clemens and Cook, 'Politics and Institutionalism', pp. 450–453.
29. A.D. Smith, *The Concept of Social Change: A Critique of the Functionalist Theory of Social Change* (Routledge and Kegan Paul: London and Boston, 1973), pp. 13–14.
30. Extension of the idea of linkages in Arthur A. Stein, 'The Politics of Linkage', *World Politics* (1980), 33(1), pp. 62–81.
31. Discussed by Lindner as on-path and off-path institutional changes, Lindner, 'Institutional Stability and Change', p. 916; also, seen as the creation of cognitive patterns in, Giovanni Dosi, Luigi Marengo, Andrea Bassanini, and Marco Valente, 'Norms as Emergent Properties of Adaptive Learning: The Case of Economic Routines', *Journal of Evolutionary Economics* (1999), 9, pp. 5–26, p. 24; also seen in the bounding nature of institutions see Geoffrey M. Hodgson, 'Institutions and Individuals: Interaction and Evolution', *Organisational Studies* (2007), 28(1), pp. 95–116, p. 110.
32. Finnemore, *National Interests in International Society*, p. 5; E. Haas, *The Uniting of Europe: Political, Social and Economic Forces 1950–1957* (Stanford University Press: Stanford, 1968), p. 14.
33. See this chapter.
34. Goertz and Diehl, 'Toward a Theory of International Norms'; Axelrod, 'An Evolutionary Approach to Norms', p. 1097.
35. Martha Finnemore and Kathryn Sikkink, 'International Norm Dynamics and Political Change', *International Organization* (1998), 52(4), pp. 887–917.

36. Ibid., pp. 896–897.
37. Ibid., p. 896.
38. The idea of norms as existing on a scale and having movement in both directions on that scale is first seen in Axelrod, 'An Evolutionary Approach to Norms', p. 1097.
39. Ibid., p. 1096.
40. Ibid., p. 1098.
41. This idea draws on the logical of organisational legitimacy in John Dowling and Jeffrey Pfeffer, 'Organizational Legitimacy: Social Values and Organizational Behavior', *The Pacific Sociological Review* (1975), 18(1), pp. 122–136.
42. Finnemore and Sikkink, 'International Norm Dynamics and Political Change', p. 901.
43. Finnemore and Sikkink acknowledge that some states are more important in a norming getting to the tipping point in their discussion of 'critical states'. Although they suggest these may change for each norm. Ibid., p. 901.
44. Barkin and Cronin, 'The State and the Nation', p. 107.
45. Ibid., p. 219.
46. Ibid., p. 220.
47. Axelrod, 'An Evolutionary Approach to Norms'.
48. See Jane Elliott, *Using Narrative in Social Research: Qualitative and Quantitative Approaches* (Sage: London, 2005), p. 111.
49. Finnemore and Sikkink, 'International Norm Dynamics'
50. Ronald M. Dworkin, *Law's Empire* (Hart, 2004), pp. 45–86.
51. Stanley Eugene Fish, *Doing What Comes Naturally: Change Rhetoric and the Practice of Theory in Literary and Legal Studies* (Clarendon: Oxford, 1989), pp. 141–150.
52. Ian Johnstone, 'Security Council Deliberations: The Power of the Better Argument', *European Journal of International Law* (2003), 14(3), pp. 437–480 and 446–447.
53. Ibid., p. 447; see also Dworkin, *Law's Empire*, p. 255.
54. Dworkin, *Law's Empire*, p. 48.
55. Kenneth W. Abbott, Robert O. Keohane, Andrew Moravcsik, Anne-Marie Slaughter, and Duncan Snidal, 'The Concept of Legalisation', *International Organization* (2000), 54(3), pp. 17–35, p. 17; Kenneth W. Abbott and Duncan Snidal, 'Hard and Soft Law in International Governance', *International Organization* (2000), 54(3), pp. 421–456.
56. Daniel Deudney and G. John Ikenberry, 'The Nature and Sources of Liberal International Order', *Review of International Studies* (1999), 25(2), pp. 179–196.
57. Jonathan I. Charney, 'Universal International Law', *The American Journal of International Law* (1993), 87(4), pp. 529–551, p. 538.

58. Ibid., p. 539; H. Lau, 'Rethinking the Persistent Objector Doctrine in International Human Rights Law', *Chicago Journal of International Law* (2005–2006), 6(1), pp. 495–510, p. 495; T.L. Stein, 'The Approach of the Different Drummer: The Principle of the Persistent Objector in International Law', *Harvard International Law Journal* (1985), 26(2), pp. 457–482, p. 458.
59. Charney, 'Universal International Law', pp. 533, p. 39, and p. 40.
60. Examples include: the use of force or the resort to the use of force except in self-defence and can also include laws against genocide.
61. Lau, 'Rethinking the Persistent Objector Doctrine', p. 498; also, UN, 'Vienna Convention on the Law of Treaties', in UN (ed.), *UN Doc A/Conf 39/27* (Vienna: UN, 1969), Article 53.
62. Andrea Bianchi, 'Ad-Hocism and the Rule of Law', *European Journal of International Law* (2002), 13(1), pp. 263–272 and 263–264.
63. Ibid., p. 270.
64. Ian Johnstone, 'Security Council Deliberations: The Power of the Better Argument', *European Journal of International Law* (2003), 14(3), pp. 437–480, p. 441; also Andrew Hurrell, 'Power, Institutions, and the Production of Inequality', in M. Barnett and R. Duvall (eds), *Power in Global Governance* (Cambridge University Press: Cambridge, 2004), pp. 42–43.
65. Johnstone, 'Security Council Deliberations', p. 442.
66. Ibid.
67. Ibid., p. 443.
68. David Beetham, *The Legitimation of Power* (Palgrave Macmillan: London, 1991), p. 3.
69. Finnemore and Sikkink, 'International Norm Dynamics and Political Change', p. 897.
70. Florini, 'The Evolution of International Norms', p. 366.
71. Wiener, 'Contested Compliance: Interventions on the Normative Structure of World Politics', p. 201.
72. Dworkin, *Law's Empire*, p. 46.
73. Ian Hurd, 'Legitimacy and Authority in International Politics', pp. 379–408.
74. Dowling and Pfeffer, 'Organizational Legitimacy', p. 122.
75. Hurrell, 'Power, Institutions, and the Production of Inequality', p. 42.
76. Clemens and Cook, 'Politics and Institutionalism', p. 459.
77. Ibid., p. 450.
78. Finnemore, *National Interests in International Society*, p. 22.
79. A.D. Smith, *The Concept of Social Change: A Critique of the Functionalist Theory of Social Change* (London and Boston: Routledge and Kegan Paul, 1973), p. 20.

80. Pepper D. Culpepper, 'The Politics of Common Knowledge: Ideas and Institutional Change in Wage Bargaining', *International Organization* (2008), 62(1), pp. 1–33, p. 2.
81. J.G. March and J.P. Olsen, 'The Logic of Appropriatness', http://www.arena.uio.no/publications/papers/wp04_9.pdf, Working Paper WP 04/09, last accessed 23 April 2013, p. 15.
82. A 'New' norm in this context is used as including new interpretations of existing norms.
83. Although it is noted that being able to control the debate and dialogue between countries will significantly impact on the types of new norms that are adopted.
84. Amitav Acharya, 'How Ideas Spread: Whose Norms Matter? Norm Localization and Institutional Change in Asian Regionalism', *International Organisation* (2004), 58(2), pp. 239–275, p. 242.
85. Johnstone, 'Security Council Deliberations', p. 444. See also Stanley Eugene Fish, *Doing What Comes Naturally: Change Rhetoric and the Practice of Theory in Literary and Legal Studies* (Clarendon: Oxford, 1989), p. 141.
86. Haas, *When Knowledge is Power*, p. 18.
87. Fish explores ways that communities can be "engines of change" through both the activities of the community and the contradictions created between groups who start with different assumptions. Fish, *Doing What Comes Naturally*, pp. 141–150.
88. Florini, 'The Evolution of International Norms', p. 376.
89. These three things are identified as being important in achieving compliance to norms in Hurd, 'Legitimacy and Authority in International Politics', pp. 387–389.
90. Acharya, 'How Ideas Spread', pp. 239–275.
91. Acharya, 'How Ideas Spread'; Finnemore and Sikkink, 'International Norm Dynamics and Political Change'; Florini, 'The Evolution of International Norms', p. 369.
92. Florini, 'The Evolution of International Norms', p. 377.
93. Hiro Katasumata, 'Mimetic Adoption and Norm Diffusion: "Western" Security Cooperation in Southeast Asia?' *Review of International Studies* (2011), 37, pp. 557–576.
94. Phrase used by Florini, 'The Evolution of International Norms', p. 369.
95. As Aggarwal notes—"New institutions are expensive to create. Thus, if actors can achieve their objectives by simply modifying an institution, this will likely be the preferred course." *Institutional Designs for a Complex World: Bargaining, Linkages, and Nesting*, Vinod K. Aggarwal, 'Reconciling Multiple Institutions: Bargaining, Linkages, and Nesting', Vinod K. Aggarwal (ed.), (Cornell University Press: Ithaca, 1998), pp. 1–29, p. 24.

96. Milja Kurki, *Causation in International Relations: Reclaiming Causal Analysis* (Cambridge University Press: Cambridge, 2008), pp. 296–297; Chapter 2.
97. Beetham, *The Legitimation of Power*, p. 3.
98. "Freedom is necessary if we are to utilise our powers to achieve our purposes but without such powers in the first place freedom will be worthless to us." Ibid., p. 43.
99. Hurrell, 'Power, Institutions, and the Production of Inequality', p. 40.
100. Thomas M. Franck, 'The Power of Legitimacy and the Legitimacy of Power: International Law in an Age of Power Disequilibrium', *The American Journal of International Law* (2006), 100(1), pp. 88–106, p. 93.
101. Dowling and Pfeffer, 'Organizational Legitimacy', p. 123; also Talcott Parsons, *Structure and Process in Modern Societies* (Free Press of Glencoe: Illinois, 1960), p. 175.
102. Beetham, *The Legitimation of Power*, p. 103.
103. Nico Krisch, 'International Law in Times of Hegemony: Unequal Power and the Shaping of the International Legal Order', *European Journal of International Law* (2005), 16(3), pp. 369–408, p. 174.
104. Ibid., pp. 173–174.
105. Robert Gilpin, *War and Change in World Politics* (Cambridge University Press: Cambridge, 1982), p. 9.
106. Ibid., p. 9; also Robert Gilpin, 'The Theory of Hegemonic War', *Journal of Interdisciplinary History* (1998), 18(4), pp. 591–613.
107. A.F.K. Organski, *World Politics* (Alfred A. Knopf: New York, 1968), pp. 363–375.
108. 1/3 of all states in Finnemore and Sikkink, 'International Norm Dynamics and Political Change', p. 901.
109. Ian Davison, *Values, Ends and Society* (University of Queensland Press: St Lucia, 1977), p. 43.
110. G. John Ikenberry, 'Liberal Internationalism 3.0: America and the Dilemmas of the Liberal World Order', *Perspectives on Politics* (2009), 7(1), pp. 71–87; Ikenberry and Deudney, 'The Myth of the Autocratic Revival'; C. Reus-Smit, 'Human Rights and the Social Construction of Sovereignty', *Review of International Studies* (2001), 27(4), pp. 519–538.
111. The suggestion here is that the absence of contest also means the absence of interaction of actors and therefore there is a limit to the social construction of the norm that is possible.
112. Jeffrey T. Checkel, 'Why Comply? Social Learning and European Identity Change', *International Organization* (2001), 55(3), pp. 553–588, p. 552.
113. Mark Leonard, *What Does China Think?* (Fourth Estate: London, 2008), p. 117.

114. Barry Buzan and Amitav Acharya (eds), *Non-Western International Relations Theory: Perspectives on and Beyond Asia* (Routledge: Oxford, 2010).
115. According to Alexander Wendt the knowledge context that emerging powers rise into is an important determinant of their ability to influence international norms: Alexander Wendt, 'Constructing International Politics', *International Security* (1995), 20(1), pp. 71–81, p. 77.
116. Florini, 'The Evolution of International Norms', pp. 363–389.
117. Ibid.
118. Johnstone, 'Security Council Deliberations', p. 450.
119. Ibid.
120. March and Olsen, 'The Logic of Appropriateness'.
121. Goertz and Diehl, 'Toward a Theory of International Norms', p. 641.
122. March and Olsen, 'The Logic of Appropriateness', p. 16.
123. Florini, 'The Evolution of International Norms', p. 378.
124. Barkin and Cronin, 'The State and the Nation', p. 114.
125. Culpepper, 'The Politics of Common Knowledge', p. 5.
126. Ibid., p. 6.
127. Ibid.
128. For discussions of the difference of China as a power distinct from other dominant states see: Martin Jacques, *When China Rules the World*; also, Daniel A. Bell, *China's New Confucianism*, p. 10; also the discussion of the possibility of a Chinese international relations theory which returns to the pre-Mao period to look at the possibility of creating a 'Chinese School' in Buzan and Acharya (eds), *Non-Western International Relations Theory: Perspectives on and Beyond Asia*, pp. 27–46; Paul S. Ropp, *China Is World History* (The New Oxford World History; New York: Oxford University Press, 2010), pp. 135–155.
129. Yaqing Qin, 'Why Is There No Chinese International Relations Theory?', in Buzan and Acharya (eds.), *Non-Western International Relations Theory: Perspectives On and Beyond Asia*, p. 37.
130. March and Olsen, 'The Logic of Appropriateness', p. 17.

PART II

Re-Interpreting Sovereignty by Contesting Norms: China and the United Nations

CHAPTER 5

Concepts of Sovereignty Their Evolution and Status

State sovereignty is a constitutive element of international order.[1] States recognise each other as entities with authority over a territory and population. This mutual recognition allows for the development of interactions between them, which subsequently flourish in international institutions. These interactions form a central part of international order.

Sovereignty is the recognition of a state, by other states, as having control over a given population and territory.[2] The element of 'recognition' of a state by other states allows for both the interpretation of the norms of sovereignty and the interpretation of reality against this interpretation. The importance of recognition makes sovereignty an inherently social concept. The 'standards' and 'criteria' by which a state's sovereignty may be tested are in themselves socially constructed, socially contested and socially interpreted; in addition, the 'facts' on the ground (the assessments of a state in regard to these standards) are socially interpreted through particular frames of reference.[3] These social interactions give sovereignty a fluid definition.

Sovereignty is, therefore, more of an aspiration of states than it is an actuality; it is not a clearly defined and delimited norm, but rather is constantly subject to interpretation and reinterpretation.[4] In consequence, norms of sovereignty are subject to the normative challenges outlined in Chapter 4. It is possible to 'interpret' sovereignty in many different ways, and for these different interpretations to have an impact on the character of international order. Sovereignty, as we shall see, can be interpreted from a number of liberal (and non-liberal) perspectives; each of these

© The Author(s) 2018
C. Jones, *China's Challenge to Liberal Norms*,
https://doi.org/10.1057/978-1-137-42761-8_5

interpretations has different implications for the activities of the agents of international order (i.e. states, collections of states and international institutions). It is not only the definition and content of 'what sovereignty is' that is changed by different interpretations, but also the role that sovereignty plays in international relations.[5]

This chapter explores how the interpretation and application of the concept of sovereignty has changed over time, becoming increasingly liberal. Following this, the main focus of the next chapter in Part II of this book, is to explore how China's engagement with debates within the Security Council (SC) has contributed to challenging this liberal interpretation of both the 'facts on the ground' and the concept of sovereignty. The reasons for choosing the UN are threefold: first, the SC is the primary institution that brings together states in dealing with matters of sovereignty and has sole authority on authorisation of the use of force (except in cases of self-defence); second, the SC is the primary institution recognised as legitimate in making (non-consensual) demands on states; thirdly, the SC's role is not limited to military matters, but is also a forum for debate, and uses coercive and non-coercive tools to implement decisions.

Following this discussion the next chapter will explore Chinese engagement in debates concerning sovereignty within the SC, this chapter draws out how Chinese engagement is affecting the liberal interpretation of sovereignty and its application. In fulfilling this function, it relates back to the possible mechanisms of normative change set out in the last chapter.

THE EMERGENCE OF LIBERAL INTERPRETATIONS OF SOVEREIGNTY NORMS

The concept of sovereignty delimits the domestic from the international. As such, sovereignty is more than a single international norm: it is a cluster of norms concerning territory, population, authority, legitimacy and the use of violence.[6] Consequently, this cluster can be separated out in a multitude of different ways to aid analysis. In the literature, it has been separated into: internal and external[7]; positive and negative[8]; human and state[9]; Westphalian, international legal, domestic and interdependent,[10] ethical and instrumental.[11] Each of these separations is analytically useful and can contribute greatly to the understanding of the basis for different interpretations of the norm; however, this discussion focuses on how the interpretations of norms of sovereignty moved from positive (political) to negative (legal) conceptions,[12] and how this shift is reflected in Daniel Philpott's three faces of authority.[13]

Changing Interpretations Since 1945

For Robert Jackson, positive sovereignty is political, it relies on recognition by states[14] and places conditions on what types of communities can be recognised—it makes claims about the appropriate relationship between states and their societies. Negative sovereignty is legally derived, based on internationally agreed criteria—'it is a formal-legal entitlement and therefore something which international society is capable of conferring'.[15] For Jackson, the international order has moved from positive to negative sovereignty in the post-1945 era.[16] However, this movement—from positive to negative sovereignty—may not be as consolidated, permanent or as universal as Jackson suggests. As Dominik Zaum argues, there is a 'Sovereignty Paradox', wherein 'communities are "forced" to be sovereign',[17] but these communities may not have the 'empirical statehood'[18] to enable them to function as a state in the international community. This paradox has then led to the re-establishment of positive sovereignty: that is, the imposition of conditions on which communities can be recognised as sovereign.

Since 1945, there have been three watershed occasions in the shifting interpretations of sovereignty. Each of these moments reflects the changes in the dominant strands of liberalism. First, decolonisation and self-determination present a fundamental reinterpretation of sovereignty within a liberal frame of reference. Starting immediately after the end of 1945 (and continuing into the 1960s), decolonisation and self-determination limited what types of states can be sovereign, as well as shaping the actors in the international order. However, this liberal interpretation of sovereignty limited the legitimate behaviours of sovereign states but also loosened some of the frames of reference for recognising states; there were more states and greater mutual recognition but there were also greater limits on their actions.

The second major shift for the interpretation of sovereignty was in the early 1990s when mechanisms for peace operations were able to be fully used after the unlocking of the stalemate in the SC during the Cold War. The initial tentative steps towards an expanded notion of peacekeeping resulted from an emerging interpretation of sovereignty as being contingent on respect for certain principles and not just on recognition. Throughout the 1990s, steps towards more coercive and forceful peace operations were sanctioned in order to protect populations against their rulers. They were justified by reference to an increasingly liberal interpretation of sovereignty.[19] Sovereignty thus became contingent on the 'social contract' between citizens and their rulers.[20] This shift created another limit on the implications of the protections granted by the recognition of states (their sovereignty and right to non-intervention). Their legitimate behaviour—domestic and international—was further limited and the requirements on them once they were recognised were also increased. In addition, classes of recognition came into being—states were classified according to their domestic organisation rather than their external attributes: 'failed' states were born.

The third major reinterpretive stage was in the mid-1990s and came to fruition in the crafting of the Responsibility to Protect (R2P). This is discussed at length later in a subsequent chapter, and its actual challenge to the interpretation and application of norms of sovereignty remains uncertain. However, the demands on states as having responsibilities that must be fulfilled in order to ensure their continued recognition again limit the sovereignty of states. This view of sovereignty calls for constant assessment and reassessment of whether a state should be recognised as sovereign based on the standards of an international community of both international and domestic actors. Under R2P states remain classified (as above) but the demands on other states have also increased. So too have the demands on the SC; the importance of the shift is in the requirements of states and the SC towards other members of the international community.

From the changing interpretations and applications of the norms of sovereignty since 1945, major developments emerged throughout the 1990s: (a) the emergence of a hierarchy between sovereign states based around liberal conditions of recognition; (b) this hierarchy is enforced through the imposition of a particular code of ethics—a normative 'good' and 'bad' emerged through the promotion of human rights and the emergence of the rule of law[21]; (c) the shifting nature of the relative importance of sovereignty and territory between sovereign states[22]; (d) these shifts then being reflected in the rights states are accorded and how they are limited and (e) what actions are demanded of sovereign states. The next section looks at how these changes have liberal dimensions.

Liberal Interpretations of Sovereignty Norms

In exploring the liberal dimensions of the changing interpretations of the norms of sovereignty, Daniel Philpott's three faces of authority provide the most useful approach.[23] Philpott proposed that sovereignty can usefully be explored by looking at three elements that make up sovereignty: what counts as a legitimate polity; who can be a member of international society; and what behaviours are allowed or precluded. Within these three elements of recognition of sovereignty, Philpott also noted that recognition has two parts: recognition of a sovereign state and recognition of a sovereign state's position in the hierarchy of states. Both of these things (statehood and hierarchy) set out what a state legitimately can and cannot do.[24]

In discussing sovereignty as a norm, Philpott notes: 'all historical uses of the term have meant a particular form of sovereignty, reflecting one or another philosophy or one or another epoch: sovereignty is never without an adjective'.[25] This section looks at the relationship of the norm of sovereignty to liberalism; how the application of a liberal philosophy to sovereignty has changed the application of the term. It specifically looks at whether there has been a gradual imposition of what counts as a legitimate polity, who can be a 'full' member of international society, and what actions sovereign states should and shouldn't perform. Within these divisions, there is room for the exploration of whether sovereignty implies rights and what those rights may be for states (understood as Jackson's negative sovereignty), as well as allowing space for different attributes or capabilities of states in claiming to be and being recognised as sovereign.

Legitimate Polities

An important shift in the evolution of interpretations of sovereignty is the issue of 'whose sovereignty'. Is sovereignty a property of states or individuals within states? How does this change the conditions under which sovereignty is granted?[26] Changes to these conditions also determine whether recognition grants political entities sovereignty as either absolute or non-absolute. Discussions regarding sovereignty might all focus on state sovereignty, but throughout the 1990s the norms of sovereignty have shifted from absolute state sovereignty, towards conditional state sovereignty but absolute popular sovereignty.[27] One dimension of the liberal interpretation of the norms of sovereignty can be seen through a discussion of the changes to what counts as a liberal polity and the relationship between these polities.[28]

As noted by Robert Jackson, the end of colonisation provoked a proliferation of new sovereign states,[29] suggesting that recognition of these new states was unconditional. However, as Dominik Zaum notes, throughout the 1990s new conditions on the recognition of states' sovereignty emerged; these conditions were based around respect for human rights and the rule of law.[30] Rather than suggesting that this has produced a sovereignty regime that is more reflective of positive rather than negative sovereignty, this account proposes that it has helped to shape and reinforce a hierarchy between sovereign states. This then fits in well with claims that '…Westphalia logic was based on the imaginary of "balance", "equilibrium", and "moderation"'.[31]

Within the grouping of liberal polities, there is a hierarchy. In the (negative) legal conceptions of sovereignty, there is equality between states, which in reality has never existed. Under a liberal interpretation of sovereignty, the rationale for the creation of a hierarchy is based around internal regime structures; which is based less around 'power' and more closely tied to states' ability to demonstrate their commitments to a particular ethical affiliation. At the top of this hierarchy were states that had flourishing liberal democratic domestic systems, where the rule of law and human rights were respected. Further down the hierarchy were states that explicitly sought to emulate these states, and therefore constructively contributed to the dialogue, and developed practices that would ensure the spread of these ideas. States like Russia and China, despite their position within the SC, were further down the hierarchy still. Hence, the 'new standard of civilisation' is not necessarily a means of determining who counts as a sovereign state, but rather what weight that status has against other sovereign states.

Thus, there is a relationship between the hierarchy of states and how that hierarchy is maintained. In order to maintain the concept of what is normatively a 'good' or 'bad' state,[32] there is a need for actors at the top of the hierarchy to actively reinforce the schemas that provide the context for others' understandings. According to Simon Reich, this needs to be done by a range of actors in a range of different settings, not only a single great power,[33] in order to provide legitimacy to both the schema and the ethics that are derived from it.

Membership and Requirements of Membership of International Society
In line with the shift in recognition of legitimate polities and the classifications of polities, there has also been a shift away from the recognition of the sovereignty of states on the grounds of population and territory towards recognition on the grounds of behaviour. This behavioural approach then links the requirements of membership of international society to the next section on the limitations and expectations of behaviour. Sovereignty viewed through a liberal lens has ethical, moral and instrumental dimensions.[34] The last element of this unbundling thus looks at the instrumental implications.

An implication of seeing sovereignty in this way is that states should respect the territorial integrity of other sovereign states, but, as discussed above, the importance of territorial integrity is less central in understanding sovereignty from a liberal perspective than it is in alternative interpretations. In place of the centrality of territory, human rights and the rule of law have become central to determining membership. As a result, if states are not seen to be upholding their agreements in respect of human rights, various types of intervention (from monitoring regimes to military interventions) are seen to be legitimate rather than a violation of state sovereignty. Hence, one of the instrumental implications of this interpretation of sovereignty is that states are responsible for protecting the rights of their own populations but also must be vigilant in observing and protecting the rights of populations of other states.

Another instrumental implication is summarised in the report of the International Commission on Intervention and State Sovereignty (ICISS),[35] which concluded that, '…sovereignty is *now understood* as embracing this dual responsibility. Sovereignty as responsibility has become the minimum content of *good international citizenship*'.[36] Thus, it recognised that the understanding of sovereignty can change over time ('is now understood') and that it is contextual ('good international citizenship'); as such, it reflects the liberal understanding of sovereignty norms (outlined above). However, in recognising changing interpretations are possible and contextual, it also recognises that it is possible for these norms in the future to be reinterpreted in a potentially illiberal or less clearly liberal way. The recommendations of this report were later discussed by the General Assembly and used in the World Summit Outcome Document 2005 (WSOD).[37] However, the recommendations outlined in the ICISS report were not wholly accepted by the WSOD. The slippage in language and intention between the two is both interesting and significant for the evolution of liberal order.

Limitations and Expectations of the Behaviour of Sovereign States
The development of liberal ethics and their impact on how 'we see sovereignty' are explored by Thomas Ward, who argues that sovereignty is an ethical norm because it is 'specifically concerned with notions of right and wrong and therefore prescribe[s] or prohibit[s] behaviour that is subject to moral praise or blame'.[38] This moral dimension to sovereignty is reflected in the ICISS report in paragraph 1.3:

> ...sovereignty is more than just a functional principle of internal relations. For many states and peoples, it is also a recognition of their equal worth and dignity, a protection of their unique identities and their national freedom, and an affirmation of their right to shape and determine their own destiny.[39]

Because of this ethical dimension of the norm, it reflects 'deep-seated moral principles'.[40] Thus, in order to change this type of norm it is necessary to change the understanding of the relationship of the moral principle and the articulation of the norm.

Another element of this discussion is that in a liberal conception of sovereignty, there is a different relationship between the state and territory. In the West in particular, there has been a diminishing importance attributed to borders, and the protection of territory. Thus, there is in a liberal interpretation a re-ordering of the hierarchy of (interstitial) norms that make up (the meta-norm) 'sovereignty' as a whole. As noted at the start of this chapter, in the broadest definitions of sovereignty, territory is central to the definition. However, in looking at liberal states, the growing willingness to relax border controls with other liberal states[41] and work cooperatively has led to liberal states repositioning territory in the hierarchy of norms of sovereignty.[42] Similarly, liberal interpretations of sovereignty are increasingly willing to breach the absolute nature of claims to territorial integrity in favour of interventions that champion the protection of human rights.[43] This position is summarised by Kofi Annan in his 2001 Nobel Peace Prize acceptance speech:

In the 21st Century I believe the mission of the United Nations will be defined by a new, more profound, awareness of the sanctity and dignity of every human life, regardless of race or religion. This will require us to look beyond the framework of States, and beneath the surface of nations or communities.

[…]

In this new century, we must start from the understanding that peace belongs not only to states or peoples, but to each and every member of those communities. The sovereignty of States must no longer be used as a shield for gross violations of human rights.[44]

The debate over the implementation of R2P and the idea of sovereignty as responsibility suggests that sovereignty is now understood in these terms by some states—predominately liberal democratic states. Furthermore, the divisions that this debate has produced have fractured rather than solidified the international consensus on a single understanding of sovereignty. Moreover, it has demonstrated that the basis for claims to sovereignty within different countries is different.

There are some important outcomes from the ICISS report and the subsequent discussions of R2P. As a result of its moral basis, the common understanding of 'what sovereignty is' must be derived from a common principle that comes from dialogue between states in order to truly be inter-subjective between them. But, although throughout the 1990s there was ostensibly a convergence of understandings around the norms of sovereignty, the hierarchies among the sovereign states and the hierarchies of the norms that comprise sovereignty, the actual convergence may have been more apparent than real.

Notes

1. Paul W. Schroeder, 'The New World Order: A Historical Perspective', *ACDIS Occasional Paper* (1994), p. 6.
2. Stephen D. Krasner, *Sovereignty: Organized Hypocrisy* (Princeton University Press: Princeton, NJ, 1999), p. 220.
3. Ashley (1984), p. 273 quoted in Luke Glanville, 'The Antecedents of "Sovereignty as Responsibility"', *European Journal of International Relations* (2010), 17(2), pp. 233–255, p. 4.
4. Reus-Smit puts it 'Sovereignty as a variable, practically constituted institution, its precise content and political implications varying with time and

context'. C. Reus-Smit, 'Human Rights and the Social Construction of Sovereignty', *Review of International Studies* (2001), 27(4), pp. 519–538, p. 538.
5. Allen Carlson, 'Protecting Sovereignty, Accepting Intervention: The Dilemma of Chinese Foreign Relations in the 1990's', *China Policy Series* (New York: National Committee on US–China Relations, 2002), p. 19.
6. The collection and codification of these norms of sovereignty are often cited as being in 1933 at the Montevideo Convention, in the treaty, 'Convention on the Rights and Duties of States', copies of the convention are available at The Avalon Project, http://avalon.law.yale.edu/20th_century/intam03.asp, accessed on 2 November 2011; for other claims of the content of the norms of sovereignty see: Allen Carlson, 'Protecting Sovereignty, Accepting Intervention'; Stephen D. Krasner, *Sovereignty: Organized Hypocrisy*; Dominik Zaum, *The Sovereignty Paradox* (Oxford University Press: Oxford, 2007), pp. 3 and 28.
7. Daniel Philpott, *Revolutions in Sovereignty: How Ideas Shaped Modern International Relations* (Princeton University Press: Princeton and Oxford, 2001), p. 18.
8. Robert H. Jackson, *Quasi-States: Sovereignty, International Relations, and the Third World* (Cambridge University Press: Cambridge, 1990), pp. 26–31.
9. Kofi A. Annan, 'Two Concepts of Sovereignty', *The Economist*, 18 September 1999.
10. Krasner, *Sovereignty: Organized Hypocrisy*, p. 10.
11. Ward Thomas, *The Ethics of Destruction: Norms and Force in International Relations* (Ithaca, London: Cornell University Press, 2001), pp. 27–28.
12. Jackson, *Quasi-States*, pp. 26–31.
13. Philpott, *Revolutions in Sovereignty*, p. 18.
14. Jackson, *Quasi-States*, p. 29.
15. Ibid., p. 27.
16. '[W]e are witnessing the emergence of a community of states with a normative, legal, and organizational superstructure that is far more elaborate than anything which existed previously'. Jackson, *Quasi-States*, p. 81.
17. Zaum, *The Sovereignty Paradox*, p. 5.
18. Ibid.
19. Fernando R. Tesón, 'The Liberal Case for Humanitarian Intervention', in J.L. Holzgrefe and Robert O. Keohane (eds), *Humanitarian Intervention: Ethical, Legal, and Political Dilemmas* (Cambridge University Press: Cambridge, 2003), pp. 93–129 and 93–96.
20. Social contract is from a strand of liberal thinking, its exact contents varies between liberal thinkers but in general it is the idea that in order for a ruler to hold authority within a state, and consequently for that ruler

to be recognised by other states as having that authority they must protect their citizens from harm that would prevail in a state of nature. Social contract works see: Thomas Hobbes, *Leviathan* (C.B. Macpherson, eds) (Penguin Books: London, 1968), Chapter 14; John Locke, *Two Treatise of Government* (Peter Laslett, eds) (Cambridge Texts in the History of Political Thought, Cambridge University Press: Cambridge, 2004), Chapter VII, para. 88–94; John Jacques Rousseau, *The Social Contract and Discourses* (G.D.H. Cole, trans.) (Everyman Classics: Vermont, 1993) in particular The Social Contract, Book II, Chapters 1–5; Fernando R. Tesón, 'The Liberal Case for Humanitarian Intervention', pp. 96–99.
21. Sovereignty is always taken in respect to a particular philosophy or idea, the result is that a hierarchy emerges. See Philpott, *Revolutions in Sovereignty*, p. 17.
22. Indeed, for some liberal interpretations of sovereignty, intervention is justified because the state has lost legitimacy to rule rather than having lost the ability to rule over a given territory and population, see, for example, Fernando R. Tesón, 'The Liberal Case for Humanitarian', p. 98.
23. Philpott, *Revolutions in Sovereignty*, pp. 15–21.
24. Ibid.
25. Ibid., p. 17; also, Tesón, 'The Liberal Case for Humanitarian Intervention', p. 93.
26. Amitav Acharya, 'State Sovereignty After 9/11: Disorganised Hypocrisy', *Political Studies* (2007), 55, pp. 274–296, p. 276.
27. Philpott, *Revolutions in Sovereignty*, pp. 18–19.
28. This approach is similar to the discussion of legitimate constituencies in Ian Clark and Christian Reus-Smit, 'Liberal Internationalism, the Practice of Special Responsibilities, and the Evolving Politics of the Security Council', *International Politics* (2013), 50, pp. 38–56, p. 44.
29. Jackson, *Quasi-States*, pp. 80–81.
30. Zaum, *The Sovereignty Paradox*.
31. Richard A. Falk, *A Study of Future Worlds* (The Free Press: New York, 1975), p. 64.
32. As noted by Mamdani, the doctrine of the Responsibility to Protect may further enshrine the different levels of 'sovereignty' between states, and there is potential that R2P may give liberal states great abilities to coerce the actions of other states, Mahmood Mamdani, 'Responsibility to Protect or Right to Punish', *Journal of Intervention and Statebuilding* (2010), 4(1), pp. 53–67, p. 65.
33. Simon Reich, *Global Norms, American Sponsorship and the Emerging Patterns of World Politics* (Palgrave Macmillan: Basingstoke, 2010), pp. 32–69.

34. ICISS, *Suplementary Volume to the Responsibility to Protect Section A: Research Essays* (Ottawa: International Development Research Centre, 2001), pp. 5–7.
35. ICISS, *The Responsibility to Protect* (Ottawa: International Development Research Centre, 2001).
36. Ibid., p. 8, para. 1.35, emphasis added.
37. WSOD GA/60/L.1, 15 September 2005, para. 138.
38. Ward Thomas, *The Ethics of Destruction*, pp. 27–28.
39. ICISS, *The Responsibility to Protect*, p. 7, para. 1.33.
40. Ward Thomas, *The Ethics of Destruction*, p. 28.
41. Significantly, this is only a feature of liberal states activities with other liberal states and in particular those states that share both a respect for the rule of law and have comparable contents.
42. For a similar argument, see: He Baogang, 'Chinese Sovereignty: Challenges and Adaptation', *EAI Working Paper*, No. 104, published 23 September 2003; also David Held, *Democracy and Global Order: From Modern State to Cosmopolitan Governance* (Polity Press: Cambridge, 1995), p. 135.
43. See, for example, Jack Donnelly, *International Human Rights* (Westview Press: Boulder, 2007), pp. 27–29.
44. Kofi Annan, Nobel Lecture, 10 December 2001, Oslo, available http://www.nobelprize.org/nobel_prizes/peace/laureates/2001/annan-lecture.html, accessed 7 November 2011; also cited in Paul Heinbecker, '*Kosovo*', in David M. Malone, *The UN Security Council: From the Cold War to the 21st Century* (Lynne Rienner: Boulder, London, 2004), pp. 537–550, p. 548.

CHAPTER 6

China's Engagement with the UN Security Council in Debates on Sovereignty

Since the People's Republic of China (PRC) reclaimed its seat in the Security Council from the government in Taiwan in 1971, China's engagement within the Council has gone through three stages. First, throughout the 1970s and early 1980s, there was a limited engagement; second, during the following long decade until the late 1990s, this developed into constructive engagement; in the 2000s, there is a clear shift towards China becoming a more 'responsible stakeholder' within the UN.[1] As noted in Chapter 2, a key element of great power status is the extent to which a power is engaged within the normative as well as the structural dimensions of international order. Throughout the 1970s, China was structurally present, but as this section explores, since the end of the Cold War, China has moved to a more substantive engagement with the normative dimensions of order. This then not only shapes its recognition as a great power, but also allows China to shape the normative dimensions of order—in this instance the normative interpretation of sovereignty.

The literature on China's engagement with the UN looks predominantly at China's approaches to peacekeeping in the context of UN operations. This literature elucidates the claims that China is becoming a more 'responsible and engaged stakeholder'. According to Marc Lanteigne '…China's views on multilateral intervention from the UN ha[ve] shifted from a blanket "no" to a "yes, but"'.[2] Miwa Hirono states that China increasingly engages with 'more robust and complex'[3] peacekeeping missions. Zhao Lei argues that '[i]n IPBOs [International Peace Building Operations], China is undergoing another process of socialization'.[4] These authors all identify a shift in China's approach to peacekeeping and peace building, but none of these authors who have discussed China and the Security Council (UNSC) have explored how peace operations, and China's broader engagement with the SC, relate to its position on sovereignty or how China's engagement is a challenge to liberal elements of the existing international order.[5]

The Security Council provides a valuable lens for exploring the interpretations of norms of sovereignty. Its debates and discussions on specific uses of force, and its role in acting as a legitimator, provide case-by-case demonstrations of the limits on state behaviour and states' claims to be sovereign. Beyond debates on the authorisation and the use of force, broader debates—such as the summit meetings or the debates within the context of the Responsibility to Protect (R2P)—illuminate the abstract notions that inform these case-by-case discussions. The UNSC (and the UN more generally) provides an excellent tool for looking at consistencies and changes in the positions expressed by a diverse group of actors over a period of time. Significantly, the UN also acts as a forum that allows for debate and contestation of both the abstract notions of interventions and limits to the recognition of a state's sovereignty, but also of the application of those notions.

The remainder of this chapter explores China's engagement with debates related to sovereignty within the UNSC, in particular focusing on debates about intervention, peacekeeping and the authorisation of the use of force. These debates crystallise the guiding interpretation of sovereignty being applied by UNSC members by demonstrating the limits to claims of sovereignty within the target states. Each of the cases discusses a different element explored in this regard. The reasons for selecting specific cases are outlined at the start of each case. In the next chapter, the abstract principles of when and under what conditions UNSC action should be taken are discussed within the context of the evolution of the R2P. Taken together, these two sections allow for explorations of the actual case-by-case application of the limits to the norms of sovereignty, as well as the broader guiding principles.

Perception–Reality Gap in Views of China and the UNSC

Before looking in more detail at specific discussions within the UNSC, an important point needs to be made. It is often suggested, in the Western press, that China is an obstacle to consensus in the

UNSC—using its veto to protect tyrannical regimes and preventing humanitarian missions taking place. However, if we look at the voting records within the SC, the picture that emerges is quite different.[6]

From 2000 to 2011, there were 752 draft resolutions before the UNSC. Ninety two percent of them were passed unanimously, a further 6.1% have been passed but either with abstentions, or votes against (from non-permanent members). Only 2% of all draft resolutions before the Council were vetoed. Thus, it is hard to claim that China is an obstacle to the agenda of the UNSC. Nonetheless, it is possible that the threat of a veto may shape the agenda or the approach towards action pursued by other states. In the period from 2011 to 2018, China's use of the veto has increased, yet, the pattern of vetoes has remained—China is yet to veto alone and maintains a position of principled objection (detailed below).

A closer look at the vetoes used in the UNSC underlines the point that China is not a major obstacle to the pursuit of peace and security: of the fifteen vetoed resolutions from 2000 to 2011, only three were vetoed by China, and on no occasion did it act unilaterally. In sharp contrast, nine of the vetoes were cast by the USA unilaterally. China does, however, have a tendency to abstain from votes rather than vote against them, thus registering a degree of disagreement but not blocking the will of the rest of the Council.

In a turn of events in the total of 12 vetoes that China has used since the People's Republic joined the Council, 6 of them have been since 2011 and all of them have related to the conflict in Syria.[7] Hence, there is a good reason to offer a critique of the narrative that it is protecting regimes; however, there is also a need to explore the particular dynamics around the Syria case. Rather than investigating this further here, I have previously presented an argument that this may be the result, of the actions and a change in approach from the Permanent three in pressing ahead with a vote that they know China and Russia will veto, rather than an altered stance by China.[8] But, it is important to note that this argument, if accepted, does mean that the negotiation with China behind the scenes of the Security Council in formulating the agenda and contributing to the drafting of resolutions requires further investigation.

Of greater interest to this discussion and the agenda of this book is the question of whether China uses its position in the UNSC to protect despotic or tyrannical regimes. Sudan is often cited as being protected by China in this way. Yet, if we look at China's record of votes on the

Sudan, we see that it has never used its veto for Sudan's benefit, but it has abstained on five of the thirty-two resolutions on Sudan. But only once has it been the only member to abstain, and the USA and Russia have also abstained on resolutions pertaining to Sudan (2000–2011).[9] Nevertheless, the voting record does not tell the whole story of Chinese engagement with the UNSC. In particular, voting records only show votes taken, it does not encompass issues or discussion not put to a vote. These dynamics will be discussed later. The voting record is indicative of the need to explore in more detail the actual rather than the assumed role of China in the UNSC.

To examine whether China has a more nuanced and constructive approach towards the UNSC and sovereignty, the next section of this chapter considers how China can affect the debates in the Security Council. The following chapter then considers China's role in UNSC debates on military interventions, and in the subsequent chapter, China's role in the development of the R2P is scrutinised.

UN Security Council and Peacekeeping

Since 1990, there have been over 50 peacekeeping operations, increasing in variety in the scope and strength of their mandates. There has also been variety in the types of force permitted, whether or not there has been host government consent, and post-facto or non-authorised missions (which were discussed within the SC, e.g. over Kosovo in 1999). The large majority of peace operations have host government consent, and the decision to deploy them does not prompt any immediate sovereignty concerns.

In looking at the changes that have taken place in peacekeeping practices since the 1990s, there is a range of literature to be explored. This literature discusses the role of the SC in PKOs,[10] or specific UNPKOs,[11] or Chinese debates around UNPKOs.[12] Clearly, all three of these literatures are relevant to the forthcoming discussion. However, it is the conclusion of this literature that is most vital to take notice of. The role of China and the approach of China to UNPKOs have been the subject of a number of studies. The highlights of these studies are Reilly and Gill,[13] Allen Carlson,[14] Stefan Stähle[15] and Taylor Fravel.[16] Each of these authors highlights that China's approach to peacekeeping demonstrates a gradual learning and adaption of China's approach to sovereignty linked with peacekeeping.

Drawing on this literature, this section looks specifically at how China's actions may challenge applications of a liberal interpretation of sovereignty. This chapter is limited to discussions in the SC that caused controversy over the respect for state sovereignty. An important contribution to this discussion is therefore made by operations that didn't have a UN authorisation but were discussed in the Council, with the issue of sovereignty raised. This section then looks at two peacekeeping operations, Cambodia (UNTAC), and East Timor (INTERFET and subsequently UNTAET); two non-UN operations Kosovo (and its post-facto acceptance), and Iraq (2003); and two places where there was an intention of either no peacekeeping mission or a limited peacekeeping action (in Bosnia and Sudan).

In this discussion, it becomes significant that the considerations of sovereignty through the lens of peacekeeping and the legitimate use of force have taken place within not only an existing institutional framework but also within an existing normative framework. How discussions are framed reflects an overarching approach that sets out the form and legitimacy of particular challenges.

This chapter makes an argument that China has presented a challenge to the existing normative framework through 'exceptionalising' its consent of peacekeeping missions (abstaining or voting 'yes' with a caveat that missions are 'special', 'particular' or 'specific'), by using its ability within the Council to limit the extent and terms of the use of force in the mandate of the mission. In adopting this approach, China acts as an ad hoc objector (there is an ostensible inconsistency in its position) and significantly its position cannot be classed as persistent objection.

The effect or the impact of this challenge can be seen in the use of a Chinese approach to Chapter 7. This was first noted to have been used in the case of Bosnia, but subsequently used to denote a specification of a mandate that goes beyond the phrase 'all necessary means'. In addition, this behaviour has been used in China's approach to the use of sanctions.[17] Thus, in looking back to the framework set out in Chapter 4, China appears to be using an approach of ad hoc objection that prevents the emergence of a precedent for a particular form of peacekeeping. In this sense, it prevents the consolidation of an alternative norm of intervention or a modified version of sovereignty becoming the pinnacle of the normative hierarchy guiding future decisions. Hence, rather than proactively championing an alternative normative approach, it is (increasingly) active in preventing the consolidation of an alternative.

China has been able to justify these actions and particularly reconcile the 'exceptions' it has made to the sovereignty of the states involved in three ways: it doesn't recognise a country as sovereign, and therefore, that country is not subject to the rights afforded to recognised states (as in the case of Somalia); it has coerced or persuaded the host state to consent and therefore doesn't violate the host state's sovereignty (such as Indonesia regarding East Timor); and finally, it recognises the state rather than a specific government as the subject of sovereignty (this is more evident in the case of Libya discussed in the section on R2P). Thus, China has used its agency in the Council debates to object to a particular framing of the issue of sovereignty. Through its justification, it elaborates on what the specific content of this challenge implies. The tool used for this challenge is to reframe the debate. This, then, shows that China is attempting to 'reframe' the debates, on sovereignty and non-interference, recalling 'traditional' understandings and usages of the terms. As such, China uses ad hoc objection with the tool of reframing.

Thus, China refocuses the issue of sovereignty. The main discussion point here is on China's role in using the tool of reinterpretation. In the case of Cambodia and East Timor, China used reinterpretation in conjunction with the tool of the population of the Association for Southeast Asian Nations (ASEAN) states as tools of ad hoc objection. In the case of Bosnia and Herzegovina, China presented an argument for limiting the use of force, acting in a manner consistent with norm entrepreneurship, which was an approach that has subsequently affected how China has approached the interpretation of the implementation of R2P (see Chapter 7). In the cases of Cambodia, East Timor, Iraq and Sudan, China presented a case that has come closest to being a persistent objector to all instances of peacekeeping that do not have host government consent.

Hence, China also uses the tools of 'populations' and 'reframing' in order to amplify its ad hoc objection, but in some instances China appears to act as a norm entrepreneur. However, as noted in Chapter 4, it can be expected that at times objection may resemble entrepreneurship in the case of reframing. Yet, the overall conclusion from all of these cases is that China uses tools of reframing and populations to amplify its ad hoc objection.

Cambodia

Examining Chinese engagement with the SC debates on intervention in Cambodia is an essential starting point.[18] Cambodia is seen as a landmark intervention.[19] It was particularly important not only because of

China's complicated relationship with Cambodia shaped by the Vietnam War and its geographical position, but it was one of the first UN missions after the end of the Cold War and the first in which China contributed peacekeepers. Importantly, it positions Chinese engagement within the evolution of the liberal interpretation of sovereignty and also sets out the role of the region in deciding these issues (and the Chinese common approach with the relevant regional organisation, ASEAN).

China has had complex relations with Cambodia during and after the Cold War, in particular because of the relationship between Cambodia and Vietnam. In 1979, China fought a war against Vietnam, following a Vietnamese invasion of Cambodia.[20] The Vietnamese finally withdrew from Cambodia in 1989, resulting in the start of a successful phase of the peace process in 1990.[21] During this, China, in conjunction with the ASEAN, was instrumental in forcing a Vietnamese withdrawal from Cambodia and securing a resolution from the SC for the United Nations Transitional Authority in Cambodia (UNTAC).[22] In this process, China was hugely important; ASEAN's efforts on its own from the 1983 'ASEAN plan' had not been successful.[23]

Cambodia is a landmark in China's UN diplomacy; it marked the start of a more constructive engagement within SC debates as well as a more nuanced approach to involvement in peacekeeping operations. UNTAC expressly promoted seven objectives including: human rights, elections, separation of the military and civilian administrations, development of a police force and the return of refugees.[24] Significantly, China was not only instrumental in bringing the issue to the SC, but also contributed military personnel to the mission.[25] Yet, China was concerned about some elements of the mission; when it came to the resolution endorsing the elections and the use of sanctions, China abstained.[26] Throughout the process, China's insistence on the Khmer Rouge being involved in the process was important in bringing all parties to the table for negotiations.[27] Thus, China's position set out respect of sovereignty of the state rather than the sovereignty of a particular government (or form of government) within a state.

Explaining its abstention, China said it agreed with some of the elements of the draft resolution, such as the call on the parties to fulfil their commitments to the ceasefire and to exercise restraint. It also contained elements that China felt were at variance with the Paris agreements: sanctions and a three-party election. The latter would increase differences and sharpen contradictions and thus could lead to new, complicated problems. The former could have possible adverse consequences, such as producing a deteriorating humanitarian situation or regional economic stability (based on major trading nations), regarding which China was deeply anxious. It added that sanctions could affect neighbouring states, in which case *their sovereignty should be respected* and their opinions on the matter fully heeded.[28] Thus, sanctions were discussed in relation to the sovereignty of other states and regional stability and not simply in regard to their effect on the sovereignty of Cambodia.[29] The adoption of this position may reflect the coordination of China's position with ASEAN and the primacy of regional concerns. It also relates to the origins of China's approach being coupled with the regional preferences (which become more evident in the discussion of R2P in the next chapter).

In terms of the conflict with the liberal interpretations of sovereignty, China in these discussions takes a stance in negotiations that requires the country to choose its own form of government rather than 'buying into' rhetoric of democratic elections. However, China's apparent concern is not the issue of Cambodia's form of government but the need to prevent the emergence of a precedent in the use of sanctions or the 'spill-over' of sovereignty issues in other parts of the region. China's ability to negotiate alongside ASEAN at Paris not only aided the Chinese approach but also limited the manner of expression. At the same time, the coordination of ASEAN and China with the UN broadened the peacekeeping mission from a regional concern.[30] But, significantly, the resolution that was reached was not biased in favour of one of the parties[31]—as such—it didn't 'interfere' but instead 'intervened'.

With regard to UNTAC and Cambodia more generally, China engaged with its region and the SC to achieve specific goals. However, Chinese involvement was limited by respect for state sovereignty, most importantly, by a particular Chinese interpretation of traditional sovereignty, requiring host government consent and non-interference into the internal affairs of states. Throughout the duration of UNTAC, China maintained relations with all parties in the Cambodian dispute[32] and thus cannot be said to have undermined the independence of the state to determine its own affairs. China then sought broad-based support for the position it advocated within the Council, giving its own position greater legitimacy. As will be explored in later chapters, China's utilisation of regional bodies to gain legitimacy, credibility and support became increasingly important for its international diplomacy.

At the same time, Chinese contributions to the peacekeeping force (significantly not a coercive force) were mostly military engineers.[33] A fundamental and striking aspect of the Chinese peacekeepers, highlighted by Miwa Hirono, was their reputation with the Cambodian population: '… Cambodians with knowledge of Chinese peacekeepers were favourably disposed towards them, […] Not all the UN troops were able to create such a popular reputation as the Chinese peacekeepers'.[34] Where China has been successful in its approach is in the respect for the demands of local populations. It links this directly to its approach to protecting the sovereignty of the state and also ties into a broader Chinese approach to development and the need to be invited and accepted as an actor with the consent of the state.

There are then legacies from China's involvement in Cambodia that stretch forward into the 1990s. Firstly, in the debates about UNTAC, China demonstrated a new willingness to be involved in discussions around peacekeeping, what types of operations should be undertaken and how concerns for the preservation of state sovereignty should limit the scope and methods of those operations. China then not only recognised a need for a multilateral international response to humanitarian, and peace and security issues, but also recognised that those responses should be limited by respect for a particular 'traditional' interpretation of state sovereignty. Secondly, it fills a gap in UN peacekeeping forces. In doing so, China can be seen as a contributing and responsible state within its own framework for peacekeeping missions contributing only troops that allow for 'traditional consensual peacekeeping missions'.[35] Thirdly, in the first instance, in dealing with the Cambodian issue, China cooperated in coordination with the relevant regional organisation. Fourthly, China's involvement with the mission reaffirmed the importance of the UN in the pursuit of peacekeeping.[36]

Bosnia and Herzegovina

The UN intervention in Bosnia is significant for the evolution of China's approach to the UN because China clearly sought (in 1993) to limit the scope of the peacekeeping forces. In this mission, China actively attempted to prevent the interveners overreaching the limits of the mandate in Resolution 816. As Stähle notes, '[w]hen the UNSC began to extend the mandates of certain missions in the 1990s, China had difficulty adapting to this new development. It felt particularly uncomfortable with the use of force in wider peacekeeping missions and with peace enforcement carried out by pivotal states'.[37]

The UN Resolution 819 of 16 April 1993 was significant and notable for a number of reasons. The first reason is the creation of 'safe areas' and the implications of the scope of the use of force to 'protect' the population. The second reason is the role of China in these discussions, but China is not particularly notable or unique in the desire to limit the scope of the use of force.[38] As Former Amb. Diego Arria notes, 'there was complicity between the Secretary General and the P5 to limit the scope of the mandate'.[39] This was done in a number of ways, but different powers used different means. For example, he noted that semantics are very important in the Council, and the term originally used by Amb. Diego Arria in the discussion in Spanish was 'protected areas'; however, the English and French translations of this phrase were, 'safe areas'. He noted that this conveyed a significantly different intention to the one he had intended. In the interview conducted, he clearly set out an agenda to try and ensure these 'safe areas' were closer to the original proposal of 'protected areas'—seeking to ensure that the populations within Srebrenica were actively protected.[40] However, this did not happen. Thus, significantly for this analysis, it is essential to point out that it was not only China that sought to limit the scope of action available to peacekeepers acting within the mandate. Yet, the approach of China was to be potentially more vocal within the Council, whereas other powers acted in coordination with the Secretary General (SG) to change the intention of the terms used—through which they limited the mandate.[41]

Nonetheless, China was instrumental in this objective—through its vocalisation in the Council. As noted in the 1994 UN yearbook, China expressly sought to limit the role of air forces to defending peacekeepers and not extending their role into actual peacekeeping activities. After the authorisation of the use of force in Resolution 816 on 31 March 1993 (on which China abstained), the UN Yearbook stated, 'China placed on record its reservations on the invocation of Chapter 7 of the Charter to authorize the use of force to ensure compliance with the ban on military flights'.[42] In Resolution 871 (1993), the resolution stated: 'Decides to continue to review urgently the extent of close air support for UNPROFOR in the territory of the Republic of Croatia as recommended by the Secretary-General in his report of the 20th September 1993'.[43] Indeed, 871 then extends the authorisation of the mission until

31 March 1994.[44] 'China stressed its understanding that air strikes were limited to UNPROFOR's self-defence and voiced concern over possible serious consequences for the safety of UNPROFOR and humanitarian organizations'.[45]

This approach then continued to be related to China in subsequent missions in the 1990s. Indeed, in the later section on R2P, this concern with 'mission creep' and clearly specified mandates re-emerges. As one interviewee noted regarding the 'Responsibility while Protecting', 'RwP balances between too rigid mandates and too flexible mandates',[46] recalling the attempts by China to specify and restrain peacekeeping missions.

Kosovo

Kosovo is a central case in the evolution of the liberal position on sovereignty as it marks the first non-UN authorised use of force by Western powers for humanitarian reasons. For China, the problem of Kosovo indicates two things: first, it highlights the importance of host government consent to the use of force; second, humanitarian intervention is not solely a domestic concern, and the international community does have a responsibility—but that responsibility is limited to non-military intervention in the absence of host government consent.

Kosovo has become emblematic for the evolution of just war principles and became the cornerstone of Tony Blair's moral foreign policy. In his Chicago speech, he claimed that there was a moral responsibility to act in cases—such as Kosovo—where genocide was taking place.[47] Following the Chicago speech and failed attempts to gain a UN authorised mission, Western powers mounted an air campaign over Kosovo and prepared to use land forces to coerce the end of the ongoing ethnic cleansing. Kosovo forms an interesting case for looking at how China engages with sovereignty debates, because China vehemently objected to the air campaign but abstained on Resolution 1244, thereby allowing what has since been seen as post-facto validation of the air campaign.[48] The Kosovan example is also important because of the SC's absence[49] and the framing of some of China's objections to action on the basis of the absence of SC authorisation to use force.

China adopted a consistent approach in saying that it wanted to deal with the humanitarian crisis through peaceful means and that any action should not violate Yugoslav sovereignty.[50] China also sought to relate its own stance to the 'purposes and principles of the United Nations Charter'.[51] Indeed, in the discussion of the Kosovo situation during the air campaign, China was keen to highlight risks to regional peace and stability, the humanitarian issues arising from the campaign and the dangers of undermining UN authority:

> What is equally of concern to us is that, bypassing the United Nations and without the authorization of the Security Council, the United States-led North Atlantic Treaty Organization (NATO) has launched military attacks against the Federal Republic of Yugoslavia and thus unleashed a regional war in the Balkans. Over the past 52 days, this war, conducted in the name of humanitarianism, has created the largest humanitarian disaster since the Second World War.[52]

This appeal to a 'higher' authority and the attempt to link the Chinese stance to principles that have long been held to be legitimate can be seen as an effective rhetorical tool within the Council.[53] But it also situates the Chinese approach within a number of legal precedents and understandings of what actions are legitimate: such as the need for authorisation of the use of force, minimum use of force and the prevention of human suffering. Furthermore, China took a moral stance against the campaign stating: 'Such perversity in NATO has outraged the entire world and should be strongly condemned by everyone who has reason and conscience'.[54] These two statements suggest an attempt to draw other states that objected to the air campaign to a particular moral and legal interpretation of events.

Over the decade since the NATO action in Kosovo, China's position has been made stronger and more appealing because of academic and practical assessments of the successes of the action, in particular the criticisms of the air campaign and the increase in humanitarian distress.[55] Claims that Kosovo was an example of a 'just war' have been criticised from both a practical perspective and a philosophical one. These criticisms both from within and outside liberal discourse have underlined the salience of Chinese insistence on the need for Council authorisation of the use of force. In terms of the evolving liberal interpretation of sovereignty, Heinbecker claims that '[t]he G8 and NATO did not create a new paradigm of international relations'.[56] Despite this, Kosovo was an impetus for the ICISS report which in turn contributed to the doctrine of R2P (discussed later). China's position contributed to the failure to systemise this liberal limited and contingent application of sovereignty with boundaries. Thus, China's ad hoc approach, in conjunction with facilitating factors such as the potential failure of the existing norms of intervention, contributes to the prevention of the evolution of the liberal interpretation of norms of intervention.

In the specific case of Kosovo, China in conjunction with Russia was instrumental in calling for an end to military action in Kosovo.[57] In looking for China's agency, in this case it is clear that China went beyond objection and hence prevention of the authorisation. China actively sought to stop the military action taking place. Through this greater display of agency, it is possible to argue that Chinese statements on Kosovo give a clearer indication of Chinese preferences. This adds to the emerging conclusion of the case-by-case and pragmatic approach that China is seemingly adopting.

This tentative conclusion is supported by China's abstention rather than veto over Resolution 1244, particularly as its abstention was accompanied by an explanation as to what aspects of the resolution were deemed unacceptable and made it clear that because of certain concessions within it (e.g. reiterating an explicit commitment to the sovereignty of Yugoslavia) China didn't feel the need to block the resolution. In particular, this case shows a need for balancing between Chinese preferences of the need to support state sovereignty, promote regional stability, act through means in accordance with ends and deal with humanitarian crises. Thus, even though Resolution 1244 had Yugoslav consent, Chinese interests were by that stage compromised: it had to balance its own response to the bombing of its embassy in Belgrade and its stated position that required Yugoslav consent for authorisation.

It may emerge that China's actions are not only case-by-case but in some instances are issue-by-issue within a broader context. This is a very sophisticated and risky approach to dealing with SC resolutions. By outlining and making it clear that China was the party that wanted certain explicit language that affirmed sovereignty and international law, China can be seen as upholding universally agreed rules and norms. Nonetheless, by not adopting the resolution, China avoids the complications of the implementation of such a resolution. Thus, China can make a claim that it didn't agree with specific actions or approaches that were undertaken.[58] Nevertheless, it can also claim that it has demonstrated support for some form of action that deals with humanitarian crises. China is thus appealing to universal norms and avoiding the particular problems.

East Timor

In looking at East Timor, the issue of host government consent re-emerges, as well as the importance of the role of the region. In addition, the case of East Timor raises issues of decolonisation and self-determination; the interpretations of which were settled in the UN before China had reclaimed its seat in 1971—thus, it is interesting to suggest whether it is 'just' norms of sovereignty in the 1990s that may be reinterpreted or whether other norms are being contested. East Timor offers a lens through which to view other issues already discussed in another context but also to tentatively explore the Chinese approaches to norms that evolved prior to Chinese engagement in the SC.

In stark contrast to Kosovo, China supported the UN resolution on East Timor and contributed peacekeeping forces. But, in showing this support, China had to reconcile these two ostensibly contradictory approaches[59] and reconcile this position with its approach to Cambodia in the early 1990s. Central to this reconciliation was the specific approach to the authorisation of the mission and the control and execution of the operation. The authorisation of the UN mission in East Timor allowed a test of whether China's interpretation to sovereignty, and the implications that have for peacekeeping missions, is consistent and durable. The significance of INTERFET, the authorised international mission that was replaced by UNTAET, is explored briefly here.

Two things are central to China's participation in the case of East Timor: participation in the operation and authorisation of the mission. First, its support was contingent on the acquiescence of the Indonesian government in the intervention, and hence, there was no challenge to Indonesian sovereignty.[60] However, it has been claimed that Indonesian consent was 'lukewarm' at best and the result of Western pressure.[61] Thus, '... East Timor did not entirely conform to the principled stance that Beijing had previously promoted'.[62] But an important element of the justification for action that made the action acceptable to China was that 'China had never recognized the 1975 Indonesian take-over of East Timor in the first place'.[63] Nor had the UN.[64] Indeed, China consistently supported the East Timorese government in exile. As Ian Storey characterises the relationship: '[f]or several years after the [Indonesian] invasion China acted as East Timor's primary patron, providing the territory's government-in-exile in Mozambique with diplomatic and financial support'.[65] China's emphasis on Indonesian consent can be seen as going above the Chinese requirement for host government consent (because Indonesia was not the 'host' government in this case given China and the international communities' previous position).

In the wake of East Timor, China has been known to exert pressure to ensure host government consent for missions. Indeed, in the Sudan, China's pressure to allow a peacekeeping force was essential.[66]

A second relevant issue arising for East Timor is the emphasis that China placed on replacing the multilateral force with a UN mission as soon as possible.[67] Thus, as in Kosovo, China sought to highlight the importance of the UN as authorising and directing missions. The importance of the UN control of the mission is also highlighted by the fact that this was the first mission (since the 1990s) that was not overseen by another force.[68]

A further issue tying the Chinese position on East Timor to Cambodia and Kosovo was the centrality they gave the views of the East Timorese. As Shen Guofang stated in the SC, '[t]hus, the principle of the East Timorese people's involvement as principal actor must be upheld and its wishes and choices respected. To the greatest extent feasible, locals should be fully involved and play their due role'.[69] Thus, China could use East Timor as a demonstration of their support for civilian rights, but only their expression within the existing agreements and limits of traditional consensual peacekeeping.

Iraq (2003)

In the case of Iraq 2003, the main issue of importance is the non-authorisation of the use of force. The Council debates reveal two clear elements of the Chinese position: firstly, the centrality of the UN as the legitimate source of authorisation for the use of force; and secondly, the relationship between the statements of China's position and that of other states in the Council at the time.

With regard to Iraq, the Chinese position against intervention could not have been clearer:

> A few days ago, the United States and a few other countries, sidestepping the Security Council, launched a military action against Iraq in the face of the opposition of an absolute majority of the international community. Such an action constitutes a violation of the basic principles of the Charter of the United Nations and of international law. War is bound to bring about humanitarian disasters ... War will also have a negative impact on safety, stability and development in the region and beyond.[70]

Buoyed by support from a number of other states, China adopted a hard line on intervention in Iraq. This is significant for two reasons. First, the language China uses in this debate is the same as the language it used for Kosovo: invoking language of political settlements, protection of sovereignty and upholding the principles of the Charter. Second, it is significant because of the range of other states adopting similar stances, most notable of which was how close the French delegation was to the Chinese position—demonstrating the case-by-case approach to the use of force applied by the 'liberal states'.

> France strove to demonstrate convincingly that the disarmament of Iraq could be achieved through the peaceful means of inspections... Our prime concern today is the civilian population in Iraq ...France reiterates its commitment to sovereignty, unity and the territorial integrity of Iraq.[71]

The subsequent problems of the invasion of Iraq and the vocal condemnation of the mission and its effectiveness have also added to perceptions that China has been 'proved right' about the potential consequences of the mission, contributing to perceived legitimacy of China's denial of UN authorisation for this use of force. However, international agreement on an intervention in Iraq was always in reality a remote prospect. China cannot clearly be seen as a leading agent in the failure of the authorising resolution. However, this intervention not only has served as an important milestone in delegitimising some types of peacekeeping actions but also has resulted in the loss of credibility of Western actors (notably the USA and UK) who act as norm entrepreneurs. As we will see in the next section, this has had a significant challenge to the promotion and acceptance of the R2P.[72]

Sudan

In investigating the mission in Sudan, issues such as the role and importance of regional actors re-emerge.[73] Similarly, the Chinese focus on consent has also become central in understanding Chinese statements.[74] However, a new issue also comes out of this case—that is how China deals with non-state actors and the changing relationships of these actors to the 'sovereign' body within the state.

A great deal has been written about China's role in Sudan.[75] Much of the dominant discourse has argued that China has been unhelpful in the progress towards peace, protecting the government in Khartoum from a UN peacekeeping force, sanctions and other forms of pressure on the government, in order to maintain its oil supply.[76] However, the discussion below argues that China's position over Sudan (both before and after separation of the country)[77] is consistent with both China's interpretation of sovereignty and its actions in other conflict zones.[78]

In 2004, China abstained from a resolution deploying UN monitors and called on Sudan to 'fulfil immediately all of the commitments it made in the 3 July 2004 Communiqué' and to aid the international community in dealing with the humanitarian disaster.[79] However, China's fingerprints were all over the resolution, with specific references to the role of the African Union and the affirmation of the 'sovereignty of Sudan'.[80] Ostensibly, this suggests that China is following the pattern it has used for the past decade. However, in looking closer at the discussion of the resolution, China has consolidated its call for a political solution with an aid package, placed emphasis on the role of the African Union,[81] and uses the language (later to be adopted in the World Summit Outcome Document) of the R2P.[82] Thus, China's rhetoric is accompanied by some affirmative action, diplomatic and economic, in trying to deal with humanitarian issues.

Significantly, China's pressure and influence in Khartoum were essential to gaining the government's consent to allow UN peacekeepers into the country.[83] For China, in this as well as other military interventions, consent of the host government is vital; however, that consent may be coerced and still be seen as conforming to a Chinese interpretation of sovereignty.

In looking at China's role in Sudan, as Miwa Hirono highlights, there is evidence of the legacies of the approach China adopted in Cambodia.[84] China has consistently put pressure on all groups party to the conflict and attempted to act as a 'balancer' between them, without unduly influencing the outcome of the conflict—stopping the humanitarian crisis without ensuring a particular political outcome.[85] In the earlier phases of the conflict, China was seen as preferring one side. China needed to ensure its supply of oil from the country, and in order to this, it needed to support the Sudanese government, but has increasingly balanced between the two sides.[86] China gives aid to both Northern and Southern Sudan[87] and has engaged other regional actors in its activities in the country.[88] Thus, at the point where Sudan could be said to have two governments with some claim to legitimately represent (semi-distinct) geographical areas and populations, China's engagement strategy shifted to reflect this. Legitimate claims to sovereignty in the country changed and in response China's position changed.

Today, China's role in Sudan continues to be heavily criticised by Western media and governments. Yet, China's use of diplomatic pressure on the government in Khartoum and regional bodies has produced some results in a situation which would (according to Daniel Large) have otherwise necessitated a military intervention.[89] But '…China's increasingly global "charm offensive" requires China to take a sophisticated approach to the principle of sovereignty of host states that are engaged in civil wars'.[90] It also forces other states around the world to take note of the increasing sophistication and nuance in the Chinese approach[91] to and discourse on sovereignty and its challenge to military interventions and debates in the SC.

Taken collectively, these cases demonstrate the application of China's interpretation of sovereignty, which gives primacy to territorial integrity and non-interference in the internal affairs of sovereign states. Within the SC, China has demonstrated that there is room for a nuanced understanding of this position. In situations where the host government's consent can be coerced, through diplomatic means outside the SC, peacekeeping and peace-enforcement activities can still be acceptable to China and are not considered a challenge to the principles of sovereignty. Furthermore, the specific ad hoc case-by-case (or indeed issue-by-issue) approach adopted by China demonstrates the need for the mission and its specification and limitations to be carefully constructed (as in the case of Bosnia); these constructions do not easily fall into separate peacekeeping and peace-enforcement categories. Objectives must be tailored to the specific mission taking into account regional and local issues. Simultaneously, all missions must take into account the host government, and as a result, missions should maintain discussions with all parties to the dispute rather than unfairly influencing the outcome (thus deviating from sovereignty conditioned on the internal regime structure). They should thus avoid 'interfering in the internal affairs of the state' or constructing a particular solution.

In the advocacy of this nuanced and case-specific approach, China has set some guidelines; as can be noted in the above discussions, Chinese diplomacy consistently emphasises host consent, regional preferences and legitimisation. China's agency is not merely ad hoc but does maintain some consistencies; nonetheless, these consistencies move the place of 'power' in deciding these issues away from a 'core' group of states—they position power with the regional group, the individual state or the UN. As a result, China has utilised its position as a Permanent SC member (an insider) as well as its position as a developing state (an outsider) in acting to permit actions and adopt the rhetoric of humanitarian intervention, whilst also being able to maintain a distance from problems caused by military action. As a result, China not only has used 'populations' as tools but also changes the relative power position of the population in order to increase the effect of the agency and tool of that population.

At the same time, as China has subtly shifted its promotion of its position, there has also been a shift in the 'interpretive attitude'[92] of the international community. The intervention of Iraq acted as a 'new event' which can be seen as allowing the international community to reconsider its frame of reference with respect to humanitarian intervention. This 'new event' coupled with the debate being stirred up by the ICISS, and questions being raised about what sovereignty is, allowed actors to consider not only new understandings of sovereignty but traditional understandings and place them in the context of actions deemed to be legitimate and illegitimate. In terms of China's specific agency in this debate, the Chinese approach has been consistent for two decades, not only in abstaining, while permitting actions to take place, but also in indicating its displeasure with elements of the action. Over time, this can be seen as planting the seed for creating an 'actual or potential disparity between the two value systems'.[93]

Conclusion

China's position within the SC gives it the opportunity to reframe existing debates. China also has used coordination with other populations—namely ASEAN and the African Union—as tools for amplifying its normative preferences. China has used these tools (reframing and populations) in acting as an ad hoc objector and a norm entrepreneur.

In its engagement with ASEAN over East Timor and Cambodia, China acted as a norm entrepreneur. China expressed its own perspective that is clearly distinct from that of ASEAN—despite the common calls for the respect of sovereignty and non-interference. In the case of Cambodia, China was distinct in ensuring that its interpretation of respect of sovereignty and non-interference meant making sure the Khmer Rouge was included in the peace process. In East Timor, China had supported the government in exile. In addition, China had persuaded Indonesia to consent to the peacekeeping mission. These actions were in line with the rest of the international community—ASEAN and the UN both sought to ensure Indonesian consent for the peacekeeping mission, and the UN also hadn't recognised the Indonesian occupation of East Timor.[94] In advocating for Indonesian consent, China also advocated for the centrality of the UN in the peacekeeping mission. This is a position that has been consistent across all of the peacekeeping operations set out above. It is also a position China advocates in the response to R2P.

China has acted as an objector in the cases of Kosovo and Iraq. China has sought to reaffirm an interpretation of sovereignty and non-intervention that gives the UN a central role in authorising and executing missions.

In the case of Sudan, China has worked alongside the African Union, using the union as a tool in amplifying China's definition of non-interference and respect of sovereignty. In this pursuit, China has been instrumental in seeking consent from the government in Khartoum. Thus, the engagement with regional organisations in this case demonstrates China using the tools of 'populations' and reframing in its agency over this issue.

It is worth highlighting a key finding of this chapter is that China has effectively acted to separate out the need to respect state sovereignty from the sovereignty of a particular government. In the cases of Cambodia and Sudan, China respected the sovereignty of the state—ensuring the government of the day was consulted, involved and in a position to grant consent—but this did not extend to seeking to support the government as sovereign. This can also be seen as the case in East Timor. This is an important finding in moving forwards and looking at Libya as a R2P case. In this instance, China separates out the moment when a particular government has lost effective control, but does not aim to explicitly guide the 'will of the state' in what form of government replaces that particular government. In this action, China has attempted to reframe the debate on sovereignty. It has done it by using ad hoc objection to prevent the consistent use of particular liberal interpretations of sovereignty. It has also attempted to invoke a more 'traditional' understanding of sovereignty. In places, this does appear to be in line with norm entrepreneurship; nonetheless, this is only the case in a few instances rather than consistently.

Thus, in ostensibly acting as an objector and reaffirming 'traditional' peacekeeping operations, China has advocated a particular interpretation of state sovereignty and non-interference. In this respect, it is significant that according to Stähle, China has abstained to all missions authorised that contained the phrase 'all necessary means' (up to 2008).[95] In acting thus, China has used reinterpretation and other populations (including ASEAN and the AU). This conclusion is in line with the observations of former Amb. Diego Arria, who stated 'China never entered into an open confrontation with anyone',[96] and this was a Chinese characteristic. In the approach set out here, this tends to confirm the role of China in abstaining rather than vetoing, in producing ad hoc objection (which avoids confrontation) and in seeking to recall traditional approaches. This conclusion is also in line with the concern of China with the long-term implications of the authorisation of peacekeeping missions: for example, Amb. Arria notes that China is conscious of the long-term picture in all its actions,[97] and in addition, in 1994, China noted the need to avoid missions setting precedents for future actions.[98]

In briefly looking back to the liberal evolution of sovereignty in Chapter 5 in conjunction with this discussion, it suggests that China is actually applying previously agreed (and liberal) interpretation of sovereignty. Across the three areas of development of sovereignty, China is essential moving the discussion of 'legitimate polities' away from 'rogue states' or from preferring liberal states as positioned higher in the hierarchy of legitimate polities, in favour of diversity of states being once again recognised and respected. Similarly, this has implications for the expected behaviours of states and the membership of international society. As China appears to move away from limiting the forms of 'legitimate polities', it also broadens and diversifies the membership of international society promoting tolerance and discussion. As such, regimes, such as Sudan's, have to be listened to and debated with using diplomatic tools rather than coercively 'bullied'. This then seems to resemble the 'liberalism' of the early 1990s rather than the 'liberalism' of sovereignty in the early 2000s.

In the next chapter, China's approach to the R2P is explored, and setting out China's actions and approach shows 'remarkable consistency'[99] with its approach to peacekeeping in the 1990s.

NOTES

1. For an excellent discussions of China at the UN see: Ann E. Kent, *Beyond Compliance: China, International Organizations, and Global Security* (Stanford University Press: Stanford, 2009).
2. Marc Lanteigne, 'A Change in Perspective: China's Engagement in East Timor UN Peacekeeping Operations', *International Peacekeeping* (2011), 18(3), pp. 313–327, p. 17.

3. Miwa Hirono, 'China's Charm Offensive and Peacekeeping: The Lessons of Cambodia—What Now for Sudan?' *International Peacekeeping* (2011), 18(3), pp. 328–343, p. 336.
4. Zhao Lei, 'Two Pillars of China's Global Peace Engagement Strategy: UN Peacekeeping and International Peacebuilding', *International Peacekeeping* (2011), 18(3), pp. 344–363, p. 358.
5. One exception here is in the work of He Yin, who wrote the leading piece of work on Peacekeeping. He Yin, China's Changing Policy on UN Peacekeeping, Asia Paper, July 2007; also, He Yin, 'China's doctrine on UN peacekeeping' in Cedric De Coning, Chiyuki Aoi, and John Karlsrud (eds), *UN Peacekeeping Doctrine in a New Era: Adapting to Stablisation, Protection and New Threats* (Routledge: London, 2017).
6. The data for this statement comes from a collation of the voting records from 2000–2010 to the 22 December 2010 same website accessed on 8 January 2011 and 5 August 2012; UN Documentation Centre, 'Meetings Conducted/Actions Taken by the Security Council', http://www.un.org/Depts/dhl/resguide/scact.htm, accessed 14 December 2010.
7. Vetoes from China since 2011: S/PV.6627, 4 October 2011 (draft resolution, S/2011/612); S/PV.6711, 4 February 2012 (draft resolution, S/2012/77); S/PV.6810, 19 July 2012 (draft resolution, S/2012/538); S/PV.7180, 22 May 2014 (draft resolution, S/2014/348); S/PV.7825, 5 December 2016 (draft resolution, S/2016/1026); S/PV.7893, 28 February 2017 (draft resolution, S/2017/172).
8. Catherine Jones, 'Regional Perspective: The Evolution of China's Peacekeeping Role', in David Curran, Larry Roeder, and Robert Zuber (eds), *New Directions and Opportunities for Peacekeeping: Expanding Stakeholders and Regional Arrangements* (Springer, 2015).
9. China abstained, on S/Res 1556, 30 July 2004 (along with Pakistan); S/Res 1564, 18 September 2004 (along with Russia, Pakistan, Algeria); S/Res 1592, 30 March 2005 (along with USA, Algeria, Brazil); S/Res 1672, 25 April 2006 (Qatar and Russia); S/Res 1706, 31 August 2006 (Qatar, Russia); S/Res 1945, 14 October 2010 (abstained alone).
10. See, for example, David Malone, 'The UN Security Council and the Post-Cold War World: 1987–1997', *Security Dialogue* (1997), 28(4), pp. 393–408; Joel Wuthnow, 'China and the Processes of Cooperation in UN Security Council Deliberations', *Chinese Journal of International Politics* (2010), 3(1), pp. 55–77.
11. These are discussed and drawn into the case specific analysis below. See also, Phillippe D. Rogers, 'China and United Nations Peacekeeping Operations', *Naval War College Review* (2007), 60(2), pp. 72–93.

12. Baogang He, 'Chinese Sovereignty: Challenges and Adaptation', *EAI Working Paper No 104* published 23 September 2003; Stefan Stähle, 'China's Shifting Attitude to UN Peacekeeping Operations', *China Quarterly* (2008), 195, pp. 631–655.
13. James Reilly and Bates Gill, 'Sovereignty, Intervention and Peacekeeping: The View from Beijing', *Survival* (2000), 42(3), pp. 41–60.
14. Allen Carlson, *Unifying China, Integrating with the World: Securing Chinese Sovereignty in the Reform Era* (Stanford University Press: Stanford, CA, 2005); Allen Carlson, 'More Than Just Saying No: China's Evolving Approach to Sovereignty and Intervention Since Tiananmen', in Johnston and Ross (eds), *New Directions in the Study of China's Foreign Policy*, pp. 217–241; Allen Carlson, 'Protecting Sovereignty, Accepting Intervention: The Dilemma of Chinese Foreign Relations in the 1990s', *China Policy Series* (National Committee on US-China Relations: New York, 2002).
15. Stefan Stähle, 'China's Shifting Attitude to UN Peacekeeping Operations', *China Quarterly* (2008), 195, pp. 631–655.
16. M. Taylor Fravel, 'China's Attitude Toward UN Peacekeeping Operations Since 1989', *Asian Survey* (1996), 36(11), pp. 1102–1122.
17. Catherine Jones, 'The Party's Over for the Use of Sanctions', Unpublished conference paper PSA Conference March 2013.
18. As noted by former Amb. Diego Arria, Cambodia was a mission that had the support of the full Council; the issues that arose were more connected to problems on the ground and particular commanders of the mission. Author Interview with Former Amb. Diego Arria [Skype] 22 February 2013.
19. Eşref Aksu, *The United Nations, Intra-State Peacekeeping and Normative Change* (Manchester University Press: Manchester, 2003), pp. 179–209.
20. It should be noted that China had a number of interests outside any concern about norm setting.
21. ASEAN had attempted to resolve the occupation of Cambodia by Vietnamese forces in 1981. Aksu, *The United Nations, Intra-State Peacekeeping and Normative change*, p. 181.
22. For a summary of China–Cambodia relations see, Ian Storey, *Southeast Asia and the Rise of China: The Search for Security* (Routledge: Abingdon, 2011), pp. 28–37; UNTAC, creation S/RES.745, 28 February 1992.
23. Aksu, *The United Nations, Intra-State Peacekeeping and Normative Change*, p. 182.
24. Yearbook of the United Nations 1992, available http://unyearbook.un.org/unyearbook.html?name=1992index.html, accessed 7 November 2011, p. 244.
25. Yearbook of the United Nations 1992, p. 247.
26. S/RES 792, 30 November 1992.

27. Aksu, *The United Nations, Intra-State Peacekeeping and Normative Change*, p. 183.
28. UN Yearbook 1992, available http://unyearbook.un.org/unyearbook.html?name=1992index.html, accessed 7 November 2011, p. 259 (author's emphasis).
29. In relation to sanctions in general—not only speaking about Cambodia— (whether sanctions related to the use of force or economic sanctions) these discussions had China's full attention in the Council—even on occasions when they had appeared to be not engaged with debates. Author Interview with Former Amb. Diego Arria [Skype] 22 February 2013.
30. Aksu, *The United Nations, Intra-State Peacekeeping and Normative Change*, p. 183.
31. Ibid., p. 185.
32. Hirono, 'China's Charm Offensive and Peacekeeping', pp. 332–333.
33. Ibid., p. 331.
34. Ibid., p. 334.
35. Courtney Richardson, 'A Responsible Power? China and the UN Peacekeeping Regime', *International Peacekeeping* (2011), 18(3), pp. 286–297, p. 290.
36. Aksu, *The United Nations, Intra-State Peacekeeping and Normative Change*, p. 188.
37. Stähle, 'China's Shifting Attitude to UN Peacekeeping Operations', p. 639.
38. Ibid., p. 644.
39. Author Interview with Former Amb. Diego Arria [Skype] 22 February 2013.
40. Ibid.
41. Ibid.
42. UNSC Res 816, 31 March 1993, see also UN Yearbook 1993, available http://unyearbook.un.org/unyearbook.html?name=1993index.html, accessed 14 February 2013, p. 464.
43. UNSC Res 871, 4 October 1993.
44. Ibid.
45. UN Yearbook, 1994, available http://unyearbook.un.org/unyearbook.html?name=1994index.html, accessed 14 February 2013, p. 541.
46. Author Interview with Simon Adams, New York, 30 January 2013.
47. Tony Blair, 'The Blair Doctrine', 22 April 1999, full text available from PBS, http://www.pbs.org/newshour/bb/international/jan-june99/blair_doctrine4-23.html, accessed 18 February 2013.
48. '…post facto validation that was widely seen as characterizing Resolution 1244 in the wake of NATO's. Kosovo intervention'. James Cockayne and

David M. Malone, 'The Security Council and the 1991 and 2003 Wars in Iraq', in Vaughan Lowe, Adam Roberts, Jennifer Welsh, and Dominik Zaum, *The United Nations Security Council and War: The Evolution of Thought and Practice Since 1945* (Oxford University Press: Oxford, 2008), p. 402.
49. Paul Heinbecker, 'Kosovo', in David M. Malone (ed.), *The UN Security Council: From the Cold War to the 21st Century* (Lynne Rienner: Boulder, London, 2004), pp. 537–550, p. 537.
50. See, for example, S/PV.3930, 23 September 1998, pp. 3–4.
51. See S/PV.3930, p. 4 see also S/PV.4011, 10 June 1999, p. 9.
52. S/PV.4003, 14 May 1999, p. 7.
53. As Cook and Clemens put it 'the most ambitious innovators may well cloak their efforts for change in appeals to restore tradition'. Elisabeth S. Clemens and James M. Cook, 'Politics and Institutionalism: Explaining Durability and Change', *Annual Review of Sociology* (1999), 25, pp. 441–466, p. 459.
54. S/PV.4003, 14 May 1999, p. 7.
55. See, for example, the discussion on the use of air power in Kosovo: Daniel L. Byman and Matthew C. Waxman, 'Kosovo and the Great Air Power Debate', *International Security* (2000), 24(4), pp. 5–38, and Robert A. Pape, 'The True Worth of Air Power', *Foreign Affairs* (2004), 83(2), pp. 116–130.
56. Heinbecker, *Kosovo*, p. 549.
57. See Rosemary Foot and Andrew Walter, *China, the United States and Global Order* (Cambridge University Press: New York, 2011), pp. 298–300, p. 48.
58. See Kosovo after the NATO bombing of Chinese embassy. S/PV.4003, 14 May 1999.
59. Ian Storey, *Southeast Asia and the Rise of China: The Search for Security* (Routledge: Abingdon, 2011), p. 276.
60. See S/PV.4043, 11 September 1999, pp. 12–13.
61. Allen Carlson, 'More Than Just Saying No', p. 228; see also Marc Lanteigne, 'A Change in Perspective', p. 320.
62. Ibid., p. 228.
63. Foot and Walter, *China, the United States and Global Order*, p. 48.
64. James Cotton, 'Against the Grain: East Timor Intervention', *Survival* (2001), 43(1), pp. 127–143.
65. Storey, *China's Rise and South East Asia*, p. 275.
66. Hirono, 'China's Charm Offensive and Peacekeeping'.
67. See point 10, S/RES/1264, 15 September 1999; also, Marc Lanteigne, 'A Change in Perspective', p. 320.
68. Marc Lanteigne, 'A Change in Perspective', p. 322.
69. S/PV.4057, 25 October 1999.

70. S/PV.4726 (Resumption 1), 27 March 2003, p. 28.
71. Ibid., pp. 28–29.
72. Alex J. Bellamy, 'Responsibility to Protect or Trojan Horse? The Crisis in Darfur and Humanitarian Intervention after Iraq', *Ethics & International Affairs* (2005), 19(2), pp. 31–54, p. 33.
73. Joel Wuthnow, *Chinese Diplomacy and the UN Security Council* (Routledge: Abingdon, 2013), pp. 105–107.
74. Ibid., p. 99.
75. See, for example: Hirono, 'China's Charm Offensive and Peacekeeping'; Jonathan Holslag, 'China's Diplomatic Victory in Darfur' BICCS Background Paper Published 1 August 2007; Daniel Large, 'China's Sudan Engagement: Changing Northern and Southern Political Trajectories in Peace and War', *China Quarterly* (2009), 199, pp. 610–626; Pak K. Lee, Gerald Chan, and Lai-Ha Chan, 'China in Darfur: Rule-Makers or Rule-Taker', *Review of International Studies* (2011), 38(2), pp. 423–444; Joel Wuthnow, *Chinese Diplomacy and the UN Security Council* (Routledge: Abingdon, 2013).
76. According to a Saferworld Report on China and Conflict Affected States, 69.9% of Sudan's exports go to China, Larry Aintree, *China and Conflict Affected States: Between Principle and Pragmatism*, January 2012, http://www.saferworld.org.uk/downloads/pubdocs/FAB%20Sudan%20and%20South%20Sudan.pdf, accessed 14 February 2013, p. 10.
77. South Sudan gained independence on 9 July 2011 reported in The Economist, 'Sudan's Separation: Their Day in the Sun', *The Economist*, 7 July 2011, available http://www.economist.com/node/18929477, accessed 14 February 2013; Xan Rice, 'South Sudan celebrates a sweet separation', *The Guardian*, 10 July 2011, available http://www.guardian.co.uk/world/2011/jul/10/south-sudan-celebrates-independence, accessed 14 February 2013; for views on how quickly China recognised the new state see: Larry Aintree, *China and Conflict Affected States: Between Principle and Pragmatism*, January 2012, http://www.saferworld.org.uk/downloads/pubdocs/FAB%20Sudan%20and%20South%20Sudan.pdf, accessed 14 February 2013, p. 17.
78. Although the most recent Saferworld Reports argue that there has been an increasing flexibility by China in its own use of the terms 'Sovereignty and Non-interference', *Saferworld, Seminar Report: China and South Sudan: New Perspectives on Development and Conflict Prevention*, 30 May 2012, available http://www.saferworld.org.uk/downloads/pubdocs/China%20and%20South%20Sudan%20Seminar%20Report%20.pdf, accessed 14 February 2013; also Saferworld, *Saferworld Briefing: China and South Sudan*, August 2012, available http://www.saferworld.org.uk/downloads/pubdocs/China-South%20Sudan%20briefing%20English.pdf, accessed 14 February 2013.

79. S/RES/1556, 30 July 2004, p. 3.
80. Ibid., pp. 1 and 3.
81. China had urged the Sudanese government to accept and cooperate with and continued to do so. Foot and Walter, *China, the United States and Global Order*, pp. 49–50; Stephanie Kleine-Ahlbrandt and Andrew Small, 'China's New Dictatorship Diplomacy: Is Beijing Parting with Pariahs?' *Foreign Affairs* (2008), 87(1), pp. 38–56.
82. S/PV.5015, 30 July 2004, p. 3.
83. Sudan Tribune, 'China Pushes Sudan to Let UN Troops into Darfur', *Sudan Tribune* published 14 September 2006, available online at http://www.sudantribune.com/China-pushes-Sudan-to-let-UN,17596, accessed on 11 November 2011; Antoaneta Bezlova, 'China Joins UN Peacekeepers in Sudan', *Asia Times Online*, published 25 September 2007, available http://www.atimes.com/atimes/China/II25Ad02.html, accessed 11 November 2011. Also Deborah Bräutigam, *The Dragon's Gift: The Real Story of China in Africa* (Oxford University Press: Oxford, 2011), p. 282; Wuthnow, *Chinese Diplomacy and the UN Security Council*, pp. 95–112.
84. Hirono, 'China's Charm Offensive and Peacekeeping'.
85. S/PV.5015, 3 July 2004; see also Wuthnow, *Chinese Diplomacy and the UN Security Council*, p. 97.
86. Wuthnow, *Chinese Diplomacy and the UN Security Council*, p. 337.
87. See, for example: Simon Tisdall, 'Follow China's Aid Lead, Sudan Urges West', *The Guardian*, published 11 March 2008, available http://www.guardian.co.uk/world/2008/mar/11/sudan.china, accessed 11 November 2011; Xinhua News Agency, 'China Helps Promote Peace, Development of North, South Sudan', 9 July 2011, available http://news.xinhuanet.com/english2010/china/2011-07/09/c_13975463.htm, accessed 11 November 2011; Hirono, 'China's Charm Offensive and Peacekeeping'; Daniel Large, 'China's Sudan Engagement: Changing Northern and Southern Political Trajectories in Peace and War', *China Quarterly* (2009), 199, pp. 610–626.
88. Hirono, 'China's Charm Offensive and Peacekeeping', p. 337.
89. According to Daniel Large, China maintained its formal agreements with Khartoum but used its influence behind the scenes, Large, 'China's Sudan Engagement', p. 619.
90. Hirono, 'China's Charm Offensive and Peacekeeping', p. 339.
91. Wuthnow, *Chinese Diplomacy and the UN Security Council*.
92. Ronald. M. Dworkin, *Law's Empire* (Hart, 2004), p. 46.
93. John Dowling and Jeffrey Pfeffer, 'Organizational Legitimacy: Social Values and Organizational Behavior', *The Pacific Sociological Review* (1975), 18(1), pp. 122–136, p. 122.

94. James Cotton, 'Against the Grain: East Timor Intervention', *Survival* (2001), 43(1), pp. 127–143.
95. Stähle, 'China's Shifting Attitude to UN Peacekeeping Operations'.
96. Author Interview with Former Amb. Diego Arria [Skype] 22 February 2013.
97. Ibid.
98. See, S/PV.3413, 31 July 1994, see also, Stähle, 'China's Shifting Attitude to UN Peacekeeping Operations', p. 643.
99. Author Interviews, New York, 1 February 2013.

CHAPTER 7

China and the Responsibility to Protect

This chapter sets out the argument that China is a key player in the interpretation and implementation of the concept of the 'Responsibility to Protect' (R2P). It makes two arguments. First, that China has used ad hoc objection in its approach to the implementation of the norm. In doing this, it has used the tools of populations (including ASEAN, NAM, BRICS and the G77). The result has been that the progress of the concept of R2P has been frustrated. Importantly, it will continue to be frustrated because of the role of China in presenting a view of R2P as related to the coercive use of force around pillar three of R2P (the role of the international community in protecting civilians). The second argument is that China has been an unsuccessful norm entrepreneur. China's presentation of 'Responsible Protection' as a way to implement R2P cannot be counted as a successful attempt at norm entrepreneurship.

Regarding R2P, it is not only China that is important. China's position as an ad hoc objector has been enhanced because of a number of facilitating conditions: changing balance of power; failure of the practice of the norm; and the reducing legitimacy of the western powers. These factors must be considered in distilling China's agency in challenging the norm of R2P.

This chapter is set out into three parts. The first considers the evolution of R2P, setting out its evolution and key features. The second reflects on China's agency (norm entrepreneurship and objection) and whether China is using any of the tools from Chapter 4. The final section highlights the facilitating factors in presenting this challenge.

© The Author(s) 2018
C. Jones, *China's Challenge to Liberal Norms*,
https://doi.org/10.1057/978-1-137-42761-8_7

The Evolution of the Responsibility to Protect

This section gives a brief—but necessary—sketch of the evolution of R2P from idea towards norm.[1] At the end of this section, there is a discussion of what type of norm R2P is. As noted in Chapter 4, understanding how a norm 'fits' within the existing normative architecture and understanding its level of acceptance are important factors in indicating how the norm can be challenged and whether that challenge has the potential to affect international order.

In 2001, the International Commission on Intervention and State Sovereignty (ICISS) published a report which attempted to establish a framework for consistently responding to mass atrocity crimes.[2] The ICISS embraced the challenge from Kofi Annan to overcome the ad hoc (or lack of) international responses to, for example, Srebrenica and Rwanda,[3] as well as the subsequent problems surrounding the narrowly held norm of 'humanitarian intervention'.[4] The result was an attempt to produce a broader and more widely accepted norm, and set of tools, to ensure that mass atrocities never happened again.

The ICISS, in putting together the report, took up the challenge that originated with the 1992 *Agenda for Peace document* (A4P)[5] and its 1995 reassessment,[6] Kofi Annan's *Two Sovereignties*[7] and Francis Deng's *Sovereignty as Responsibility*.[8] Moving on from these starting points, the ICISS initiated a number of international discussions around the world concerning the concept of 'sovereignty as responsibility'.[9] The final document submitted by the ICISS advocated the concept of the 'Responsibility to Protect'. The report set out clear lines of responsibility for governments and international organisations. In particular, it maintained that responses should not be limited in scope to the use of force and that they should not be restricted in sources of authority in order to overcome potential deadlock in the Security Council (SC).[10]

Following the ICISS report, the UN worked towards the acceptance and implementation of R2P. This culminated in the *World Summit Outcome Document* (WSOD). Prior to this document, results from these activities included: the High Level Panel report in 2004, *A More Secure World: Our Shared Responsibility*,[11] which resulted from the High Level Panel created by Kofi Annan on *Threats, Challenges, and Change*[12]; and Kofi Annan's Secretary General Report *In Larger Freedom* issued in September 2005.[13] Furthermore, prior to the 2005 outcome document, there was a process of negotiation and discussion regarding the content and the position of the paragraphs (138 and 139) that related to the Responsibility to Protect.[14]

In the 2004 High Level report, *A More Secure World*,[15] it was made clear that despite general acceptance of the concept of 'sovereignty as responsibility', 'the concept of State and International responsibility to protect civilians ... has yet to truly overcome the tension between the competing claims of sovereign inviolability and the right to intervene'.[16] However, it made its disapproval of current attempts to protect civilians clear in paragraph 42, which states 'we have been struck once again by the glacial speed at which our institutions have responded to massive human rights violations'.[17] The mood of this report thus provided the impetus for the production of the WSOD.[18]

The WSOD is interesting in two ways: first, for the differences between this document and the ICISS report; second, for the consensus around the ideas contained within it. The differences between these documents have been elaborated by academics[19] and international lawyers[20] and need not be expanded on here. The main point, from these discussions, is that the motives for international action in the ICISS report were partially (but not solely) related to crimes already identified in international law. But in the WSOD the scope of R2P was limited to four crimes: 'genocide, war crimes, ethnic cleansing and crimes against humanity'.[21] This made it easier for states to agree on the crimes that R2P should be applied to. Furthermore, the ICISS document noted that the permanent members should try to avoid the use of their veto powers in R2P cases.[22] Whilst this was reflected in the draft of the WSOD,[23] it was removed from the final document.[24]

Since 2005, the Responsibility to Protect has continued to evolve as a norm. It has developed in two main ways. First, through the invocation of the concept in Resolutions 1674[25] and 1894,[26] which both concern the protection of civilians in armed conflict, in Resolutions 1970[27] and 1973[28] (Libya), 1975[29] (Cote D'Ivoire), 1996[30] (South Sudan), 2014[31] (Yemen) and 2016[32] and 2040[33] (Libya) and 2056[34] (Mali).[35] Second, it has evolved within the UN through the annual General Assembly Debates,[36] and the Secretary General's reports on implementation.[37]

Within the process of evolution, the aim of the Secretary General has been to move the abstract concept of R2P to an implementable norm associated with specific actions and expected responses. Both the practical attempt to implement the norm and the conceptual discussion around how to create mechanisms and tools in order to systematise consolidation are significant for the process of evolution of the norm. As a result, both the attempts to use R2P and the attempts to systematise the UN responses are important in challenging and shaping the context and application of the norm.

From the view of the conceptual specification of the norm, the most significant driving force has been the Secretary General's (SG) reports. The first SG report separated R2P into three pillars. Pillar one stated that the state has the primary Responsibility to Protect its population; pillar two, that the international community has a responsibility to assist where necessary; and pillar three, that the international community has a responsibility to intervene if a state is unable or unwilling to protect its people in a 'timely and decisive manner'.[38] These three pillars have been further elaborated in the SG reports of 2010,[39] 2011[40] and 2012.[41]

There are a number of significant elements to this specification of implementation.[42] First, these three pillars (although numbered) do not have to be followed sequentially—that is it is not necessary to try and aid a state if it is evident that the target state is unable to fulfil its responsibility. Second, the majority of the discussion of R2P has revolved around the third pillar—seen as the most problematic for implementation. Third, in separating out these three pillars, there have been discussions as to whether R2P is becoming 'R2Plite',[43] regarding whether all three pillars will continue to be seen as a unified whole. As such, an objection to an interpretation, or an implementation, of one of the three pillars needn't necessarily be an objection to the norm. Thus, there is significant mileage to be gained by separating out these pillars to locate what exactly is under challenge. Fourth, there are regional dynamics at play. Regions are important for the implementation of R2P and arguably offer a place for contesting the norm.

Beyond the SG's reports, there have been two noteworthy additions to the discussion of implementation. The first is the Brazilian proposal, 'Responsibility whilst Protecting'[44] (RwP). This specifies the limitations of the use of pillar three within the SG's implementation strategy. It arose from the concern of a number of states following the action in Libya, and it is particularly concerned with the use of force and the oversight of missions by the SC. RwP was further discussed in an interactive debate held by the GA in 2012. It has been noted that RwP may aid the progress of R2P, but there is also the potential that it may hinder future consensus on whether to intervene.[45] In particular, in the GA discussion, a number of states highlighted the need for the pillars to be applied sequentially and that it was unfair not to give states the opportunity to protect before intervention was authorised.[46]

RwP not only refocuses attention of R2P on prevention, but also sets out some clear criteria on intervention practices. In particular, one of the issues a number of states had with recent UNPKOs was the subcontracting of missions to Western groups of states. As one interviewee noted that because of the lateness that 'all necessary means' was added, 'some states were concerned that the UNSC was outsourcing implementation of a coercive mandate AND ensuring that the mandate would operate on the broadest terms possible. They felt this was a recipe for possible abuse'.[47] One attempt of the RwP was to reposition the role of oversight to be more directly within the remit of the SC.[48] Nonetheless, as discussion of RwP developed, a number of problems with the initial outline emerged (particularly in relation to the sequencing of the pillars); as a result, it seems to have moved from being seen as a potential norm in itself[49] to the note and informal discussion providing 'an opportunity for Member States as well as regional organisations and civil society groups to raise and address concerns related to the concept note and the larger questions on the subject of implementation strategies'.[50]

The second significant proposal on implementation is the Chinese concept of Responsible Protection (RP). RP sets out that the people of the state should be protected, by 'legitimate' protectors, whose actions are 'limited', and protection duties should be defined, protection should also include reconstruction, and all actions must be supervised by the UN.[51] This document sets out conditions on which R2P should be invoked and on how actions are implemented. It was written by an influential scholar in China, Prof. Ruan Zongze. In this document—that has been published by the China Daily[52] and the China Institute for International Studies[53]—a central theme is that 'Responsible Protection' is the best means for implementing R2P in accordance with the UN Charter.[54] The author argues that this is how China should approach the notion of R2P and advocate it internationally.[55] Nevertheless, a key problem with seeing this as a challenge from China is that the concept does not seem to have made any headway among the UN bodies, or even among civil society groups.[56] Hence, China may be seen to be developing an alternative interpretation of R2P, but at present it appears to lack the capacity to develop an alternative interpretation and then propel it towards international acceptance.[57] Consequently, as noted in Chapter 4, in order for entrepreneurship to be possible, there is a need for not only a capacity within the state, but also the capacity to drive a new interpretation. In this instance, it seems that at most, China's 'Responsible Protection' idea merely specifies a particular view within China. Although there are some elements of RP that appear in China's statements at the UN, for example, Beijing stresses the need for 'prudent' action in crises.[58]

In attempting to put the norm of R2P into practice, there have been some significant actions. The first of these was the first use of the norm in Resolution 1674.[59] Nonetheless, the norm's most significant progress towards implementation is related to Resolutions 1970 and 1973 on Libya,[60] and the failed resolutions on Syria[61] (particularly the debate on 31 January 2012 and the vetoed resolution on 4 February 2012).[62]

Importantly, for the first five years of the norm's existence, the academic community seemed astounded by its success and rapid acceptance.[63] Conversely, since 2011, the progress of the norm has been greatly frustrated. The problems associated with implementation since 2011 link this discussion back to the problems of peacekeeping in the 1990s (discussed in the previous section). However, it is imperative to recall that the implementation and scope of R2P were intended to be, and still is, broader than just peacekeeping activities. As a result, in the following section, concerning China's challenge to the norm, the distinction between pillar one, two and three (non-use of force actions), and pillar three's implementation with the use of force, is made evident.[64]

In summary, there has been a shift since 2005 from whether the norm has been accepted to how to implement it. Nevertheless, as will be noted below, implementation and specification of the concept pose their own challenges to the norm.

Implementation and Conceptualisation

There are two main factors enabling the consolidation of R2P: conceptual clarification and implementation. These two are necessarily linked. However, it is helpful to separate them in order to clarify the nature of China's challenge.

The first part of this section focuses on whether China has attempted to challenge the abstract concept of the norm. Specifically, it considers China's responses to the ICISS report, the WSOD, the SG reports and the subsequent conceptual discussions on implementation.[65] This section argues that China has used ad hoc objection to the evolution of R2P and its liberal specification. Where able, it has linked this objection to other states of a similar predisposition; in doing so, it has used the tool of populations.

The second section focuses on China's responses to particular uses of R2P. It sets out whether China has sought to adopt R2P or reinterpret it, through application of the norm. This section considers Resolutions 1674, 1970, 1973, and the failed Syria resolution. It concludes that China has attempted to be a norm entrepreneur in its interpretation and implementation of R2P. But that a lack of capacity in China,[66] as well as a lack of experience, has (so far) meant this entrepreneurship has been unsuccessful. Yet, China has been more successful in stymieing a particular liberal interpretation of how the international community should react to R2P crimes (particularly concerning which tools are effective as pillar three responses). Interestingly, China has aided the progress of pillars one and two. Accordingly, it is not forming a challenge to these elements of R2P per se. In particular, in actions coordinated with ASEAN, China has been instrumental in supporting activities that could be classed as R2P pillar one and two actions. But, because these actions are not viewed as invocations of R2P, they perpetuate the perception that R2P is related to pillar three coercive activities. Hence, China's actions with ASEAN regarding pillars one and two actually aid a misleading perception of 'what R2P is'—relating it to coercive action and regime change. This has the effect of reinterpreting the norm because it deprives R2P of a source of legitimacy (in terms of successful pillar one and two activities in Asia) which is necessary for its further consolidation.

China's Challenge to the Concept of R2P

This section argues that—whilst not explicitly objecting to R2P as a norm—China's actions frustrate the ability for consensus to emerge around it. This section makes three points. Firstly, China is instrumental in ensuring that R2P discussions remain in the GA (rather than these discussion taking place outside the UN or within the SC),[67] thus making consensus more difficult to achieve. Second, China's presentation of its views in accordance with the Non-Aligned Movement (NAM) and the G77 making use of the flatter and more democratic structure of the UN within the GA. China's engagement with these groups which ensures a constant voice in the SC and a significant voting bloc in the GA. Finally, China's participation in events, such as the informal dialogue on RwP, ensures that little action actually happens.

The first notable element of this challenge is the use of the conservative bias of the GA. The SC and the UN more generally have a tendency to lean towards inaction.[68] China, in seeking to change and influence the norms of sovereignty, through the debates around R2P within legitimate offices of the UN, has been able to present itself as a responsible actor. Significantly, this change in recognition of China as 'responsible', and the related change in its influence, enables China to act as a persistent objector. In being able to act as a persistent objector, China is preventing the consolidation of a new interpretation of the norms of sovereignty rather than producing a new rival to them. As Foot and Walter put it: 'China has been able to help shape that norm's interpretation and content, relatively sanguine in the knowledge that its more conservative approach to R2P will find support among the other UN member states'.[69]

In setting out China's position as a persistent objector, China can capitalise on the reality that in the expression of sovereignty as a liberal norm (see Part I of this chapter), there are many inconsistencies both in application and in theory. A part of China's challenge to the consolidation of R2P utilises these inconsistencies and contradictions.[70] Moreover, the attempt to use the norm in Libya has allowed China (along with other powers) to claim that the norm is being used to justify Western interventionism rather than pursuing peace and security.[71]

As noted in Chapter 4, new interstitial norms must fit within larger meta-norms, and this can either occur by new norms slightly adapting the interpretation of the meta-norms or new norms failing to become a part of the international normative order. Indeed, highlighting these persistent problems helps prevent the consolidation of R2P until R2P advocates can consistently overcome these issues. For example, R2P faces challenges in overcoming the hesitancy of states regarding intervention— in particular R2P addresses an increasing challenge to reconcile R2P with the meta-norm of state sovereignty. As noted above, there has been a move to limit state sovereignty so that it is no longer used to justify the prevention of violence against civilians. China's actions thus prevent both the specific use of the interstitial norm of R2P (in the implementation of pillar three) and prevent the reframing of sovereignty through the interstitial norm.

As a result of this inability to make progress in the discussion of R2P at the broadest international level, the discussion of the norm has found a home within more regional contexts, as will be discussed in more detail later. The focus here is on the issue of the 'post-interpretative' stage, as a driver of the evolution of the norm, in particular the role post-interpretative changes have in driving the norm from 'hard' to 'soft' in its expression.[72]

The claim here is that for the norm of R2P to be consolidated it needs to develop consistency and coherence within the network of existing norms. However, as the network of existing norms regarding sovereignty lacks coherence with each other, this is difficult to achieve—especially when there are resistance and contestation to both the new norm and the existing dominant interpretation of established norms. As a result, it is much easier for a state unhappy with the concept of R2P to resist its consolidation as a 'hard' norm by exposing that it doesn't 'fit' within the existing practices and frameworks guiding the international community. Given the acceptance at the GA, that resistance may only be able to make the implementation of R2P 'softer'.

Looking at this claim more closely, it is clear that the documents that discuss the R2P have a common central element: the continuation of the recognition of the sovereignty of a state is contingent on that state protecting its civilian population from harm. Despite the acceptance of this as an abstract issue, the application and consolidation of this norm had not yet taken place in 2005. As noted by the SG in 2005:

> We must also move towards embracing and acting on the "responsibility to protect" potential or actual victims of massive atrocities. The time has come for Governments to be held to account, both to their citizens and to each other, for respect of the dignity of the individual, to which they too often pay only lip service. We must move from an era of legislation to an era of implementation. Our declared principles and our common interests demand no less.[73]

Nevertheless, since 2005, the concept of R2P seems to have gone backwards in terms of the norm hierarchy and acceptance.[74] Challenging the norm of sovereignty was always going to be difficult, but at present even making addenda to the norm seems almost impossible. For China's position, this works well on two counts; not only does a more traditional Westphalian interpretation better suit Chinese pragmatism, but also the door to debating sovereignty and intervention has been blown wide open by R2P. As Bellamy states, the loss of momentum over R2P allowed for its opponents to put together credible and coherent arguments, couched in the language of R2P, to use against it. Furthermore, more debates on humanitarian intervention have also weakened the 'partial consensus on these questions [which] was established in the 1990s, [but] there is now deep division'.[75]

A significant blow to R2P was dealt in 2008 when a committee meeting of the GA stated that 'the responsibility to protect itself which was not accepted or approved as a principle by the General Assembly'.[76] This issue was discussed in relation to the appointment of Edward Luck as a Special Advisor to the SG on the R2P. Within the context of this budgetary meeting about UN staffing, China made three things clear: firstly, that it stood with the 'group of 77',[77] secondly, that it was seeking to maintain its leadership by explicitly championing the needs of developing countries,[78] thirdly, that it favours changes that proceed in a 'cautious and incremental manner'.[79] China's position on the evolution of R2P is consistent with its approach to the development agenda and the way that it engages with its region (as will be made clearer in Part III).

China's position then 'falls in line' with that of a number of countries sceptical about the evolution of a norm of R2P, and it has used its seat on the SC, and groups within the UN system, to stall any progress on the norm. However, the norm has also undergone changes, and reinterpretation at a regional level, in a part of a process that Prantl and Nakano[80] describe as a feedback loop—highlighting the role of regional bodies in creating consistency between new norms and existing practices. The ability to link ASEAN states' concerns about R2P, such as protection from Western intervention, is significant. Even if, as noted by Noel Morada and others, that in terms of practical adoption and acceptance of R2P, the region has been more accepting than the banner headline of 'non-intervention' would suggest.[81]

China can also be seen to be utilising its regional influence to shape the regional interpretation of the norm and thus contributing to the experiences that regional states draw on when they act at the international level. In looking at China's role in this process, Prantl and Nakano clearly attribute considerable agency to China at both a regional and international level in the reinterpretation of the norm: 'China has actively deconstructed RtoP ... The reconstructed norm was then fed back to the global level where Beijing co-shaped the RtoP norm throughout the discursive enmeshment of RtoP, in line with Chinese foreign policy principles'.[82] In using China's role within regional bodies, China has been able to join up with an existing community to reinterpret R2P.

In looking to the region in reinterpreting the norm, China reinforces statements of the centrality of the region in deciding courses of action for intervention.

Furthermore, China's ability to position itself within a group gives China the opportunity to further its own foreign policy agenda of not showing leadership and 'peacefully rising', and as Sarah Teitt suggests, it also prevents it from having to stand alone in showing opposition.[83]

The use of regional organisations and the G77 demonstrates the significance of populations in interpreting and reinterpreting international norms. These collections of states develop a common (and legitimated) interpretation and can then act in coordination to promote their interpretation. As a result, the G77 plus China, whilst not providing a majority in the General Assembly, do present a sizable population with its own legitimated interpretation of R2P.

China's Challenge to the Implementation of R2P

China's contestation concerns the coercive use of pillar three, rather than pillars one and two. Indeed, as noted later, China has been supportive of a number of actions that constitute, or can be seen to constitute, pillars one and two.[84] However, the contest and the importance of the development of the norm surround whether pillar three can be specified and implemented. This discussion addresses these two issues, focussing on what China does and *how* it presents a challenge.

China and Resolution 1674

In Resolution 1674 of 28 April 2006, the R2P was invoked for the first time.[85] This presented the first test for implementation of the abstract norm. It has been noted that both China and Russia voted in favour of Resolution 1674. Nevertheless, the extent of acceptance by these powers is a matter of debate.

Most notably, the resolution used the exact language of the WSOD: '*Reaffirms* the provisions of paragraphs 138 and 139 of the 2005 World Summit Outcome Document regarding the responsibility to protect populations from genocide, war crimes, ethnic cleansing and crimes against humanity'.[86] China and Russia would only agree to the same phrasing that had already been agreed in 2005. Thus, it should not be regarded that China and Russia were becoming increasingly comfortable with the use of R2P as a norm. Rather they agreed that it hadn't made more progress, or been specified to a greater degree, than it had been in 2005.[87] Significantly, China's position was secured by British negotiators before Russia was brought on board, but their position remained sceptical about the scope and acceptance of R2P.[88] There was not only no attempt to reinterpret R2P, but also no move to increase implementation or produce a specific and specified norm.

In these debates around 1674, it has also been suggested that the use of the exact language was important in bringing China and Russia on board with the resolution. Indeed, according to one report, China tried to get all references to R2P removed from the report.[89] This, having been unsuccessful, in order to gain China's agreement, meant that the resolution used the same phrasing as in the WSOD. Moreover, '[t]he shift in China's position was also important in bringing Russia on board'.[90] Neither Russia nor China likes to veto alone, so converting one may be the key to converting the other. This helped with the adoption of the resolution. Yet, as will be noted later over Syria, this link in voting may also frustrate the norm. But, this link can be overstated; both states have vetoed alone.[91]

The G77, BRICS and Regional Organisations: The Use of Population of Actors as Tools for Normative Change?

As noted in the SG's 2011 report on the follow-up to the Millennium summit, there is a role for regional organisations to play in the implementation of R2P.[92] In particular, the SG notes that ECOWAS and OSCE 'were in the vanguard of international efforts to develop both the principles of protection and the practical tools for implementing them'.[93] Indeed, ECOWAS has been important in the implementation of the resolution on Mali.[94] This demonstrates the role that is currently being explored with regard to the role that regional organisations can play in the implementation and interpretation of international norms.[95] As noted by the SG, this presents an opportunity to propel the implementation of the norm of R2P, but it also presents an opportunity to prevent the cascade of the norm.

This section looks at how China, by tying its position to that of regional groups and the G77, frustrates the progress of pillar three of the norm. This section does not suggest that China is advocating for a new interpretation of the norm, but by linking China's position to the NAM or G77, China's preference in challenging the Western interpretation of the emerging norm of R2P is enhanced.

Within large and complex institutions, there is potential for some interactions between different groups to become relatively more intense; an example of this is explored in terms of informal groupings acting as 'groups of friends' within the UN.[96] These groups then form units through which changes become possible and promoted: '[g]roups of friends constitute a platform for quiet diplomacy, [...] making up like-minded countries that lend leverage to the efforts taken by the secretary general'.[97]

There are limitations in the use of this approach in relation to the G77 as it is a formal rather than informal and temporary grouping; however, the idea of groups of states acting together is a useful starting point for exploring the G77.[98] The G77, in addition to acting collectively, can also lend leverage to efforts of the major powers. This is in part because institutions promote certain individual (state) actions. These actions 'interlock' with the actions of other individuals, creating small groups of actors acting in similar ways. Thus 'any attempt to create or develop an organization, or to change its strategy, partly but necessarily involves the development of accordant individual habits'.[99] Thus, in order to initiate changes to organisations, how they work or interpret events and actions, there is a need to alter or shape how individual group members develop habits.

Thus, a final element of China's challenge to the development of R2P can be seen as the linking of China's position to that of the G77 countries. In this linking exercise, China increases the credibility and legitimacy of its own position and therefore gives its interpretation a greater chance of being internationally accepted or at least of reducing the chances of alternative interpretations being adopted. It also gives China the opportunity to influence the development of the habits of a group of individual states that then have the ability to shape how these habits 'fit' with the broader interpretation of norms. In terms of the development of R2P, this was a crucial element in shaping the development of the norm as the discussion of R2P in the GA.

The claim here is not that China has managed to switch the preferences of all of the states of the G77 to adopting China's position. Rather, that China's position is amplified by being able to utilise and maintain a correlative stance with the G77. As noted by Axworthy and Rock, in the evolution of international norms—in particular the R2P—it has been shown that it is important to bring on board 'partners from newly emerging states who are members in good standing of the new coalitions and regional organizations'.[100] Thus, there is a need to cultivate and maintain support from international organisations. As Rock and Axworthy note, it is important for the progress of the norm, who speaks for the key populations in the UN.[101]

This is important not only in driving forward the agenda of R2P but also in objecting to it. In looking back at the framework in Chapter 5, this demonstrates China acting as an ad hoc objector, using the pathway of new populations and new issues. China's agency and the challenge of China are in using the G77 to 'ventriloquize' for China. Nevertheless, some interviewees claimed this takes China's position too far.[102] Yet, it seems fair to suggest that the truth of China's relationship with the G77 is somewhere in between these positions. That is, China is the G77's 'most reliable friend among the P5'.[103] Whether this position is the result of some discussions and persuasion on each side is not clear. However, one thing is clear: as a more democratic era in the UN dawns, China plus the G77 are a key voting bloc. Thus, this permanent member, in combination with a majority in the GA, is a recipe for guiding the future direction of the UN. China is a very significant component in this mixture. Without it, the G77 would have all the potency and agency of water rather than a wine.

Does China matter in this cohesion and in this grouping? It matters for the presentation of China's stance that it can link its statements and its position to the G77 as it legitimises and amplifies its stance. This, in looking back at causation in Chapter 1, is enough to demonstrate that there is a causal chain that links China to the group. In this case, there is a need to highlight that it is not China that actively brings together actors (in the case of forming new population and institutions), but rather that it can enhance its agency through their use.

China and the BRICS—Concerted Action or Coincidence?

In 2005, as Sarah Teitt notes, China was far from being the most outspoken of the BRICs[104] grouping in objecting to R2P.[105] Indeed, she noted that one rarely sees China as the main objector to R2P actions and that it hasn't taken a leadership role in frustrating R2P.[106] Rather, China prefers to take a stance alongside other actors. On the one hand, this is connected with a form of free-riding and cost reduction for the advocacy of China's position. However, there is a structural issue here too—China lacks a capacity to focus attention on a peripheral issue and really push hard for its interpretation to be accepted.[107] This is a problem for most (if not all) of the BRICS states. Brazil, despite the proposition of RwP, has found that it may not have the capacity to push the concept forwards. 'Since the dissemination of the document on RwP there has been on-going discussions and consideration of the purpose of the document. Indeed after the initial burst of enthusiasm to discuss it there has been a decrease in these discussions in UN meetings'.[108] In particular, with the lack of enthusiasm from civil society and the P3 (UK, USA and France), Brazil's proposal may not go much further. Thus, for all the BRICS countries, there is a structural limitation in their ability to be entrepreneurs in regard to R2P. However, in the case of RwP and RP, there are indications of where these countries are unhappy with the concept, and thus a clear idea of what actions they are likely to object to or seek to frustrate. The core issues here are around pillar three, particularly who does the intervening and what means are used.[109] As a result, we have a clear idea of what within the concept is likely to be challenged by the group.

Thus, we move on to the possibility of the BRICS acting as objectors to particular actions. Here, the issue focuses largely on China and Russia within the BRICS grouping as the veto holding powers. However, in the case of Libya, all the BRICS were in the SC. Nevertheless, according to Simon Adams, as a group, they 'didn't have all their ducks in a row', suggesting that there was at best weak coordination between them.[110] In reality, he saw more coordination between the IBSA (India, Brazil and South Africa) than between the BRICS.[111] Indeed, the mixture of regime types in the BRICS as a group and the different public and private positions that they express, suggests that political and security cooperation is not likely to endure, although the economics might.[112]

By contrast, according to Gareth Evans, BRICS have taken a particular stance over the intervention in Libya stating that:

> Leading the critical charge have been the "BRICS" (Brazil, Russia, India, China, and South Africa). Their complaints are not about the initial military response – destroying the Libyan air force's infrastructure, and air attacks on ground forces advancing on Benghazi. Rather, they object to what came after, when it rapidly became apparent that the three permanent Security Council's members driving the intervention (the United States, the United Kingdom, and France) would settle for nothing less than regime change, and do whatever it took to achieve it.[113]

Moreover, he goes on to note that the BRICS countries were unhappy with the interveners' rejection of offers for a ceasefire.[114] A key issue among these states was how intervention was undertaken (as noted above). Thus, RwP was seen by these states as a positive step forward in gaining some agreement on the mechanisms for intervention and action, once it has been determined that international action is necessary. However, the initial reaction from the west to these proposals—according to Evans—was very sceptical.[115] Nonetheless, there has been some further discussion on the proposal, and it has potentially opened up a bridge between the Western powers and the more sceptical powers.

There are several noteworthy actions of China and the BRICS over R2P. Firstly, their joint challenge is over pillar three, in particular concerning who intervenes and with what tools.[116] This is a position that demonstrates a significant consistency of China. As noted in the section on China and peacekeeping (above), China has been a consistent advocate of increasing monitoring, and the feeding back to the SC, on PK missions. The BRICS' 'critical clarification' of R2P pillar three owes some intellectual heritage to this position. Nonetheless, the leadership within the BRICS on this issue is not coming from China. But, the presence of the BRICS as a group is important for the expression of China's preferences. As noted in many places in this section, China does not like to act alone, it has an aversion to leadership, and as a result, its challenge to any international norm is likely to be in coordination with other actors. This presents a challenge to the norm—because it faces the opposition of a group rather than a single actor. Yet, it also presents an opportunity for converting and bringing China on side through the persuasion of the group and then China. As will be noted on the section on China and ASEAN, this approach may prove to be very effective.

China and the ASEAN States

As noted above, the UN Charter in Chapter 8 reserves a special place for the role of regions in maintaining peace and security. Similarly, the WSOD and SG's reports and practice of implementing R2P have all declared and saluted the importance of the regions. This section explores the role of China's relationships with the ASEAN region. It sets out an argument that in its regional engagements, China is broadly supportive of actions that are considered to be pillar one and two actions.

This tells us three things about China's challenge to R2P. First, China is at best ambivalent to the use of the norm—a number of its actions could be seen as R2P, but it seems to have a preference for them not to be considered as such. Second, China has used—whether consciously or not—regions to help justify, legitimise and amplify its own position. Third, China contributes to the problems facing R2P. That is that R2P success stories are not claimed as R2P stories, and yet R2P controversies are across the newspaper headlines around the world for days. Thus, China's regional relations help the reinterpretation process of the R2P norm. On the one hand, China acts as an ad hoc objector, and on the other hand, China acts as an entrepreneur in its actions in coordination with regions. Consequently, China creates a continuing challenge for the acceptance of the norm of R2P across the region—even states considered a part of the international 'friends of R2P' group are less vocal in their regional avocation of the norm.[117]

In drawing out these outcomes, this section addresses three issues. First, that the states across SEA have different levels of acceptance of R2P.[118] Thus, there is room for the norm to achieve greater or lesser acceptance across the region. Second, the regional approach to R2P is fuelled by misconception of the norm and a low level of awareness. This is aggravated by the dominance of the events in Libya and Syria in guiding regional impressions of the implications of the norm. Third, there are problems in restoring regional consensus around the norm of R2P. This may continue if the P3 (UK, USA and France) remain 'dismissive' of the concept of RwP. In this sense, China may become important for the regional actors' preferences being heard in the SC.

The claim here is that China is important in these regional dynamics for two reasons. China acts as a key enabler in the engagement with Myanmar that enables R2P-like actions. China's position in advocating for consideration and dialogue at the international level is enhanced because of the broad base of support for this position among the ASEAN states.[119] Indeed, China advocating for RP or RwP presents an opportunity for creating regional consensus on R2P: this is a possibility rather than a reality.

There are a number of challenges facing R2P in Southeast Asia (SEA). Among these are the issues around ensuring that governments and populations understand that R2P is not intended to challenge sovereignty, but rather to ensure that states enjoy sovereignty to the fullest extent[120]: both popular sovereignty and international recognition of sovereign status. However, many states in SEA are sceptical regarding R2P. This is not helped by the intervention in Libya which is seen as regime change. Yet, some governments have been open to workshops and training on R2P (Philippines in particular), and once governments, civil society groups and other actors have engaged with the whole concept, they have become more accepting of it.[121] Highlighting the African success stories of pillars one and two (e.g. Kenya in 2008)[122] has proved successful.[123]

Nonetheless, misconception of the norm or a lack of understanding is a problem for the norm of R2P. Indeed, the Philippines' actions in Mindanao are a good indication of a level of acceptance of pillars one and two.[124] However, although Mindanao can be seen as a success for pillars one and two, it is not called R2P. Even the regional supporters of R2P have not claimed it as an R2P success.

Exploring China and the regional usages or potential use of R2P, China has been a constructive and contributory partner, but only in terms of dealing with pillar one and two actions. Nevertheless, these events and activities are not called 'R2P' incidents. In part, this is because they have been successfully dealt with by the region and have not been required to be referred to the SC. Yet, this creates a problem for how R2P evolves, despite Edward Luck's claim that 'it doesn't matter if it is called R2P or not'.[125] If the goal is to prevent individual mass atrocities, this is indeed true. However, if in order for *all* mass atrocities to be prevented it is necessary to create a new 'frame of mind' regarding sovereignty, then this still presents a problem. This is because if R2P success stories are not attributed to R2P, then the norm is driven by the less successful uses.

In 2007, the French foreign minister attempted to invoke R2P in the case of Myanmar after Cyclone Nargis. However, this use of R2P was resisted, not only by regional organisations and individual states, but also by western powers. These states made it clear the R2P was not to be used in the case of natural disasters.[126] However, Cohen makes the claim that in the aftermath of Nargis, the humanitarian disaster makes it an R2P case.[127] However, Noel Morada notes that the cyclone could be seen as an R2P case, if there had been failure on the part of the government to withhold humanitarian assistance from particular groups.[128]

The potential to see the cyclone and the subsequent human disaster as an R2P case has some value for seeing the region as more comfortable with R2P pillar one and two actions—even if the consent or the request for assistance from the international community is coerced rather than voluntary. Indeed, in this respect, China and the region may be seen as R2P advocates, as China was instrumental in persuading Myanmar to allow in the SG's envoy to inspect the situation.[129] In addition, the aid was coordinated by ASEAN rather than being provided by the UN alone.[130] Moreover, according to Cook and Gong's conclusions, regarding the lessons and legacy of the Cambodian situation, the region is fertile land for the application of the norm of R2P in the region.[131] There is a clear suggestion, that in Southeast Asia (with the coordination of China), the norm of R2P may be undergoing a reinterpretation, to focus on pillars one and two.

The final element of the significance of the region is how it fits in with South–South dialogues. As noted above, RwP and RP may not have the necessary national capacities to propel their discussion beyond this point. Conversely, they do offer a point around which South–South consensus can coalesce. The fact that within ASEAN even 'friends of R2P' don't talk about R2P within ASEAN groupings and bearing in mind that 'once ASEAN states have agreed something at the national level they are unlikely to renegotiate at the international level'[132]; it is important to note if there is a point of consensus with a P5 member and south hemisphere partners, this will be a significant challenge for the norm.

China and R2P After the Libya Decisions (Resolutions 1970 and 1973)

It is not a difficult claim to make that China's hesitancy over R2P became more pronounced following the Libya action. Indeed, as noted by Tiewa Liu, it was only after the Libyan invocation that academic discussions of R2P in China become more prominent.[133] In addition, this has been noted by a number of interviewees, as well as in the academic literature, both within and outside China. At a conference on R2P in Beijing run by the United Nations Association (UNA), Prof. Shi Yinhong, commenting on the international community's move towards R2P as a norm, noted: 'I don't want to let this progress to be abused, or let something like legal interventions become something which has no strict, legal, moral and political limitations'.[134] Indeed, later in the same paper, he states that there is a clear distinction between the norms of sovereignty and the R2P: 'There is a difference in these two sides of the principle through comparison. One is most fundamental. Another compared with sovereignty, is submissive. So they have no equal basis and equal status'.[135]

Thus, following Libya, there is a palpable shift backwards within China on R2P. But, other participants demonstrated that the issue with R2P in China is around the implementation rather than the concept.[136] 'I acknowledge this is a clear step forward in the protection of human rights. It is an ideal concept. But when it comes to implementation, an ideal concept needs an ideal world for its implementation in the ideal way. ... The world we see now is not ideal, should I say far from ideal'.[137] As such, this move is instep with the rest of the international community. Where the shift that has taken place following Libya is around *how* to implement the norm rather than whether the norm exists.[138] As such, at present, it would seem that China is not acting to present an alternative to R2P or that it is frustrating its progress as a norm. But, China is seeking critical engagement on its application of the norm, for example in its constructive abstention in Resolution 1973.[139]

China's primary concern is in the coercive use of pillar three tools. This is not new. Indeed, as an interviewee in New York noted: 'there is surprising consistency in China's position'.[140] This consistency, as this chapter has shown, flows from the peacekeeping missions in the 1990s. It shows that now—as then—China has a huge problem with missions being hijacked or mandates of the SC being exceeded by the intervening forces.

In the past, we have seen that China has quietly acted to try and prevent mission 'creep' or mission overreach. Thus, we can expect that China will act in the future to ensure that there are safeguards on R2P pillar three activities. It is likely to be a power that abstains from or authorises this type of limited mission. It is also likely to be a power that seeks to ensure that mandates are curtailed and that feedback mechanisms to the Council are in place to ensure the limitations to mandates are respected.[141] This approach, as in the case of Rwanda, could lead to its own disaster.[142]

Nevertheless, other participants in China also noted that success of PK missions was also linked to the respect of state sovereignty and the need to acquire host government consent.[143] Undeniably, Zhang notes 'The reason [for success] is so simple that the military means is not a good solution for conflicts'.[144] This has international resonance. However, it does not clearly address the issue of what to do when non-coercive methods of R2P are unsuccessful. Indeed, this discussion presents a significant problem for R2P as a norm. That is, it is increasingly associated with coercive tools of pillar three. This is in itself a limited interpretation of R2P.

The norm in the ICISS report was intended to limit the extent to which sovereignty was used to guard against regimes committing atrocities. This version of R2P clearly seeks to ensure that sovereignty remains the prime element in the international community. It also limits the use of the terminology of R2P to being linked with coercion and regime change. This approach, when linked to the role of China with ASEAN, shows that China does not challenge all elements of R2P, but rather challenges—alongside other powers—the coercive use of pillar three, in cases where the mission exceeds the mandate of the UN.

In the post-Libya world, this discussion has shown that China has attempted to develop a distinct approach to R2P. Both in the report from RCUNIO and in Responsible Protection, there have been attempts to enunciate this position. This is an element—recognised in Chapter 5—as being essential for norm entrepreneurship. Still, China lacks international advocacy.

Thus, China may be making what it objects to clearer, it may engage more critically with international debates on R2P, and this position when stated in the SC (e.g. in the case of debates on Syria)[145] presents a significant challenge to the evolution of R2P. In particular, China's objection in Syria draws on these positions, setting out its view that 'the draft resolution is seriously flawed, and its unbalanced content seeks to put pressure on only one party. Experience has shown that such a practice would not help resolve the Syrian issue'.[146] This has echoes of Cambodia for China, when—as noted earlier—China objected to the specification of how many parties should contest the elections in Cambodia. China's statement then goes on to reaffirm the importance of credibility to the UN and the need to respect sovereignty and non-intervention.[147] However, in a surprising note, China indicated that it had come under international pressure and condemnation for its position in Syria and made a committed and very forthright stand in its commitment to the Annan plan as a root to a political settlement.[148] As noted by one interviewee: China is not being disingenuous in this presentation. It may genuinely believe that an alternative is better. The central problem for China is that it has not, or cannot, set out what it thinks that alternative should be.[149]

In addition, there has been adjustment and increasing concern on the use of force within China. Prior to Resolution 1973, China clearly made a case that the decision on the use of force should be left to the relevant regional body. Yet, in the case of Libya, the two regional bodies of which Libya was a member disagreed over the action that should be taken.[150] It then chose to adopt the position of the Arab league. Since then, China has demonstrated, 'buyer's remorse' as it didn't want to be seen as an outlier.[151] It may feel it should have joined forces with the African Union.

China has baulked at the use of force in pillar three since Libya. There is a recognition that it needs to reconcile its position on various actions. In the case of Syria, it could be said to be 'region shopping'[152] for a position that agrees with China's own preference. For example, it is suggested that because of China's rhetoric of deferring to regional preferences over the use of force, it has had to adjust its position on deference to the regional preference. This is because the Arab league has called for action from the international community regarding Syria. However, very significantly, in the case of Syria, the Arab League has called for 'regime change'. In all of China's statements on peacekeeping and R2P, it has openly and consistently stated that it doesn't want R2P to be used as a pretext for 'regime change'.[153] As a result, there is a case to suggest that China has a hierarchy of preferences (or challenges) with regard to R2P: China will defer to regional preferences, but not if those preferences directly contradict China's 'red line' on regime change or interference.

China presents a challenge within the SC on the authorisation of missions that seek justification through the invocation of R2P, particularly when those missions are to be implemented through coercive measures related to pillar three. Even this challenge to R2P may be muted if there is a clear regional preference for international action, so long as that intervention is not intended to produce regime change. Because of China's position on the SC, as a veto-holding member, it doesn't need to use other populations, or other institutions, or new issues, to present its objection. However, it does gain a benefit from being able to tie its objection in this specific area of R2P to that of other states. In particular, it does this with Russia, so that China does not have to veto alone.

One counterfactual lingers over this conclusion: Would China object if Russia didn't also veto? This cannot be known. A number of interviewees suggested that China tends to 'follow' Russia (on the issue of Syria)[154] and a lot less is known about Russia's understanding and preferences in R2P than is known about China.[155] However, it is instructive and significant that China's current objections are centred on the same issues that led them to seek to limit SC missions in the 1990s—a move that appears to have been independent of Russia. Nonetheless, it remains possible that China would have abstained on Syria, if not for Russia.

Conditions Facilitating Challenges to R2P

This section of this chapter looks at the facilitating factors for the frustration of R2P. As noted in this section, China's position adjusted following Libya, as did the preferences of a number of other powers, making the discussions around implementation more vibrant and aiding any voices that called for a reassessment of R2P.

Legitimacy

In the process of evolution of R2P, the progress of the norm may have been further stymied by the invasion of Iraq in 2003 and the actions in Libya and Cote d'Ivoire in 2011, as the credibility of some of the key proponents of this new interpretation of sovereignty was called into question, making it harder for them to 'build consensus' around the new norm.[156] The action in Iraq split the partial consensus that had previously existed,[157] increasing the political plurality of actors considered legitimate on this issue, as well as the number of interpretations that were credible. In addition, the response to the crisis in Libya has created further problems for developing a consensus on the implementation of the norm.

Under the norm of R2P for a state to be recognised as sovereign over its population and territory, it has to protect its own population; if a state was unable or unwilling to do so, it has to allow an intervention,[158] whether those powers were other states, regional or international organisations.[159] This moved away from traditional understandings of articles 2(1) and 2(4)[160] of the UN charter that are still defended by many states, most notably for this discussion, China. Attempts to take the idea of 'Responsibility to Protect', from a nascent and niche concept to a fully recognised international norm have been frustrated by growing competition in the norm pool, as well as challenges from attempting to apply the idea to peacekeeping operations. Moreover, it has exposed the different justifications for states' claims to sovereignty and the roles that sovereignty as a norm plays in international order. According to Sarah Teitt, 'Although China's constructive and cooperative engagement in UN peacekeeping over the last decade is now widely recognized, China's support for, or at the very least acquiescence in, the UN endorsement of R2P seems to test the limits of its flexibility on sovereignty and non-interference'.[161] Importantly, this is not just the case for China—other states also needed to be gradually guided towards the concept of R2P.[162]

Balance of Power

As noted previously, humanitarian intervention had the benefit of emerging as a norm at a point when the balance of power, between great powers, favoured liberal states. R2P has not been so lucky. It is not only China that is growing in power, but also Russia has become more vocal since the 1990s. Indeed, the split between the P3 and the P2 in the SC is a significant problem for the evolution of the norm, especially for some events where some members of the P5 have key strategic interests.[163] India and Brazil have grown in power and, although they are democratic states, they are not clearly in support of R2P.[164]

Added to this, there is a 'flattening of the UN structure'[165] resulting in more small and medium powers taking leadership and ownership of particular issues and gathering support for their position. Key in this is how they bring on board 'reliable' partners among the P5. Thus, although China may not be the entrepreneur for a particular reinterpretation of R2P, it can be seen to be instrumental in the presentation of that challenge. The challenge is aided by the agency of China in the SC in combination with a changing balance of power dynamic.

Failure of the Norm?

As noted in numerous places in this chapter, Libya has presented numerous problems for the norm of R2P. As noted above, it presents a legitimacy problem not only for the norm but also for the legitimacy of the entrepreneurs. Yet, the norm has not yet received a fatal blow. It hasn't completely failed. Thus, there are significant limits to the ability to reinterpret the whole concept of the norm. Indeed, there seems to be little appetite within China or elsewhere to do this. Even Syria, as it is now civil war situation, it has moved beyond being clearly an R2P situation.

Conclusion: China and R2P

The challenge to the norm of R2P concerns the implementation of pillar three. In this regard, China has acted as an ad hoc objector to the use of force. This position has been made more legitimate by regional support for China's position, including support from the NAM and the G77. China has played an effective role in stalling the cascade of the norm by seeking dialogue and discussion around the implementation of pillar three.

It should be noted that international power matters. China is a key element to the consensus in the Global South. Without the support of the Global South, the authorisation of the use of force will remain unlikely (China's position in the SC is central in ensuring this). Without clear guidelines on the implementation of pillar three, and clear safeguards on its use, consensus is unlikely.

China's attempt to be an entrepreneur, in reinterpreting R2P, through the concept of RP, has not yet been successful. Indeed, the lack of capacity in China around this issue makes it unlikely that it will be successful.

Nevertheless, China does not object to all elements of R2P. Indeed, regarding pillars one and two, China has been instrumental in some successful actions that can be considered to fulfil pillars one and two, such as Myanmar. It has worked effectively with regional organisations in these respects. The willingness of China to engage with debates around pillar three may result in a positive reinterpretation of this aspect of the norm. China's potential to hold the key to progress on R2P results from its position as a P5 power, its ability to link into the dominant views within the Global South and its potential to act as a bridge between the West and Russia. There is room for some optimism. However, the problems China identifies with R2P pillar three are the same problems that China identified with UNPKOs earlier in this chapter.

Notes

1. For further discussion of this process see: Carsten Stahn, 'Responsibility to Protect: Political Rhetoric or Emerging Legal Norm?', *The American Journal of International Law* (2007), 101(1), pp. 99–120; Jennifer Welsh, Carolin Thielking, and S. Neil Macfarlane, 'The Responsibility to Protect: Assessing the Report of the International Commission on Intervention and State Sovereignty', *International Journal* (2002), 57, pp. 489–512.
2. In the ICISS, these crimes were broader than current discussions of R2P to include 'Prevention of deadly conflict and other forms of manmade catastrophe'. ICISS, *The Responsibility to Protect* (International Development Research Centre: Ottawa, 2001), p. 19.
3. UN SG Press Release SG/SM/7136 GA/9596, 20 September 1999; Kofi Annan, *We the Peoples: The Role of the United Nations in the 21st Century* (United Nations: New York, 2000), para. 368; see also, Jennifer M. Welsh, 'From Right to Responsibility: Humanitarian Intervention and International Society', *Global Governance* (2002), 8, pp. 503–521.

4. Ramesh Thakur and Thomas G. Weiss, 'R2P: From Idea to Norm—and Action?' *Global Responsibility to Protect* (2009), 1, pp. 22–53; also Welsh, 'From Right to Responsibility'.
5. UNGA A/47/277-S/24111, 17 June 1992.
6. UNGA A/50/60-S/1995/1, 3 January 1995.
7. Kofi A. Annan, 'Two Concepts of Sovereignty', *The Economist* (18 September 1999).
8. 'Until a replacement is found, the notion of sovereignty must be put to work and reaffirmed to meet the challenges of the times in accordance with respected standards of human dignity'. Francis M. Deng, *Sovereignty as Responsibility: Conflict Management in Africa* (R.R. Donnelley: Virginia, 1996), p. xi.
9. For reports of these discussions see: ICISS, 'Suplementary Volume to the Responsibility to Protect Section A: Research Essays' (International Development Research Centre: Ottawa, 2001).
10. ICISS, 'The Responsibility to Protect', pp. 53–55 (sets out conditions on authority and who should act).
11. UNGA GA/59/565, 2 December 2004.
12. Details of the panel, the members, and the press statements from the panel are available from: http://www.un.org/secureworld/, accessed 5 February 2013.
13. UNGA A/59/2005, 21 March 2005.
14. For example, see the R2P paragraphs in the first draft (pre-edited) version of the WSOD, A/59/HLPM/CRP.1/Rev.2, 5 August 2005, where it notes in para. 118 '[w]e stress the need to continue consideration of the concept of the responsibility to protect within the sixtieth session of the General Assembly'. In addition to in this draft of the document, there is an emphasis that the permanent members of the UNSC should 'We invite the permanent members of the Security Council to refrain from using the veto in cases of genocide, war crimes, ethnic cleansing and crimes against humanity' (para. 119) which is removed in the WSOD.
15. GA/59/565, 2 December 2004.
16. Ibid., para. 36, p. 23.
17. Ibid., para. 42, pp. 36–37.
18. This was made crystal clear in paragraph 240 'Members should use the opportunity provided by the Millennium Review Summit in 2005 to forge new consensus on broader more effective collective security'. Ibid., p. 65.
19. Bellamy, 'Responsibility to Protect or Trojan Horse?'; Alex J. Bellamy, 'The Responsibility to Protect and the Problem of Military Intervention', *International Affairs* (2008), 84(4), pp. 615–639;

Jennifer Welsh, Carolin Thielking, and S. Neil Macfarlane, 'The Responsibility to Protect: Assessing the Report of the International Commission on Intervention and State Sovereignty', *International Journal* (2002), 57, pp. 489–512.
20. Carlo Focarelli, 'The Responsibility to Protect Doctrine and Humanitarian Intervention: Too Many Ambiguities For a working Doctrine', *Journal of Conflict and Security Law* (2008), 13(2), pp. 191–213; Susan C. Breau, 'The Impact of the Responsibility to Protect on Peacekeeping', *Journal of Conflict and Security Law* (2006), 11(3), pp. 429–464; Jutta Brunnee and Toope Stephen, 'Norms, Institutions and UN Reform: The Responsibility to Protect', *Journal of International Law and International Relations* (2006), 2(1), pp. 121–137; Carsten Stahn, 'Responsibility to Protect: Political Rhetoric or Emerging Legal Norm?', *The American Journal of International Law* (2007), 101(1), pp. 99–120.
21. UNGA, GA/60/L.1, para. 138.
22. ICISS, 'The Responsibility to Protect', p. xiii, p. 51, para. 6.21.
23. A/59/HLPM/CRP.1/Rev.2, 5 August 2005.
24. UNGAGA/60/L.1, paras. 138–140.
25. S/Res 1674, 28 April 2006.
26. S/Res 1894, 11 November 2009.
27. S/Res 1970, 26 February 2011.
28. S/Res 1973, 17 March 2011.
29. S/Res 1975, 30 March 2011.
30. S/Res 2006, 8 July 2011.
31. S/Res 2014, 21 October 2011.
32. S/Res 2016, 27 October 2011.
33. S/Res 2040, 12 March 2012.
34. S/Res 2056, 19 December 2012.
35. A table of these resolutions including their relationship to R2P is available from Global Responsibility to Protect, 'UN Security Council Resolutions', available http://www.globalr2p.org/resources/335, accessed 8 January 2013.
36. UNGA, A/RES/63/308, 7 October 2009, available http://responsibilitytoprotect.org/Resolution%20RtoP%283%29.pdf, accessed 1 February 2013; UNGA, A/64/864, 14 July 2010, available http://responsibilitytoprotect.org/Resolution%20RtoP%283%29.pdf, accessed 1 February 2013; 2011 and 2012 reports not yet available.
37. UNSG, 'Implementing the Responsibility to Protect', A/63/677, 12 January 2009; UNSG, 'Early Warning, Assessment and the Responsibility to Protect: Report of the Secretary General', A/64/864, 14 July 2010; UNSG, 'The role of regional and Subregional arrangements in implementing the responsibility to protect: Report of the

Secretary General', A/65/877-S/2011/393, 28 June 2011; UNSG 'Responsibility to Protect: Timely and Decisive Response: Report of the Secretary General', A/66/874-S/2012/578, 25 July 2012.
38. UNSG, 'Implementing the Responsibility to Protect', A/63/677, 12 January 2009.
39. UNSG, 'Early Warning, Assessment and the Responsibility to Protect: Report of the Secretary General', A/64/864, 14 July 2010.
40. UNSG, 'The Role of Regional and Subregional Arrangements in Implementing the Responsibility to Protect: Report of the Secretary General', A/65/877-S/2011/393, 28 June 2011.
41. UNSG, 'Responsibility to Protect: Timely and Decisive Response: Report of the Secretary General', A/66/874-S/2012/578, 25 July 2012.
42. For a commentary on the report and its implications for implementation see Monica Serrano, 'Implementing the Responsibility to Protect: The Power of R2P Talk', *Global Responsibility to Protect* (2010), 2, pp. 167–177; Furthermore there are already some academic discussions of the problems of implementation see for example: Jennifer M. Welsh, 'Turning Words Into Deeds? The Implementation of the Responsibility to Protect', *Global Responsibility to Protect* (2010), 2, pp. 149–154; In the case of Libya Bellamy and Williams note the 'exceptional factors' that enabled implementation, Alex J. Bellamy and Paul D. Williams, 'The New Politics of Protection? Cote d'Ivoire, Libya and the Responsibility to Protect', *International Affairs* (2011), 87(4), pp. 825–850.
43. R2Plite in this instance refers to its use by Noel Morada in terms of separating sections of R2P and excluding the use of force. Author Interview with Noel Morada [Skype], 15 January 2013. Although it is noted that this phrase is also used by Thomas Weiss in Thomas Weiss to distinguish the WSOD and its lack of specification from the ICISS report Thomas Weiss, 'R2P after 9/11 and the World Summit', *Wisconsin International Law Journal*, 24(3), available http://hosted.law.wisc.edu/wordpress/wilj/files/2012/02/weiss.pdf, accessed 8 February 2013.
44. A/66/551-S/2011/701, 11 November 2011.
45. There have been a series of working papers and discussion documents as to whether RwP is compatible with R2P or whether it challenges it. For example, A/66/874–S/2012/578, para. 49–58; Andreas S. Kolb, 'The Responsibility to Protect (R2P) and the Responsibility While Protecting (RwP): Friends or Foes?' Global Governance Institute CGI Analysis Paper 6 (2012); Also noted in Francis Deng's 'The Responsibility While Protecting (RwP) Talking Points for Remarks', available http://www.un.org/en/preventgenocide/adviser/pdf/FD%2021%20February%20remarks%20-%20English.pdf, accessed 8 January 2013.

46. For examples see Statement by Amb. Hussein Haniff, Permanent Representative of Malaysia to the United Nations, 5 September 2012, available http://responsibilitytoprotect.org/Malaysia.pdf, accessed 8 January 2013; Amb. Albert Chua, Permanent Representative of Singapore to the United Nations, 5 September 2012, http://responsibilitytoprotect.org/Singapore.pdf; Amb. Pham Vinh Quang, Deputy Permanent representative of the Socialist Republic of Vietnam, 5 September 2012, http://responsibilitytoprotect.org/Vietnam.pdf.
47. Author Interview with Simon Adams, New York, 30 January 2013.
48. 'Enhanced Security Council procedures are needed to monitor and assess the manner in which resolutions are interpreted and implemented to ensure responsibility while protecting'. A/66/551-S/2011/701, 11 November 2011, para. 11(h) see also para. 11(g).
49. Andreas S. Kolb, 'The Responsibility to Protect (R2P) and the Responsibility While Protecting (RwP): Friends or Foes?', *Global Governance Institute CGI Analysis Paper* (2012), 6.
50. Author Interviews, with Members of an R2P NGO, New York, 29 January 2013.
51. Zongze Ruan, 'Responsible Protection', *China Daily*, 15 March 2012, available http://www.chinadaily.com.cn/cndy/2012-03/15/content_14837835.htm, accessed 1 February 2013.
52. Zongze Ruan, 'Responsible Protection', *China Daily*, 15 March 2012, available http://www.chinadaily.com.cn/cndy/2012-03/15/content_14837835.htm, accessed 1 February 2013.
53. Zongze Ruan, 'Responsible Protection: Building a Safer World', *CIIS*, 15 June 2012, available http://www.ciis.org.cn/english/2012-06/15/content_5090912.htm, accessed 1 February 2013.
54. A key problem in the debate that emerged around RwP was that the Brazilian Proposal whilst consistent with the broad statement of Chapter VII, it is not consistent with Article 42, see Alex Bellamy online YouTube Interview http://www.youtube.com/watch?v=et3joawfUe8 (five part interview this is one of the links); also Author Interview with Alex Bellamy [phone], 16 January 2013.
55. It should be noted in the position paper on UN reform in the section on R2P this phrase is not in the document, but this paper was published before the phrase 'Responsible Protection' was used by Ruan Zongze. Indeed this is backed up by the criticism China had to the Libyan intervention see Liu, 'China and the Responsibility to Protect'. Author Interview with Amb. Diego Arria, 22 February 2013; also, Catherine Jones, 'Regional Perspective: The Evolution of China's Peacekeeping Role', in David Curran, Larry Roeder, and Robert Zuber (eds), *New Directions and Opportunities for*

Peacekeeping: Expanding Stakeholders and Regional Arrangements (Springer, 2015).
56. Some civil society groups hadn't heard of RP when asked, for example Author Interview with Simon Adams, New York, 30 January 2013.
57. At time of writing the academic and other debates in China, focusing on the specific topic of R2P was limited to a very small group of scholars. However, there was a greater literature on the specific implementation and critiques of individual cases of R2P use—most notably surrounding Libya and Syria.
58. Zhenmin Liu, 'Statement by Ambassador Liu Zhenmin At the Plenary session of the General Assembly on the Question of "Responsibility to Protect"', 24 July 2009, available http://www.china-un.org/eng/lhghyywj/smhwj/2009/t575682.htm, accessed 22 April 2013; see also Micheal Fullilove, 'China and the United Nations: The Stakeholder Spectrum', *Washington Quarterly* (Summer 2011), pp. 63–85; also Sarah Teitt, 'China and the Responsibility to Protect', Asia-Pacific Centre on R2P, 19 December 2008, http://responsibilitytoprotect.org/files/China_and_R2P%5B1%5D.pdf, accessed 22 April 2013.
59. UN Res 1674, 28 April 2006 notes '*Reaffirms* the provisions of paragraphs 138 and 139 of the 2005 World Summit Outcome Document regarding the responsibility to protect populations from genocide, war crimes, ethnic cleansing and crimes against humanity'.
60. Although it is noted that R2P has been invoked in other cases indicated above.
61. The failure of the Syrian Resolutions contributes to implementation by aiding the specification of when and with what response R2P can be used.
62. S/PV.6710, 31 January 2012 and the failed resolution UNSC S/2012/77, 4 February 2012 (vetoed by China and Russia).
63. Thakur and Weiss, 'R2P: From Idea to Norm'; Thomas G. Weiss, Ramesh Thakur, Mary Ellen O'Connell, Aidan Hehir, Alex J. Bellamy, David Chandler, Rodger Shanahan, Rachel Gerber, Abiodun Williams, and Gareth Evans, The Responsibility to Protect: Challenges and opportunities in the light of the Libyan Intervention, e-international relations, November 2011, available http://www.e-ir.info/wp-content/uploads/R2P.pdf, accessed 8 February 2013.
64. As Tiewa Liu states China's main problem with R2P is concerned with the use of force connected to some pillar three activities, Tiewa Liu, 'China and the Responsibility to Protect: Maintenance and Change

of Its Policy for Intervention', *The Pacific Review* (2012), 25(1), pp. 153–173.
65. It should be noted that in the 2005 Chinese position paper on UN Reforms, the paragraphs dedicated to R2P restated the position of the WSOD and reiterated the need for all actions to be in line with the Charter, see, FMPRC, 'Position Paper of the People's Republic of China on UN Reforms', 7 June 2005, available in English from http://www.fmprc.gov.cn/eng/zxxx/t199318.htm, last accessed 8 March 2013.
66. Capacity in China in this instance relates to the ability to generate a concept, explore the implications of the concept, educate diplomats who are then able to advocate in the international arena.
67. This is also noted Sarah Teitt, 'China and the Responsibility to Protect', Asia-Pacific Center on R2P, 19 December 2008, http://responsibilitytoprotect.org/files/China_and_R2P%5B1%5D.pdf, accessed 22 April 2013.
68. Joel Wuthnow, 'China and the Processes of Cooperation in UN Security Council Deliberations', pp. 55–77.
69. Rosemary Foot and Andrew Walter, *China, the United States and Global Order* (Cambridge University Press: New York, 2011), p. 61.
70. For example, China consistently advocates that the norm should be applied in line with the Charter, making the suggestion that other interpretations are not in accordance with the charter. For example, Zongze, 'Responsible Protection'; it has also strenuously objected to when it perceives missions to be going beyond the mandate see Tiewa Liu, 'China and the Responsibility to Protect: Maintenance and Change of Its Policy for Intervention', *Pacific Review* (2012), 25(1), pp. 153–173 and 167–168.
71. See, for example, Eduarda P. Hamann and Robert Muggah, *Implementing the Responsibility to Protest: New Directions for International Peace and Security?* (IGARAPE Institute: Brasilia, Brazil, 2013); Liu, 'China and the Responsibility to Protect', it should also be noted that there even prior to Libya authors were noting that there were a number of challenges to implementation of the norm and on-going discussions for how it should or could be implemented see for example: Jennifer Welsh, 'Turning Words into Deeds: But, What of Implementation?' *Global Responsibility to Protect* (2010), 2(1–2), pp. 149–154; Rebecca Hamilton, 'The Responsibility to Protect: From Document to Doctrine—But What of Implementation?' *Harvard Human Rights Journal* (2006), 19, pp. 289–296; it as also discussed at the RSIS conference on 'Regional Consultation on the Responsibility to Protect', report published by NTS RSIS, Singapore 2010, available

http://www.rsis.edu.sg/publications/conference_reports/RtoP_240810.pdf, last accessed 24 April 2013.
72. See Chapter 5.
73. GA/59/2005, para. 132, pp. 34–35.
74. Discussed as a move from a hard to a soft norm in Prantl and Nakano, 'Global Norm Diffusion in East Asia: How China and Japan Implement the Responsibility to Protect' (Working Paper), p. 6.
75. Alex J. Bellamy, 'Responsibility to Protect or Trojan Horse? The Crisis in Darfur and Humanitarian Intervention after Iraq', *Ethics & International Affairs* (2005), 19(2), pp. 31–54, p. 34.
76. The Egyptian statement quoted in the Press Statement in Fifth Committee Sixty-Second General Assembly, 28th Meeting 'Press Statement: United Nations Human Resources Structures Must Be Adapted to Meet Growing Demands of Peacekeeping, Other Field Operations, Budget Committee Told', http://www.un.org/News/Press/docs/2008/gaab3837.doc.htm (Department of Public information: United Nations News and Media Division: New York, 2008).
77. The spokesman for China stated that 'subscribed to the statement made earlier on behalf of the Group of 77'. Ibid.
78. China emphasised the 'The report of the Secretary-General had indicated that the number of staff from developing countries in decision-making posts within the Secretariat had been decreasing. That was a cause for serious concern'. Ibid.
79. Ibid.
80. Prantl and Nakano, 'Global Norm Diffusion in East Asia: How China and Japan Implement the Responsibility to Protect', p. 2.
81. Noel M. Morada, 'The ASEAN Charter and the Promotion of R2P and Southeast Asia: Challenges and Constraints', *Global Responsibility to Protect* (2009), 1, pp. 185–207; see also Cook and Gong, 'Cambodia's Legacy'.
82. Prantl and Nakano, 'Global Norm Diffusion in East Asia: How China and Japan Implement the Responsibility to Protect', p. 13.
83. Sarah Teitt, 'The Responsibility to Protect and China's Peacekeeping Policy', *International Peacekeeping* (2011), 18(3), pp. 298–312, p. 309.
84. See, for example, Teitt, 'China and the Responsibility to Protect' (2008).
85. UN Res 1674, 28 April 2006.
86. Ibid.
87. Indeed as Chin and Thakur note the insistence of China that R2P should not be expanded beyond the agreement in 2005 they note is 'one way that China is shaping global norms and rules'. Gregory Chin and Ramesh Thakur, 'Will China Change the Rules of Global Order', *The Washington Quarterly* (October 2010), 33(4), pp. 119–138.

88. Alex Bellamy, *Responsibility to Protect* (Polity: Cambridge, 2009), p. 137.
89. Maria Banda, *The Responsibility to Protect: Moving the Agenda Forward* (Canadian UN Association, March 2007), p. 26.
90. Author interviews with Sarah Teitt [Skype], 10 January 2013.
91. Russia vetoed alone on S/2009/310 and S/2004/313; China vetoed S/1997/18 and S/1999/201 alone. Although China's lone vetoes were both in the 1990s.
92. A/65/877, 28 June 2011; indeed there has been an important role set aside for regions in the Charter since 1945.
93. Ibid., para. 4.
94. Author Interview with Alex Bellamy, 16 January 2013.
95. For example see: Prantl and Nakano 'Global Norm Diffusion in East Asia'.
96. Jochen Prantl, 'Informal Groups of States and the UN Security Council', *International Organization* (2005), 59, pp. 559–592, p. 561; Jochen Prantl, *The UN Security Council and Informal Groups of States: Complementing or Competing for Governance?* (Oxford University Press: Oxford, 2006).
97. Prantl, 'Informal Groups of States', p. 561.
98. Moreover, as noted by one interviewee the formality of the G77 can easily be overstated. Author Interview New York, January 2013.
99. Geoffrey M. Hodgson, 'Institutions and Individuals: Interaction and Evolution', *Organisational Studies* (2007), 28(1), pp. 95–116, p. 110.
100. Lloyd Axworthy and Allan Rock, 'R2P: A New and Unfinished Agenda', *Global Responsibility to Protect* (2009), 1, pp. 54–69.
101. Ibid., p. 63.
102. Author Interview with Simon Adams, New York, 30 January 2013.
103. This can be seen in China and G77 statements and also the presentation of China's position alongside the G77 in both SC and GA Debates.
104. South Africa only became a BRICS member in 2011 up to that point the appropriate acronym should be BRICs. After 2011, the correct acronym should be BRICS.
105. Author interview with Sarah Teitt [Skype], 10 January 2013.
106. Ibid.
107. Author interview [Skype], 25 January 2013.
108. Author interviews New York, with Members of an R2P NGO, New York, 29 January 2013.
109. This is particularly the case with China. Author Interview with Sarah Teitt [Skype], January 2013.
110. Author interview with Simon Adams, New York, 30 January 2013.
111. Ibid.
112. Ibid.

113. Gareth Evans, 'Responsibility While Protecting', Project Syndicate, 27 January 2012, available http://www.project-syndicate.org/commentary/responsibility-while-protecting#MKc0ZIeBPQ6YeY2z.99, accessed 8 January 2013.
114. Ibid.
115. Ibid.
116. Author Interview with Simon Adams, New York, 30 January 2013.
117. Author Interview with Noel Morada [Skype], 15 January 2013.
118. Author Interview with Noel Morada [Skype], 15 January 2013; Author Interview with Alex Bellamy [phone], 16 January 2013; see also Alex Bellamy and Sara E. Davies, 'The Responsibility to Protect in Southeast Asia: Progress and Problems', *Security Dialogue* (2009), 40(6), pp. 547–574.
119. This does not claim that China is persuading ASEAN states to adopt China's position.
120. Author Interview with Noel Morada [Skype], 15 January 2013.
121. Ibid.
122. Although Kenya in 2008 was at most retrospectively an R2P case.
123. Author Interview with Noel Morada [Skype], 15 January 2013.
124. After a massacre in Mindanao Philippines called for assistance from the region.
125. Author Interview with Noel Morada [Skype], 15 January 2013.
126. Roberta Cohen, 'The Burma Cyclone and the Responsibility to Protect', *Global Responsibility to Protect* (2009), 1, pp. 253–257, p. 254.
127. Ibid., p. 255; also Alex J. Bellamy and Catherine Drummond, 'The Responsibility to Protect in Southeast Asia: Between Non-interference and Sovereignty as Responsibility', *The Pacific Review* (2011), 24(2), pp. 179–200, p. 190.
128. Author Interview with Noel Morada [Skype], 15 January 2013.
129. Alex J. Bellamy and Sara E. Davies, 'The Responsibility to Protect in the Asia-Pacific Region', *Security Dialogue* (2009), 40, pp. 547–574, p. 557.
130. Alex J. Bellamy and Catherine Drummond, 'The Responsibility to Protect in Southeast Asia: Between Non-interference and Sovereignty as Responsibility', *The Pacific Review* (2011), 24(2), pp. 179–200, p. 191.
131. Alistair D.B. Cook and Lina Gong, 'The Cambodian Legacy and the Responsibility to Protect in Asia', *Peace Review*, 23(4).
132. Author Interviews with ASEAN secretariat officials, Jakarta, 14 September 2011.
133. Tiewa Liu, 'Is China Like Other Permanent Members? Governmental and Academic Debates on R2P', in Monica Serano and Thomas Weiss

(eds), *Rallying to the R2P Cause: International Politics of Human Rights* (Routledge: London).
134. Shi Yinhong, Statement at RCUNIO Conference on R2P at Beijing University, March 2012 conference report, p. 87.
135. Ibid., p. 88.
136. Tiewa Liu and Haibin Zhang, 'Debates in China About the Responsibility to Protect as a Developing International Norms: A General Assessment', *Conflict Security and Development* (2014), 14(4), pp. 403–427.
137. Ambassador Chen Jian, RCUNIO Report, p. 85.
138. Author Interview with Alex Bellamy [phone], 16 January 2013.
139. Despite misgivings about the mandate for the use-of-force in the resolution, China recognised 'the need to do something' as such it can be seen as a constructive abstention rather than an abstention aimed at preventing action. Author Interview with Simon Adams, New York, 30 January 2013.
140. Author Interview, New York, 1 February 2013.
141. Amb. Chen Jian, RCUNIO report, p. 86.
142. Famously, the Rwandan Peacekeepers were not authorised to step outside their mandate to protect the civilians targeted.
143. Jiang Zhenxi, noted missions in Cambodia, Sudan, and Somalia, as showing signs of success. Jiang Zhenxi, RUNCIO, p. 77.
144. Ibid., p. 77.
145. UNSC S/2012/538, 19 July 2012.
146. UNSC S/PV.6810, 19 July 2012, p. 13.
147. Ibid.
148. UNSC S/PV.6810, 19 July 2012.
149. Author Interviews with Alex Bellamy [phone], 16 January 2013—please note in particular this relates to Syria.
150. African Union: Thomas Alberts, 'African Union and Libya, on the Horns of a Dilemma', *African Arguments*, 2 November 2011, available http://africanarguments.org/2011/11/02/the-african-union-and-libya-on-the-horns-of-a-dilemma-by-thomas-alberts/, accessed 7 February 2013; Anna Fifield, 'Clinton Warns the African Union over Libya', *Financial Times* [online edition], 13 June 2011, available http://www.ft.com/cms/s/0/176ecd08-95fa-11e0-ba20-00144feab49a.html#axzz2KD-0nPzfl, accessed 7 February 2013; Mike Pflanz, 'African Union Refuses to Recognise Libyan Rebels as "Legitimate Authority"', *The Telegraph*, 28 August 2011, available http://www.telegraph.co.uk/news/worldnews/africaandindianocean/libya/8726486/

African-Union-refuses-to-recognise-Libyan-rebels-as-legitimate-authority.html, accessed 7 February 2013—it should be noted that in Res 1973 all members of the AU voted in favour of the resolution. Arab League: Ethan Bronner and David E. Sanger, 'Arab League Endorses No-Flight Zone Over Libya', *New York Times*, 12 March 2011, available http://www.nytimes.com/2011/03/13/world/middleeast/13libya.html?pagewanted=all&_r=0, accessed 7 February 2013; Colin Freeman, Nick Meo, and Patrick Hennessy, 'Libya: Arab League Calls for United Nations No-Fly Zone', *The Telegraph*, 12 March 2011, available http://www.telegraph.co.uk/news/worldnews/africaandindianocean/libya/8378392/Libya-Arab-League-calls-for-United-Nations-no-fly-zone.html, accessed 7 February 2013.
151. Author Interview with Sarah Teitt [Skype], 10 January 2013.
152. Author interview with Alex Bellamy [phone], 16 January 2013.
153. Author Interview with Noel Morada [Skype], 15 January 2013.
154. One noted that 'the Russians hold the key on Syria' suggesting that China is not the obstacle to action, Author Interview with Alex Bellamy [phone], 16 January 2013; Author Personal Interview [Skype], 25 January 2013.
155. Author Interview with Alex Bellamy [phone], 16 January 2013.
156. Gareth Evans, 'Responsibility While Protecting', *dlx*, 27 January 2012, available http://www.project-syndicate.org/commentary/responsibility-while-protecting#MKc0ZIeBPQ6YeY2z.99, accessed 8 January 2013.
157. Ibid., p. 34.
158. ICISS, 'The Responsibility to Protect', pp. 53–55 (sets out conditions on the authority and who should act).
159. ICISS, 'The Responsibility to Protect', pp. 53–55.
160. Article 2(1) 'The Organization is based on the principle of the sovereign equality of all its Members'. Article 2(4) 'All Members shall refrain in their international relations from the threat or use of force against the territorial integrity or political independence of any state, or in any other manner inconsistent with the Purposes of the United Nations'. UN Charter, available http://www.un.org/en/documents/charter/chapter1.shtml accessed 8 March 2011.
161. Sarah Teitt, 'The Responsibility to Protect and China's Peacekeeping Policy', *International Peacekeeping* (2011), 18(3), pp. 298–312, p. 298.
162. Author Interview with Sarah Teitt [Skype], 10 January 2013.
163. Author Interview with Simon Adam, New York, 30 January 2013.
164. Indeed some interviewees suggested that the IBSA group of states was more coordinated among its members and also more critical of R2P.

Author interviews [Skype], 10 January 2013; author interview New York 30 January 2013.
165. In the sense that more states are taking responsibility and ownership for issues outside the grouping of the P5, an example of this is within the C34 meetings.

CHAPTER 8

Conclusion: China and the Norms of Sovereignty

This discussion of China's interpretation of sovereignty and its actions in the Security Council (UNSC) has several very interesting implications for China's engagement with the liberal international order. At the end of the fourth chapter, four tools for normative change were identified: reframing existing debates; creating new institutions; using 'new' issue areas; and creating new populations. By the use of these tools, states can express their agency in challenging international norms. The agency of states could take the form of: persistent objection; ad hoc objection (or consent); or norm entrepreneurship.

In China's interaction within the SC on issues of sovereignty, China can be seen as adopting all three types of agency; although the dominant narrative set out above demonstrates a tendency to use objection. China also uses the tools of populations and reframing debates. In challenging international norms, China's challenge is facilitated by a changing balance of powers and the perceived failure of existing interpretations of norms.

In conclusion, this section looks at how successful China has been in using these tools, and then goes on to examine how much of a challenge this represents to the liberal international order.

Tools for Challenging Liberal Interpretations of Norms

In the debates on the Responsibility to Protect (R2P) and debates on intervention in the Security Council (SC), China has been a crucial contributor to the reframing of the original interpretation of both the concept and the application of R2P. Linking the current debate to previous interpretations of sovereignty, China specifically seeks to uphold the consistency between previous and current interpretations of sovereignty and in so doing, prevents the acceptance of R2P in its liberal formulation. The desire of China to promote more debates and dialogue before this norm progresses along the life cycle, is reminiscent of a continuing approach of China concerning norms of sovereignty, which is clearly seen in the 1995 SC debate reconsidering the Agenda for Peace. The Chinese delegate, Wang Xuexian stated '[t]he report has provided us with some new and thought-provoking views and ideas which deserve our in-depth consideration and extensive discussion'.[1] Furthermore, he went on to state that the SC needs to ensure the protection of the purposes and principles of the Charter. The primary purpose of which, for China, is the protection of state sovereignty and non-interference.[2]

In reframing this debate, China's approach has been to utilise the benefits of adopting a position of persistent objection from early on, and gathering support for its position, by couching its own position in relation to existing interpretations of sovereignty and practices of international intervention. In garnering support for this position, China has clearly benefited from the 'fractures in the liberal paradigm',[3] and the subsequent divisions appearing in the liberal core. That is, as liberal interventions have experienced problems, disagreements about the purposes and methods of intervention have emerged between the liberal democratic states, as with France's and Germany's objection to the invasion of Iraq in 2003, and Germany's objection to military intervention in Libya in 2011.[4] The norm of liberal interventions has not failed, but these divisions contribute to exposing some of the inconsistencies in the rhetoric of liberal interventions protecting civilian populations, and the actual outcomes and damage to communities.

The exposure of these contradictions helps to create an environment in which an alternative that has consistency between the interpretation of sovereignty and potential outcomes is more likely to be accepted; if an interpretation and means to achieve the limitations of sovereignty include the protection of human life, the consistency between intention and means will make that interpretation more acceptable. However, if the aim is to protect civilian life, but the execution of the norm in fact endangers human life, then this inconsistency will reduce the chances of acceptance.

In acting collectively, liberal states can marshal the debate (through their majority in the Permanent 5 (P5) in the SC they can limit information and help to limit the content of debates) in order to prevent the exposure of any inconsistencies. This is because these liberal states when acting collectively form '[t]he inner circle [that] consists of all the individuals directly or indirectly responsible for the formulation, negotiation, conclusion, implementation and application of a particular legal norm'.[5] If a norm, that has not yet been internalised by all actors, or reached the tipping point of the norm life cycle, is supported by a collective and cohesive group its progress towards the tipping point is more likely. Nonetheless, if this group contains different interpretations of the norm that increases divisions within the group over time, the progress of the norm is less likely. But it is more likely that an alternative schema or an 'alternative script'[6] that remedies the problems highlighted will be increasingly accepted. This is exemplified by China's role in the development of R2P and the debates within the Council on military interventions. China has not actively promoted a 'new' interpretation of sovereignty; it has actively reached backwards to previous applications of the norms of sovereignty to legitimise its own position.[7] By abstaining, China also limited the detrimental effects to its own credibility by not blocking the use of the norm of R2P. Thus, it adopted a position that is closely related to the idea of ad hoc acceptance, that is, individual council decisions are 'exceptional' rather than precedent forming.[8]

Complementing this reframing activity, enhancing China's success and aiding China's ability to be a norm entrepreneur in other areas are the development of a 'shared logic'.[9] China has reframed the debate in such a way that its interpretation of sovereignty appeals to other actors, both in the abstract and in the real implications.[10] In looking at the R2P the debates around RwP, these reflect the issues raised in the 1990s regarding humanitarian intervention. The use of common phrases and ideas binds a group of individual states more closely together,[11] but it also increases the chance that they will adopt similar positions in different debates because they employ similar schemas or frameworks to understand new issues.

How successful have China's actions been in reinterpreting the norms of sovereignty? These discussions suggest that China has been partially successful. China's position is increasingly supported by other states, and the language it uses in the SC is consistently adopted by others in arguments around sovereignty. One area China has been particularly successful is stalling the cascade of R2P. Nonetheless, China's approach is only ad hoc rather than demonstrative of persistent objection. In some certain situations, it is successful, when its position can be closely aligned to that of other states, or when it makes efforts to demonstrate consistency and clarity over the issue of the consequences. This can be viewed in two ways: either China is not yet a significant enough power within the SC to 'get its own way' or there are lessons to be learnt from the 1990s about how to get an interpretation of a norm to endure. Simon Reich argues that norms are more likely to endure for a long period of time if they are seen as coming from a group of actors.[12] Furthermore, actors are more likely to be committed to an interpretation if they see themselves as being a part of the process of creating it. There is a greater chance of a Chinese interpretation of sovereignty and its correlative activities enduring for a long time if other actors are actively engaged in determining the contents of that interpretation; China's engagement in the SC gives the greatest potential for this being the case, by framing but not overtly determining the outcome of debates.

CHALLENGES TO LIBERAL INTERPRETATIONS OF SOVEREIGNTY

This section makes three points: (a) China engages more constructively than is commonly perceived; (b) China's challenge is nuanced and sophisticated, targeting specific elements of the liberal interpretation of sovereignty and (c) China is reforming sovereignty away from coercive liberalism, but it is doing so through liberal means, and as such upholding a different form of liberalism.

China engages more constructively than commonly perceived. Indeed, the discourse of China's engagement in the Western press in particular actively tends towards delegitimising China's engagement by promulgating the idea that China consistently blocks actions within the SC. But very few debates in the SC result in a veto by any power, and taken in comparison with the use of the veto by other powers, China is one of the less obstructive members in the Council (both Russia and the USA have used the veto more often in the last decade). In looking more closely at China's involvement within debates in the SC, China increasingly contributes to debates, justifying its own voting actions by relating them to its own conception of sovereignty and expressly linking its votes to what it perceives to be the 'right and proper' thing to do with respect to commonly agreed norms. As a result of this level of engagement, China's challenge to liberal elements of international order and sovereignty in particular are more nuanced and sophisticated than frequently professed.

8 CONCLUSION: CHINA AND THE NORMS OF SOVEREIGNTY

China challenges specific elements of the liberal interpretation of sovereignty. In particular, it challenges the diminishing importance that liberal states attribute to territorial integrity, and the related norm of non-interference. Yet, the emergence of a new core or the potential of new significant groups all unified in their position forms not only a method of challenge but also a key element of change from the liberal interpretation of sovereignty. In the outline, it was noted that within the liberal conception of sovereignty a hierarchy has emerged, with liberal states being preferred to others because of their domestic systems. However, in the emergence of divisions between liberal states, the potential has been created for the emergence of a new 'democracy' and new equilibrium to emerge.

Furthermore, China challenges the 'code of ethics' of a liberal interpretation of sovereignty that privileges individual rights above the right of the state to sovereignty. But, crucially China does not make a claim that human life should not be respected, or that violations of human rights should be ignored; rather, they should be respected alongside the respect for the sovereignty of the state. As was the case in the Sudan and East Timor, in order to uphold the respect for sovereignty, but take action on the humanitarian issues, China put pressure on the government in question to force consent. China's solution to protecting civilians and state sovereignty is to situate them side by side, rather than one above the other; if this approach is increasingly adopted, it may also produce contradictions and tensions—but at present it lacks the drawbacks of recent experience.

Finally, China's challenge to the liberal interpretation of sovereignty is to ask what the international community should do as a result of its interpretation and whether the international community has a Responsibility to Protect. It would seem that China's interpretation of the doctrine is that all states should be pressured to protect from outside. If this does not work, they should be pressured to consent to a UN force protecting their citizens. But the liberal interpretation of R2P would have far-reaching implications that would undermine the structure of international laws and norms that would be undesirable and harmful to international peace and security. Therefore, every effort must be made to maintain the sovereignty of states, so that they are then empowered to uphold these international agreements.

Thus, there is an irony in China's position on sovereignty and its actions in the SC. China, in actively trying to uphold sovereignty, and the primacy of the UN as an organ of international order, is upholding a type of liberal international order, but it is different from the liberal order that was advanced through the late 1990s and early 2000s.

Notes

1. S/PV.3492, 18 January 1995, p. 12.
2. Ibid., p. 13.
3. Miwa Hirono, 'China's Charm Offensive and Peacekeeping: The Lessons of Cambodia—What Now for Sudan?', *International Peacekeeping* (2011), 18(3), pp. 328–343, p. 331.
4. *Reuters*, 'China Reaches Out to Germany on Libya', *Reuters.com*, 25 March 2011.
5. Ian Johnstone, 'Security Council Deliberations: The Power of the Better Argument', *European Journal of International Law* (2003), 14(3), pp. 437–480, p. 450.
6. Elisabeth S. Clemens and James M. Cook, 'Politics and Institutionalism: Explaining Durability and Change', *Annual Review of Sociology* (1999), 25, pp. 441–466, p. 445.
7. Courtney Richardson takes this claim further by arguing that China has actively framed the discourse and set out the parameters for what is seen as legitimate and illegitimate actions. Courtney Richardson, 'A Responsible Power? China and the UN Peacekeeping Regime', *International Peacekeeping* (2011), 18(3), pp. 286–297, p. 288.
8. Andrea Bianchi, 'Ad-Hocism and the Rule of Law', *European Journal of International Law* (2002), 13(1), pp. 263–272 and 263–264.
9. Shogo Suzuki, 'Why Does China Participate in Intrusive Peacekeeping? Understanding Paternalistic Chinese Discourses on Development and Intervention', *International Peacekeeping* (2011), 18(3), pp. 271–285, p. 273.
10. Marc Lanteigne, 'A Change in Perspective: China's Engagement in East Timor UN Peacekeeping Operations', *International Peacekeeping* (2011), 18(3), pp. 313–327, p. 324.
11. This is the idea of a collective identity, Karen Cerulo, 'Identity Construction: New Issues, New Directions', *American Review of Sociology* (1997), 23, pp. 385–409.
12. Simon Reich, *Global Norms, American Sponsorship and the Emerging Patterns of World Politics* (Palgrave Macmillan: Basingstoke, 2010).

PART III

Evolution or Revolution in International Aid Practices? China and International Development

CHAPTER 9

Liberal Development: The Practice and Assumptions of Aid

The focus here is on whether and how liberal interpretations of 'development' differ from Chinese interpretations; the subsequent chapter then utilises these differences to determine whether it can be plausibly argued that Chinese approaches are challenging liberal development practices. Accordingly, it explores the implications of the UK's former Development Secretary Andrew Mitchell's proposition that 'Chinese investors, Brazilian social entrepreneurs and Indian bloggers now rival Oxford and Oxfam in setting the development agenda'.[1]

China's role in the developing world has met with two distinct reactions: as Stephan Halper characterises them, the 'panda huggers' and the 'panda bashers',[2] perceiving China as an opportunity and a threat, respectively. Nonetheless, this discussion does not aim to attach any normative value to China's engagement with developing countries, but rather to revisit a languishing debate[3] and assess whether there is a 'Beijing Consensus' (BC) on development, what form it takes, and whether it is challenging the current liberal international order.

Traditionally, the development debate encompassed both the issue of how development can be achieved and what a developed state 'should' look like.[4] In contrast, as this chapter shows, the Beijing Consensus on development only contains norms regarding development practices, not direction on what a developed state 'should' look like.

In this exposition, development is discussed as a collection of norms that, in the case of the Washington Consensus (WC), are held by a group of actors that implicitly or explicitly conform to the same understandings

© The Author(s) 2018
C. Jones, *China's Challenge to Liberal Norms*,
https://doi.org/10.1057/978-1-137-42761-8_9

and practices that have an underlying liberal ideology. Resulting from this underlying ideology, there has been an emergence of the norms, modalities and practices of development, in particular practices of aid allocation. The emergence of China as a donor has the potential to challenge both the liberal content of the norms of development and the related practices and modalities. However, in parallel with the emergence of China as a donor, the persistent evaluation of existing aid practices facilitates potential normative changes.

In looking at the failure or resilience of the WC, aid is used as a lens through which to view change or stability. The relationship of this concept of aid to the way in which it is supposed to produce growth and therefore development is vital for understanding the criticisms of some aid practices, and most significantly the challenge that China may pose. As Deborah Bräutigam explains, the role of ideas and concepts is central to understanding aid, the politics at play in development, and most significantly, to the broader question of China's challenge to the liberal international order.[5] As a result, China's challenge to the liberal international order through aid may become more apparent when considered alongside the types of states produced by certain aid practices and ideologies.

This chapter advances two parallel arguments. The first is that China's rise has illuminated the pre-existing fractures in the liberal logic of the existing collection of norms, facilitated by the Global Financial Crisis and the ongoing assessments of the aid system from within the Organisation for Economic Cooperation and Development (OECD). Secondly, China, through the provision of alternative sources of aid and different ideological underpinnings for aid, is triggering responses in the practices and architecture of the OECD. Hence, it is a catalyst for changes already needed and identified rather than a cause of them.

Likewise, this argument is presented in two parts. The first explores the theoretical assumptions and practices of aid donations before exploring the concept of the Beijing Consensus (BC—also known in the literature as the China Model) and its implications for aid practices. This book part then explores what China is doing in terms of aid donations and loans. It also evaluates how China is engaging with existing multilateral institutions of development (the World Bank, United Nations Development Program—UNDP, International Monetary Fund—IMF, and World Trade Organisation—WTO). It seeks to explore whether Chinese approaches to aid differ from their Western liberal counterparts, and assesses the challenge presented by the emergence of China as an aid donor to the practices of Western donors. The key question in this part is whether China's actions in providing aid present a challenge to the ideology, and practices, or are merely provoking a temporary reorganisation of international development practices.

Herein, the argument is made that 'development' offers the best demonstration of China acting as a norm entrepreneur. In pursuing a course as a development actor, it uses the tools of new institutions (FOCAC) as well as reinterpretation and new populations (within the high-level forum at Busan) to get its approach to aid more widely used. This challenge to the WC is also facilitated by the criticisms and the failures of the WC practices and the fracturing of the liberal consensus around aid.

The Washington Consensus

The 1970s left an enduring legacy in the form of 'New Institutional Economics' (NIE) with the subsequent policy prescriptions termed the 'Washington Consensus'.[6] The WC, promoted through the IMF, WB and General Agreement on Tariffs and Trade (GATT), later to become the WTO, was founded on a particular logic that established a link between liberalism and capitalism.[7] Broadly speaking, the WC promoted economic development at the same time as political development, highlighting the link between good governance, reducing corruption and respect for human rights as essential for economic development. Central to the WC is a shrinking role of the state and liberalisation of the economy (increased privatisation and deregulation). This link is important not only for seeing the current world order as liberal but because it represented a shift in how we see development; WC changed *what* development is as well as *how* it was to be achieved.[8] Importantly, the WC made claims, about how states could not only achieve economic success—through interaction with the markets—but also link these developments to an image of what constitutes 'the good life' and how it should be achieved. The rapid adoption and promotion of the WC through international institutions changed the development debate entirely. It broadened the concept of development by applying normative standards of good governance and financial assessments as a part of development.[9] These institutions, in line with the logic of WC, adopted policies such as Structural Adjustment Policies (SAPs), which further consolidated the link between capitalism and liberalism.[10]

This shift meant developing nations had to contend with increasing debt, crisis management and growth problems, whilst at the same time producing domestic institutional change in line with ideals of 'good governance'. In some countries, these prescriptions created success stories, but in others their implementation had dramatic consequences.[11] The WC made claims (that are contested) about the type of governance structure that is essential to economic success. Development is best achieved in environments that have: competitive elections, accountability, democratic institutions and functioning systems of the rule of law.[12] In seeking to make aid more effective, practices should encourage the creation of these types of environments. Despite the growing recognition throughout the 1990s that the WC was flawed, there was no alternative to this approach to development.

What Does the Washington Consensus Mean for Aid?

The Washington Consensus (WC) is a broad collection of policies that form a toolkit for developing countries framed within a particular ideology and logic.[13] Thus, there is a great deal of flexibility in the WC; it can produce a range of policies, as has been demonstrated over the past four decades, but crucially all of these policies are coordinated with an overarching framework that sees development as both an economic and political aspiration. Moreover, the aims of development are focused on producing political and economic freedoms that are inseparable from each other. However, in the practices of aid agencies, these broad policies and range of realities find a particular expression. As a result, there is a need to understand whether it is the practices of aid or the guiding ideology (of the WC) or both that have failed or faltered.

What Is Aid?

This section sets out what China presents a challenge to; it thus explores the criticisms and problems of OECD countries' aid practices. This is significant because in order to explore whether the Washington Consensus has failed it first needs to be separated out into the underpinning liberal ideology and the application of the theory through practices of institutions and donors. Following this, these criticisms of the Washington

Consensus are put together in looking at whether the norms or practices (in whole or in part) have failed.

The Washington Consensus was so called because it was a consensus about how development was to be achieved that existed between the major institutions of international development and international financial institutions in Washington. The liberal logic of the WC has had clear implications for aid, in both how it is defined and practised.

According to the OECD 'Aid', or Official Development Assistance (ODA), is:

> Flows of official financing administered with the promotion of the economic development and welfare of developing countries as the main objective, and which are concessional in character with a grant element of at least 25 percent (using a fixed 10 percent rate of discount). By convention, ODA flows comprise contributions of donor government agencies, at all levels, to developing countries ("bilateral ODA") and to multilateral institutions. ODA receipts comprise disbursements by bilateral donors and multilateral institutions. Lending by export credit agencies—with the pure purpose of export promotion—is excluded.[14]

This definition needs to be unpacked in order for it to be useful in understanding whether China is challenging the practices or underlying assumptions of development. The OECD has a focus on poverty reduction and economic growth, so any definition of aid needs to be coupled with an understanding of whether the objectives that create a standard for assessing effectiveness are appropriate to achieve the desired outcomes. Tables or definitions of aid flows are essentially meaningless in the absence of an understanding of how they relate to these objectives. For the OECD, particularly the DCD-DAC (Development Cooperation Directorate) in addition to the WB, IMF, and many bilateral and other multilateral sources of aid, attention has been focussed on not only how to increase the volume of aid, but also how to make it more effective. As a result, an extensive literature has been produced around aid effectiveness and the theoretical underpinnings of both what development is and how it can be achieved.

Criticisms of Aid Effectiveness and Its Implication for the Failure of the WC (A Formal Cause)

One significant methodological issue in identifying China's agency in challenging the WC is being able to identify the other causes. This section sets out a major facilitating condition (a formal cause) of the challenge to the WC. The clear identification of what constitutes this formal cause is essential in being able to distil China's agency.

This section explores two things: first, it looks at aid effectiveness, and how (or whether) criticisms of how aid works in producing growth have challenged practices over time; second, it looks at how this is reflected in discussions of whether the Washington Consensus has failed.

In all the literature on aid effectiveness, there are problems with the selectivity and the collection of data available. So whilst unpacking the data available would provide the best analysis for understanding the dynamics of aid, and despite the significant improvements in the quality of information about aid flows in the past decade (the OECD tracking flows and more recently the International Aid Transparency Initiative— IATI—tracking receipts),[15] the current state of the literature is still limited to long-term studies that explore aid effectiveness. As a result, the same or similar data sets can be (and are) used to confirm or decry contrasting claims about what makes aid effective.[16] Indeed, the most interesting analysis is frequently produced as a result of different definitions rather than any differences in the inputs into regressions.[17]

Despite the weaknesses in the data, and the ability to tell numerous different stories about the effectiveness of aid in producing development and reducing poverty, there are important themes within the debate on aid effectiveness that are crucial: good policy environments; institutionalisation; overhead costs; fragmentation; fungibility; transparency; short- or long-term aims. Importantly, the reasons for which these issues limit aid effectiveness in part relate back to a particular understanding of the role of the state in development and economics, and thus to an economic view conditioned by the dominance of the WC.

The WC and its criticisms can be clearly seen in the manifestation of three central debates of aid effectiveness. First, the shrinking of the state: the effectiveness of aid has been linked to a logic first set out by Burnside and Dollar and has been reiterated frequently by both bilateral and multilateral aid agencies, and that aid produced growth in 'good policy environments'[18] defined by Burnside and Dollar as countries with 'sound economic policies'.[19] This links back to the 'good states' and 'bad states' of the Washington Consensus. Identifying these 'good policy environments' should lead to selectivity criteria being applied in the decisions of where to give aid; indeed, they have led to the creation of the Country Policy and Institutional Assessment (CPIA).[20] However, as Dalgaard et al. indicate, this is not a 'fair' system of aid distribution because of a number of biases built into the model.[21] In addition, it is not the only criterion that multilateral and bilateral aid agencies use in their assessments to decide who receives aid.[22] Thus, the selectivity of the recipients of aid according to the data produced should favour donations to countries that have 'good policy environments', but what a good policy environment is remains underspecified in the literature and the impact of these environments on development is therefore questionable.

Second, the level of institutionalisation within a target country has an effect on the ability of a state to handle the flows of aid. Decreasing the tools available for the state—through deregulation, reducing controls over markets and an increasing focus on the impartial distribution of aid flows—disables the ability of the state to produce these types of environments. The WC produces two central concerns around this issue. A central element of the WC requires the restructuring of domestic governance and a shrinking of the state apparatus, reducing the capacity of the state to manage financial flows whilst simultaneously increasing the volume of money going into the country. As a result of the increasing volume of money going into a country, highly skilled individuals are working to direct the flows of aid (because of higher wages possible) rather than promoting in-country growth.[23]

There is a logical tension within the WC revealed by the experiences of developing states. In order to produce growth, the liberalisation of the economy requires a stronger rather than a weaker state. In particular, the state needs to have a central role in regulating the functioning of markets and creating an effective rule of law.[24]

Third, other outcomes from the WC that have undermined the provision of aid include differences in optimal levels of overhead costs.[25] This problem is a result of the shifting role and function of institutions as a response to the demands of state reform within the WC. Undertaking these reforms has an impact on the level of institutional efficiency needed to cope with disbursing the aid and also assessing effectiveness. Other issues in aid effectiveness—exacerbated by the prescriptions of the WC in relation to the reform of the state—include: fragmentation and coordination among donors[26] and the ability of an ineffective state to counter this problem[27]; the ability to effectively manage tied and untied aid[28]; the problem of aid fungibility; and the impact on government budgets of the inflows of specific and targeted aid requiring the ability to track and hold to account institutions and individuals.[29] These concerns are not directly related to the WC but rather demonstrate that challenges or criticisms of international aid may focus on practices rather than demanding a change in the underlying ideology.

As the discussion of aid effectiveness demonstrates, the challenges to the WC have been to its policy prescriptions, but some also relate to its underlying logic. Challenges to its underlying logic include a realisation from other nations about the implications of the WC, which has an impact on the legitimacy of these actors to ensure development. As other nations have learnt and adapted, or succeeded within, or perhaps failed because of, the WC, understanding of the implications of the WC has also increased. Furthermore, criticisms of the bias of the WC in favour of already developed nations have also increased.[30] The WC forced other states to 'get rich' (resulting in some very rich individuals) on the terms of the already rich, through methods outlined by the developed world. Developing nations have learnt that '[d]eveloped countries ... did not get where they are now through the policies and the institutions that they recommend to Africa today'.[31] Consequently, questions are being asked as to why developing nations should accept the conditions placed on loans and aid by international institutions. Aggravating this position is the fact that because of China's rise these nations now have a place to go and ask for money without conditions.[32] In addition to the assessments of what makes aid more effective presenting a practical challenge to how aid works, these assessments also challenge the underlying ideology of the WC that these practices are imbued with. According to Charlie Gore, 'the Washington Consensus has cracked in the practical sense'.[33]

Within the norms of the WC, states should be trying to: achieve fiscal discipline; control and manage public expenditure; seek tax reforms; control interest rates; float exchange rates; liberalise trade; seek foreign direct investment; pursue privatisation; deregulate industries; and seek to advance property rights.[34] This is evidenced not only by attempts to select recipients of aid but also by the conditions placed on aid. Indeed, because of these conditions, developing states found it impossible to resist this approach; their need for both trade and aid meant that they had no alternatives.[35]

In addition to the practical failures of the WC, there has also been a realisation that modernisation is not a linear process; there is not just one path to modernisation as liberal thinkers would have states believe.[36] Thus, the framework of norms in which policies are created and followed is vital in determining the pathway to modernisation; and therefore, changes to the existing norms of development are likely to change views of what modernisation is and how it is achieved. The most successful stories of modernisation have been the Asian Tigers,[37] who have at best become 'semi-democracies' or 'quasi-democracies'.[38] These countries have pursued 'market or soft authoritarianism',[39] combining a free market economy with authoritarian rule.

There is controversy as to whether this is a perversion or development of the original WC. Williamson has been keen to claim the success of these economies as a testament to the WC,[40] but there are also claims that these economies demonstrate the failure of the WC, not only because of their systems of government but because of their 'cherry-picking' of the prescriptions of the WC. Similar claims are also made by Williamson about the causes of the Asian Financial Crisis (AFC). He claims that the AFC was caused by exactly this 'cherry-picking' attitude towards the WC. However, the countries that were most badly damaged by the AFC were those that seem to have stuck most rigidly to the WC's key prescriptions. Evidently then, there is confusion as to how much deviation is permissible whilst still being able to suggest that a country is following the WC. The problem that arises is that because the WC is such a broad church of practices linked to a loose guiding idea, it is difficult to claim that it has failed or that it has succeeded.

If the Washington Consensus—or elements of it—has failed, and if there are specific recommendations for making aid more effective, the question arises as to why changes have not yet taken place. The answer in some of the literature is that there has been no new ideology with which to replace the Washington Consensus, and there has been no real catalyst to improve aid effectiveness. The rise of China changes both of these things, structurally and agentially.

The pressure within the WC to reduce the role of the state and increase growth through liberalisation of markets contributes to making the BC attractive to developing states: it makes no demands for internal changes. 'The Chinese have subsequently walked through an open door with an alternative philosophy that makes few demands on the internal root and branch of client states'.[41] This statement oversimplifies the reality. Crucially for China, this absence of 'interference in the internal structures of the state' fits well with the approach to sovereignty and non-interference outlined in the previous chapter. It demonstrates a 'need' for China to challenge the existing aid architecture and framework.

This section has set out the elements of the WC that are challenged through the formal cause of the failure of the WC. The aspect of the discussion explores whether there is a discernible 'Beijing Consensus'; if so whether it presents a challenge to what is considered as aid and how it is distributed; whether China offers an ideological alternative; and whether China is an alternative source of funding for developing states. A subtext to this discussion is the issue of whether China is an agent in this challenge. As a result, the next segment moves on to look at China as an efficient and final cause of a challenge to the WC; specifically, it looks to set out if China is a norm entrepreneur.

THE BEIJING CONSENSUS/THE CHINA MODEL

The concept of the Beijing consensus is key to being able to identify whether China is a norm entrepreneur with respect to aid. As noted previously, capacity is important in determining its status as a norm entrepreneur. A state must be able to develop an idea and then to get it accepted by other actors. This was a key stumbling block for China and R2P. In setting out this argument concerning development—that there is a clear attempt for China to be a norm entrepreneur—China must be able to be seen as having a new approach, and be seen to be using some of the tools outlined in Chapter 4 to get its norm accepted.

This concept was first proposed by Joshua Ramo in his 2004 book '*The Beijing Consensus*',[42] but prior to Ramo, Randall Peerenboom had already argued for the existence of a distinct Chinese approach to development in 'China Modernises'.[43] Furthermore, since 2004 the idea has been developed and criticised by many authors.[44] Moreover, since the announcement of the Asian Investment Infrastructure Bank (AIIB) and the One Belt One Road (OBOR) (or more recently 'Belt and Road') policies, China's development strategies have received further consideration.[45] Yet, despite all of this discussion and debate, there remains confusion over whether the Beijing Consensus or a uniquely Chinese approach to aid exists, who it is a consensus between and perhaps most importantly whether it is persuasive as an alternative.

The literature on the Beijing Consensus suggests one clear distinction from the WC: the BC has a different understanding of the role of the state in respect to the markets and the management of the economy.[46] As a result, the BC suggests that there is an advantage for developing states in an authoritarian government because a strong central power is in a better position to be able to effectively manage financial flows, push through social changes that may be unpopular, and—by virtue of a consistency of approach within the government—is more able to develop and use leverage in a state's relations to aid donors. Consequently, conditionality of aid donations is an aberration; the state and the government of the state should be able to negotiate and pursue approaches that it sees as the most appropriate. In addition, this approach and this view of the state fit in with China's approach to sovereignty and non-interference. An important point to note here is that this idea is also present in some of the literature on the criticisms of aid practices discussed earlier.[47]

The presence of China quantitatively changes the number of choices a state faces: aid with conditions, no aid, or aid without or with different conditions. Significantly, the rhetoric of aid without conditions supports negotiation and a discussion—giving greater ownership to the target state of this development path. In looking back over the criticisms of aid practices, they also identify the inability of these criticisms to effect changes in the absence of catalyst.[48] In part, this is a problem that those making appraisals of projects' success or difficulties are those who implemented the project.[49] The proposition is that China is the catalyst.

A further proposition about the Beijing Consensus is that opening-up should be incremental; it is not efficient to open up markets, deregulate, float currencies, and privatise all at once.[50] Rather there is a need to pursue these policies gradually and under the watchful eye of the state. But, such a recommendation is also possible with the Washington Consensus; there is an overlap between the two. It is agreed that these reforms are important, but the timeline of implementation is different.[51] Within the context of either consensus, the conclusion that strong centralised governments are most capable of producing development may only be true at a certain stage of development; as financial and economic deregulation is implemented decentralisation of the state apparatus may also become necessary.

A final supposed difference between these two approaches is who they are a consensus between. The Washington Consensus earned its name because it was a consensus between the major multilateral aid agencies in Washington; this consensus was then expanded to include many state aid agencies. But, from the literature regarding criticisms of aid practices and criticisms of the Washington Consensus itself,[52] it is clear that any consensus that might have existed on this approach is now considerably contested.[53] The same problem emerges when looking at the Beijing Consensus; it is supposed to be a consensus between the different elements of the aid establishment in Beijing. Yet, the extent of consensus in Beijing is also disputed. In part, this is because there is limited knowledge of the level of coordination between the practices of these institutions,[54] but there is also disagreement even about the idea of the 'Beijing Consensus' and especially there is a leadership denial of whether China's approach to development is suitable for other states.[55]

The nub of the difference is the role of the state. The difference between the policies they each recommend is that development and growth should be within the control of the state and a state should be able to negotiate and set out its own agenda for its development, but it should have a range of options to choose from. In practice, this produces different definitions of what aid is and therefore how aid practices are pursued.

What Does the Beijing Consensus Mean for the Definition and Practices of Aid Donations?

This section sets out what implications the BC has on the provision on aid. As such, it describes the areas in which a challenge to the practices of the WC would be expected to emerge. It therefore offers essential guidance for the subsequent chapter which looks at the tools that China is using to challenge the WC. This is important in piecing together the steps of China's challenge, linking the idea of the BC, to practices, and then through entrepreneurship to challenging the practices of the existing aid architecture through the use of the tools reinterpretation, new institutions, and new populations.

What Is Aid?

According to the 2011 Chinese white paper on foreign aid:

China's foreign aid policy has distinct characteristics of the times. It is suited both to China's actual conditions and the needs of the recipient countries. China has been constantly enriching, improving and developing the Eight Principles for Economic Aid and Technical Assistance to Other Countries - the guiding principles of China's foreign aid put forward in the 1960s.[56]

These eight principles are: "building self-development capacity"; "no political conditions"; "Equality"; "Mutual Benefit"; "Common Development"; "remaining realistic"; "keeping pace with the times"; and "paying attention to reform and innovation."[57]

Further elucidation of China's aid orientation can be found from the Ministry of Commerce People's Republic of China (MOFCOM), the main provider of aid by China, where it states one of the aims of the ministry is:

To formulate and implement China's foreign aid policies and plans, facilitate the reform on foreign aid provision modalities, compile foreign aid programs, select foreign aid projects and organize their implementation. To manage funds in the nature of China's official foreign assistance, the grant aid provided to China through multilateral and bilateral channels (excluding the grants provided by foreign governments and international financial institutions under the framework of fiscal cooperation) and other development cooperation programs.[58]

The 'forms of aid' discussed in the 2011 White paper include: complete projects; materials and goods; technical cooperation; human resource cooperation; Chinese medical teams; overseas volunteers; humanitarian aid; and debt relief.[59] This means that China does give aid in some of the same ways as the DAC countries, but the part of Chinese donations along these lines that can be counted as ODA is quite small, because of the confusing overlap between what is seen as commercial and what is counted as official. The China Export-Import Bank (EXIM) is one of the main providers of Chinese aid, and some of EXIM's activities do correlate with the practices of the OECD-DAC countries, but only a part of EXIM's activities can be treated as OECD-ODA.[60] Indeed a part of EXIM's work is related to the Ministry of Finance rather than MOFCOM. Because of its intention to invest in future growth, 'China's expansion into other developing countries is not mainly about aid but about all the other instruments of economic engagement'.[61]

If one looks at this approach to 'overseas assistance' in combination with the vagaries of the Beijing Consensus, one can see this as a different interpretation of aid; China can be seen as redefining aid—or perhaps it would be more accurate to suggest that China's approach is not changing aid, but rather is reshaping how development is best pursued: reducing the component of aid and increasing commercial and economic cooperation. But the extent to which the activities of 'commercial' elements of China's activities in Africa are actually commercial is also contested. There remains a grey area where it is unclear what kind of returns China's EXIM gets on the loans it makes not within the structures of the OECD-ODA. It is difficult to draw a clear line between what is actually 'commercial' and what is not. Commercial loans that are written off do not count as a part of ODA because the original loan was commercial, but the decision to write off the loan may have been officially sanctioned.[62] As a result, it is also problematic to draw a line between what is 'official' and what is commercial.

In addition, some of China's donations in terms of material goods and infrastructure projects do count as a part of OECD-ODA, but many do not because they are either provided by commercial enterprises or are commercial in character. Where China funds technical cooperation there is a distinction between the 'rates' charged by Chinese providers and those charged by Western donors. That is, a Western donor country lists in the tables of aid the value of the donation as the market price in the donor country whereas the Chinese approach is different focusing instead on the value in the recipient country. China also includes military assistance and subsidised loans for joint projects as aid, but doesn't count training of students or debt relief (thus overcoming one problem about what type of debt has been relieved).[63] As a result of different ideas of what development is and how it should be achieved there is a different definition of aid, and subsequently a difference in aid practices and approaches.

Hence, we have a range of considerations for understanding how, why and with what effect China could be considered to be a distinctly different aid actor: what is and what isn't included in aid; whether it is seen as being 'developmental' in character; whether China's practice or definitions are related to the experiences of China's own path to development; and whether they are in part an expression of the Beijing Consensus.

These differences then reflect an approach to aid that gives a central role in managing the economy to the state—carving out deals with China is a part of the process[64]—and that development comes from using FDI in a targeted way. Although this is a plausible understanding, these differences could also be the result of demands from recipient countries, in reaction to the perceived failed aid practices of the OECD. The presence of a 'tried and tested' alternative that can relate directly to the current experiences of recipient countries grants greater legitimacy to China's approach. At the same time, China's need for new markets creates interdependence between donor and recipient that is different to the OECD. As a result of this particular expression of a dissimilar definition of aid that speaks directly to China's own experience, it is plausible that China has a significant role in the determination of these relationships.

This discussion has presented a view of what a Chinese 're-interpretation' of aid would look like and therefore provides a set of indicators to identify challenges to the aid architecture that could be specifically Chinese. In particular, for China it is important that aid links to the development of trade. Consequently, the 'risks' of development strategies are born by both donor and recipient. In Part II this reinterpretation can be seen as being attempted in the case of Busan.

How Much Aid?

As noted above it is important for China to be 'able' in presenting a challenge as a norm entrepreneur. It must have the capacity to develop an idea (set out above) and a means to propel that idea towards international acceptance. This therefore presents significant constraint on China's role in challenging the aid architecture—the fact that it remains a relatively small aid contributor—even bearing in mind the problems of identifying how much aid China gives (set out below). Thus, it would be expected that in order to act as a norm entrepreneur it would need the support of other populations of states as well as reinterpretation. This is because the support of other states would reduce the capacity (of a single state) needed to get the norm accepted.

In attempting to provide some idea of the scale of Chinese aid donations, this section attempts to use as much of the available data as possible to produce a comparison with OECD-DAC donations. In 2011 China published its first White Paper on aid. Included in it is some evidence for what types of projects Chinese aid supports[65] and some data on how much aid China gives.[66] At the Forum on China-Africa Cooperation, China promised to double its aid to Africa over the following three years to US$3 billion in concessional loans and a further US$2 billion in preferential export buyer's credit.[67]

According to newspaper reports, by 2011 China had over-taken the World Bank in terms of aid donations.[68] But, crucially, in the comparison of the WB and China's donations, there is an absence of a sophisticated analysis of what elements of Chinese aid have been included in these figures. A much more reliable approach is produced by Bräutigam who estimates that about US$1.2 billion can be counted as ODA for the year 2008 (based on both official statements and her own interviews with officials).[69] Assuming that this figure is somewhere near the 'actual' aid donation of China to Africa, it is small in contrast to the OECD. According to Bräutigam, this compares with UK at $2.6, France at $3.4, and the US at $7.2 billion (in USD).[70] But, it also suggests that China in 2008 gave around a quarter of the amount of funds directed to Africa by the World Bank.[71]

Another way of gaining an impression of the extent of Chinese funding is in carefully comparing emergency relief fund donations; according to Global Humanitarian Assistance's database on humanitarian aid, in 2009 China contributed 0.04%, France donated 4.2%, Germany 6.1%, the UK 9.1%, and the US 15.3%.[72] Nevertheless, these figures are more problematic because of China's different definitions of aid. Therefore, it is necessary to go on and look at what China's aid practices are and whether they are different.

What Are the Modalities of Chinese Aid?

This section moves on from looking at the abstract challenge of China to WC informed aid and looks specifically at what practices are different between China and the OECD. This helps this part to overcome one of the methodological challenges of this subject by specifying what practices can be linked with China, and therefore what challenges to these practices can be separated out and attributed to China. Thus, this aims to distil China's agency from the facilitating factors (the formal causes), of perceived challenges to the practices of the OECD.

In the terms of what can be seen as 'aid' following the OECD-ODA definition there is very little difference in the practices of China and the OECD. One DFID official notes that in terms of 'good donor practices' and how they seem to fit with sovereignty and non-interference it is surprising that China is not closer to the OECD approach.[73] Indeed, much of Chinese aid that is within the OECD definition takes the form of concessional loans, donations, interest-free loans, debt relief, preferential rates and joint ventures. The similarities of Chinese aid and OECD aid are expertly demonstrated by Bräutigam. However, the definition of OECD aid constrains the amount of variety that is possible. The reality is that because of the different underpinnings of China's approach to development, what is considered 'development assistance' opens up a much broader range of tools to produce these types of outcome. This is where the overlap between aid and investment re-emerges. However, if one looks more broadly at what China sees as 'aid' there are in fact many differences.[74]

The major difference is that Chinese aid is nestled in bigger commercial projects and takes the form of 'turnkey' projects: blurring the distinction between aid and investment.[75] This is further complicated because the same companies (and particularly the same banks) fund both investments and aid—often termed the policy banks (EXIM and The Bank of China and the China Development Bank). However, it should be recognised that OECD aid is also often given in the context of other investments and economic linkages. The key difference is that the distinction between the two is apparently unimportant—or unnecessary—for China.[76] Additionally, the turnkey projects that China funds are often projects which OECD donors have been reluctant to fund; such as the Bui dam in Ghana.[77]

A second crucial distinction is that China focuses on the need to ensure an 'equal footing' between the partners in aid and investment (donor and recipient); both FOCAC statements[78] and the Chinese 8-point approach[79] include references emphasising the equality between partners. However, similar language can be seen within the OECD—Chinese statements are supported in the presentation of aid—that is, Chinese aid (like its Japanese and Korean forerunners)[80] is recipient-driven. China makes a clear attempt to move away from the perception of the paternalistic nature of OECD aid donations. Aid—particularly Western aid—is perceived as charity. Indeed, this view is enshrined in the very OECD definition of aid which demands an amount of the donation be 'charity'. Whereas the fuzziness of what constitutes aid for China, and the way aid is packaged within a Chinese approach, as part of larger commercial deal, means that there is space for seeing equality between developing partners. This perception is enhanced because China doesn't have the baggage of a colonial history in Africa.[81]

The element of Chinese aid that gains the most international attention is that it is given with 'no strings attached'; there are no political conditions on China's aid. However, because China's aid is often nestled within broader economic projects it does place economic conditions on its aid. For example, where China makes deals about longer-term projects there are specific details about the returns and the access that China should have to resources and output from the project; China is investing in what it hopes will become a fruitful industry. However, the important difference is that China doesn't gain as many benefits and will continue to incur costs if the industry fails to flourish. So China is tied into making its aid and linked economic packages successful—at least for China.

An additional feature of Chinese provision of aid is that there seem to be conditions on the donor in addition to the recipient. The volume of Chinese aid is relatively small and China is an aid recipient as well as a donor, and it remains keen to claim it is still a developing country. Indeed much of its foreign policy agenda depends on that label. As is frequently noted in the literature on the history of Chinese aid, Deng Xiaoping's 'going out' policy was to find new markets that would be essential to the success of China. Thus China's aid donations have different limitations placed on where and on what it is spent and the expected and needed outcomes: China requires a return on its investments to support its own growth. In the short term, the Chinese can afford to make losses as a result of investments in African infrastructure, in expectation of long-term benefits from cultivating new and dynamic markets for their goods, and sources of raw materials. There are also greater constraints on China in ensuring that its aid donations are fiscally responsible—less of a concern in the OECD.[82]

A final major difference between China and OECD is the formation and role of FOCAC. Whilst similar groupings exist, such as New Partnership for African Development (NEPAD), The European Commission's Quintennial Conferences, and AGOA, FOCACs approach has been different and more successful. The first thing of note in the creation of FOCAC and China's subsequent engagement with African states, is that the Beijing statement asserts that it is a part of the 'establishment of a just and equitable new international political and economic order'.[83] As a part of this creation, the declaration outlines that this just and equitable order requires the development of 'close consultation between two sides on international affairs which is of great importance to consolidating solidarity among developing countries and facilitating the establishment of a new international order'.[84] This new international order should reflect a 'democratic principle governing international relations'.[85] Thus FOCAC is a part of the endeavour on the part of developing states to change the current international structures by bringing themselves together in cohesive units. The next sub-section explores the significance of FOCAC in more detail.

This discussion has set out five areas of contest between China's approach and the OECD's approach to aid practices. These five elements form the basis for China as a norm entrepreneur in challenging the practices of the OECD. These areas can be seen to be separate—but facilitated by—the formal causes of challenges to the OECD practices set out above. The next section sets out how China is using the tool of a new institution to amplify its agency as a norm entrepreneur.

Forum on China and Africa Cooperation

FOCAC was launched in 2000 with the Beijing declaration; its aim was to streamline China's role in African states. In its first years, it was a forum for declarations of China's commitments to Africa—with big policy statements on aid and infrastructure projects. However, its role has developed throughout the past decade, becoming a more useful forum for the coordination of China's and Africa's development practices—the launch of the Addis-Ababa action plan is one example that shows some of the more specific commitments on both sides. Its creation is an instance of the increasing plurality in terms of political institutions that China is creating within the liberal international order. But it is also a demonstration of a particular grouping of states within a population being held together by common experiences and interpretations of norms.

In this endeavour, China's agency is apparent; FOCAC is the brainchild of China; the Five Principles of Peaceful Co-existence are given the same status in the Beijing declaration (and subsequent summit meetings) as the UN Charter.[86] The asymmetry between the agency of the partners ensures China's ability to direct and shape relations: China has a clear Africa policy[87] 'whereas "Africa" does not have a China policy'.[88] Thus, China has the ability to exert greater influence over the increasingly coordinated relationship between China and the developing world.

The second important aspect of the creation of FOCAC is that 'it implicitly showcased China as a possible model for Africa with regard to reform and development'.[89] China's influence in Africa is not just evident in the creation of FOCAC but also in its numerous bilateral relations with African states. However, China receives an increasingly poor press both from Western media[90] and academics.[91] FOCAC, then, is not just the opportunity to see China as a development model; but it is explicitly a method for generating good press for China in Africa.[92]

A third important element that comes out of the creation of FOCAC is that the declaration clearly sets out ambitious responsibilities for both developing and the developed countries. The developing world has the responsibility to cooperate, peacefully, through dialogue and building consensus, working to 'harmonise our [the Developing World's] positions on international affairs and enhance mutual support so as to uphold the legitimate rights and interests of China and African countries'.[93] These rights and interests are respect for state sovereignty and non-interference so that states may determine for themselves the best pathways for development. In China's approach, it sets out its own model as a possible pathway, but doesn't overtly coerce other states to emulate it. The drawing out of these common approaches extends the importance of FOCAC beyond the provision of a new institution—it highlights the creation of a new 'population' of states around a particular and distinctive identification with a particular interpretation of sovereignty and non-intervention. In the common agreements of the roles and responsibilities of different actors this population attributes identities to the developing world and clearly sets it apart from developed states.

The responsibilities of the developed world are to 'provide financial, technological and other assistance to developing countries, African countries in particular'.[94] Moreover, as the dominant group within international financial institutions that agree the distribution of aid, developed states should respond to the calls by the developing world to adjust aid policies and 'adopt more concrete measures aimed at debt relief and reduction'.[95] As such, China—through FOCAC—aims at setting out the roles and responsibilities of various powers within international order, reshaping that order in favour of developing states with China coordinating the position of the developing world. In the second instance the formation of a self-legitimating and (potentially successful) grouping formed around different (if not always competing) norms of development, challenges the legitimacy and authority of the OECD as a development framework. In particular, within a small group of like-minded states, the potential for norms to develop and 'cascade' quickly is increased; and the effect of these new norms may be difficult to change—as a result, the recipient may be operating in a different normative framework to the donor.

Since the first summit and the Beijing declaration in 2000, there have been three subsequent summit meetings. Each of these has broadened the activities of FOCAC, extended the connections between China and Africa (and China and individual African states), and increasing the roles and responsibilities of both sides.

Throughout the past ten years, FOCAC has played a progressively important role in giving some form and structure to China's engagement with Africa. Through a process of the harmonisation of policies both of Africa and China, the constant aim has been stated to be the development of practices that are win-win.[96] As a result, China and Africa aim to work closely together in international forums in order to reshape international order into a fairer and more just society.[97] The irony of this statement is that because of the asymmetry in the relationship (noted above) what a fairer and more just society looks like—within this population—is more likely to reflect Chinese preferences with African support than being a clear expression of consensual and balanced agreements between China and Africa.[98]

Importantly, in the FOCAC documents the rhetoric used, particularly by China, unites China's approach to aid and development with its stance on sovereignty and its actions in its own periphery. For example, in his address in 2000, Jiang Zemin stated that peacekeeping operations had to have consent,[99] that the UN was the central body to promote international peace and security,[100] and that toleration is essential to ensure peaceful development.[101] China's FOCAC policy is then a part of a broader Chinese strategy of change which is being pursued through organising support in the developing world. As Jiang Zemin went on to say:

> China and African countries should increase consultation, coordination and cooperation on the bilateral and multilateral fronts, participate actively in the management of international affairs and formulation of international rules and promote the reform of the international political, economic, financial and trading systems. In this way, the voice of developing countries will be heard more clearly in the world, a fair international environment

will be created and the legitimate rights and interests of developing countries will be effectively safeguarded.[102]

In this search for change, the FOCAC documents clearly establish a link between the need to respect sovereignty and territorial integrity (Part II) and the path to peaceful development. 'Peace-threatening and development-hampering factors continue to exist. Interference in the internal affairs of other countries, particularly developing countries, has occurred from time to time'.[103] Indeed throughout all the FOCAC documents, there is an emphasis on the protection of sovereignty and the principle of non-interference. Importantly, there is also a link to the UN system and the role that the UN must play in legitimising international actions. There are also many rallying calls within FOCAC for unified action at the UN. Such an action would then seek to ensure that rules and laws are modified in such a way that any changes in the interpretation of international norms rectify the bias of the current international economic order.

The Addis-Ababa action plan (2004) makes the first concrete steps towards the evolution of FOCAC beyond a talking shop, but its tangible promises will take a long time to implement. The plan was the result of the 2003 summit meeting and a series of high-level talks subsequently. It sets out ambitious plans for the development of FOCAC as an institution—FOCAC should embrace efforts in terms of peace and security, multilateral cooperation, economic development, social development, and also develop follow-up mechanisms.[104] China's approach was spurred by the continual affirmation that change needs to happen, and happen now. For example, statements like this are common: 'how to build a world where all nations shall be winners and where dialogue, cooperation and mutual benefit shall prevail is an important, urgent and practical issue before us all'.[105]

How Are Chinese Aid Practices Different from the OECD?

In looking at contrasts in technical practices the differences help to reveal how Chinese aid is different from traditional ODA—thus sets out a program of China's entrepreneurship. Indeed a number of authors note that there are many benefits to China in being able to be seen as being different from the OECD.[106] In seeking to demonstrate differences there is a need for China to have substantially different practices, and preferably a different underlying ideology that supports those different practices as indicated through China's approach to what counts as aid and who provides it. This section will look back over the problems of aid effectiveness identified in regard to OECD-DAC practices and seek to draw out how Chinese aid practices attempt to resolve or deal with some of these issues (identified above); finally, it provides a set of hypotheses about what types of changes could be expected drawing on the evidence set out above.

Tracking the effectiveness of Chinese aid is almost impossible, not least because effectiveness is intimately linked to aims and objectives, and this suggests that there are problems in coordinating aid policies between different branches of the government or policy banks. However, there does seem to be some distinction between the different roles of MOFCOM and the Ministry of Finance, and between the China Development Bank and EXIM; MOFCOM apparently taking the lead in aid decisions. However, the lack of transparency in the reporting of aid also has a knock-on effect on assessments of whether it is effective. Although, as noted by Grimm et al., there are mechanisms in place in Exim's structure to make assessments about effectiveness, it remains unclear how any of these assessments play out.[107] But Chinese development strategies are looking for long-term profits and therefore any assessment and monitoring will be skewed towards different development outcomes.

Furthermore, what is meant by transparency is different. For the OECD, transparency is about more in-depth information about what aid is given, in what form, by whom, and for what purpose, in order to achieve more effective aid in the future. However, China believes itself to be being transparent in its approach—declarations of volumes of aid in Presidential statements are transparency from a Chinese perspective. As a result, even though both China and the OECD might agree that transparency is necessary, what transparency is and what function it performs are different.

China does not include administrative costs as a part of its aid provision.[108] It also costs the work done by Chinese workers in Africa in the 'development state' rather than Chinese or Western rates, so the overall costs for the same number of personnel are much lower.[109] This is described in the literature as China's 'low-cost way of doing things'.[110] Significantly, the perception of the Chinese by Africans is different from their Western counterparts: 'Africans generally perceive Chinese who work in Africa as less privileged and exploitative than Western expatriates'.[111]

In looking at China as a single donor it is easy to claim that there is less fragmentation in China's approach than that of Western donors. Indeed there is less fragmentation in aid given by China, but that is not to say there is none. The difficulties in assessing how much aid China gives suggest an endemic lack of coordination between the various branches of the government and the different providers of aid in China. Yet, there is evidence to suggest that China's presence in the aid arena is actually producing greater fragmentation among the traditional aid partners.[112] The coordination problems between OECD-DAC donors may become worse as the presence of China removes political incentives to make changes in their aid policies, especially changes that would favour policies that enable donors to deliver on their commitments at Accra and Paris (made clear because of the specified nature of these commitments), thus discouraging a new conception of aid effectiveness that was in fact emerging.[113] If so, the presence of China, rather than any particular Chinese action, causes an effect in the existing group of development partners.

In contrast to the conditional loans and projects from international institutions and through bilateral aid agencies, 'China does business with the good, the bad, and the ugly—as long as they pay'.[114] China's approach to aid has been that achieving development is up to the government of the state. The role that outsiders can play is in providing the resources, information, technology, or money requested by those governments.[115] It is up to those governments to ensure that benefits from these donations are effective.[116] In reality, this has meant that how effective Chinese aid depends on the recipient's ability to use the aid and economic assistance effectively.

Like the OECD countries, China does give aid donations and 'development assistance' for political as well as economic and security reasons. However, China has started giving aid to countries where these benefits are not as easy to see.[117] Furthermore, infrastructure projects (such as building roads, stadia, government buildings or the African Union building) that seem to have become the hallmark of Chinese aid practices are less likely to be funded by OECD-DAC states because they are seen as less effective. In looking back at the different types of projects that China donates resources to they are clearly different to the types of projects funded by OECD countries.

It seems a strange claim but it is noted by a number of authors that the way China gives aid prevents rulers from buying expensive cars or enriching themselves.[118] Because much of Chinese aid is delivered through infrastructure programs (that are often managed by Chinese companies) and through the provision of medical services, it leaves little excess money in the state in the hands of the elites. Rather the money goes to the local people in the form of pay. However, there are significant drawbacks to this approach in particular. Not as many Africans are employed in Chinese projects than in OECD projects. So there are fewer Africans being paid for the work and the presence of a large Chinese expatriate population may produce an inflationary impact on food prices and commodities. The positive is that at the end of the project the Chinese leave and the people have the benefit of a new road or building which they can continue to derive economic benefits from; the key difference is that under the patterns of OECD aid, when and how infrastructure projects happen is a much more truncated process. The approach or the aims of this type of aid may not be different to the aims of OECD aid programs; the significant and stark difference is the involvement and speed at which the Chinese make things happen.

Similarly, China has a focus on training and invests in education at the tertiary level rather than school age level.[119] This did not help African states to meet their Millennium development goals; however, it does help them produce a more vibrant economy with a greater number of highly educated Africans able to take up economically beneficial jobs in the country. Indeed, the brain drain that tends to occur when Africans move to the West to study does not yet seem to be happening when Africans study in China; few remain in China. As a result, it is their home country that benefits from their overseas education.[120]

The most significant element of the Chinese approach to aid—informed by the ideology of the Chinese development experience—can be seen in the change of language: Chinese aid is 'economic development assistance'. In the OECD it is 'Official Development Assistance'. The change might seem a small one, but it is significant as the approach from China is to develop economies into effective trading partners. The focus is on promoting bilateral trade where institutional reforms are a by-product. The focus within the WC, by contrast, is on multilateral forums that tie countries into a wider program of economic engagement.

In order to achieve these reforms, the OECD focuses on institutional reforms, and the change in the role (and form) of the state is a part of the process. As a result, Chinese aid provision has a different teleology.

Identifying China as a Norm Entrepreneur and as a Cause for the Challenge to the OECD Practices

Important in achieving change in the development agenda and practices is a catalyst; although as noted above there are many criticisms of both the theories and practices of OECD-DAC aid: how it is distributed; to whom; and under what conditions. Changes to any of these things have been slow or non-existent. Is it fair then to attribute any changes by African states, in their practices or in their preferences in who is to receive aid, to China? Importantly, is China's approach shaped by the demands of African states and the need of China to have access to their raw materials; or is it the presence of China as a 'different' aid partner that is directing any changes?

This section summarises and clarifies the claims set out above that led to the assertion that China is a formal and efficient cause of these particular challenges to OECD practices and the logic of the WC. In looking back to the discussion in the introduction, this section sets out how this chapter has so far contributed to overcoming the methodological challenge of identifying China's agency.

The ambiguities of the BC allow for a large amount of flexibility in individual interpretation; the broad and loose character of the BC almost demands this type of approach. It requires a dialogue between partners in making deals and importantly it supports a more equal relationship between the partners (at least superficially). This has been a key element to China's appeal in Africa: giving Africans ownership of their development. Although none could deny that China is the more powerful and dominant partner, the approach that China takes gives Africans some leeway in determining the nature of joint endeavours.

Indeed China's position in relation to the OECD is enhanced because 'In many ways China is uniquely positioned to tackle poverty alleviation and the global "development divide'."[121] There is a perceived difference between the legitimacy of China and the OECD; facilitating China's ability to create normative change. Without a doubt, there does appear to be movement in Africa towards a Chinese approach to development. For example, the 2012 State of the Nation address by President

Zuma of South Africa made clear that there are many frustrations within Africa about the role that aid is playing and the need to adopt a different approach.[122] He stated that there was a need for a more central role for the government to play in managing the economy and that there was a need to develop the connections between the government and business.

> Informed by some of these difficulties and the need to move away from piecemeal planning, we took a decision in 2009 to establish the National Planning Commission and asked them to produce a national development plan for the country, informed by the Constitution of the Republic. ... we strengthened social dialogue and cooperation between government, business and the community sector.[123]

In a more explicit expression, the President of the African Development bank stated at the World Economic Forum in 2006:

> Some welcome the emergence of China because it is a major donor and is less intrusive in domestic politics. But we can learn from them how to organize our trade policy, to move from low to middle income status, to educate our children in skills and areas that pay off in just a couple of years.[124]

Thus, China isn't just an alternative donor but is perceived by some as having a different approach to aid.

If China is presenting a challenge in terms of wooing African leaders away from Western approaches to aid, by adopting a slightly different approach with a distinctly different rhetoric, then the next question is whether this is shrinking the liberal international order in the area of development and reducing it to just being liberal among the OECD donor countries (so international development would not be globally liberal); and whether the arrival of China on the scene challenging their practices.

In general, China also has the ability to present itself as a more credible development partner. One of the emerging themes from African countries' criticisms of the way aid and development are pursued is that Western donors prescribe paths to development that are different from the paths by which they themselves achieved development. By contrast, if China has a discernible approach it is to lead others along the path that it did, in fact, pursue; and so African states seek to mimic China's development. In this sense China contributes to both the facilitating condition of the criticisms of the WC and OECD, as well as, acting as an agent for presenting a challenge as a norm entrepreneur.

Notes

1. Andrew Mitchell, 'Emerging Powers', Speech at Chatham House, 15 February 2011, text available http://www.dfid.gov.uk/News/Speeches-and-articles/2011/Emerging-powers/, accessed 28 November 2011.
2. Stefan A. Halper, *The Beijing Consensus: How China's Authoritarian Model Will Dominate the Twenty-First Century* (New York: Basic Books, 2010), p. 174.
3. Since 2012, the debate around the Beijing consensus has lost academic attention in preference for discussions of the BRICS, New Rising Powers, and the more specific debates on China in Africa.
4. There has been a dominant view in Western Aid programmes to see development as linear and teleological; Jacques argues that there is now a contested modernity rather than the dominant perception of a singular modernity, see Jacques, 'When China Rules the World', pp. 117–168; Stiglitz argues that the one size fits all is not appropriate anyone (if it ever was); Joseph Stiglitz, *Globalisation and Its Discontents* (Penguin: London, 2002); Sen, demonstrates the need to move away from a particular conception of modernity and development and embrace the concept of freedom Amartya Sen, *Development as Freedom* (Oxford University Press: Oxford, 2001).
5. Deborah Bräutigam, *Chinese Aid and African Development* (Macmillan Press: Basingstoke, 1998), p. 14.
6. The term Washington Consensus was coined by John Williamson in 1989 as a reflection of the link between currency development strategies and institutions based on the Washington style. John Williamson, 'A Short History of the Washington Consensus', *Law and Business Review of the Americas* (2009), 15(1), pp. 7–23, p. 7.
7. Halper, *The Beijing Consensus*, p. 55.
8. "Appropriate institutional change has been elevated by the NIE to a central place in theory of development, by contrast with neo-classical growth theory's central focus on saving and population growth." John Toye, 'The New Institutional Economics and Its Implications for Development Theory', in John Harriss, Janet Hunter, and Colin M. Lewis (eds), *The New Institutional Economics and Third World Development* (Routledge: London, 1995), pp. 49–68, p. 61.

9. Ibid., p. 66.
10. Samuel P. Huntington, 'Political Development and Political Decay', *World Politics* (1965) 17(3), pp. 386–430; Colin Leys, *The Rise and Fall of Development Theory* (James Curry: Oxford, 1996), pp. 3–44; Paul Moseley, Jane Harrigan, and John Toye, *Aid and Power* (Routledge: London, 1991); Douglass C. North, 'The New Institutional Economics and Third World Development', in John Harriss, Janet Hunter, and Colin M. Lewis (eds), *The New Institutional Economics and Third World Development* (London: Routledge, 1995), pp. 17–26.
11. The NIE has been claimed to have brought about the successes of the Asian Tigers (South Korea and Singapore in particular) but it failed to produce lasting economic growth in much of Africa, particularly Sub-Saharan Africa where its effects in opening up nascent local businesses to economic competition has been a total disaster. For claims that the Washington consensus was a success see for example: John Williamson, 'A Short History of the Washington Consensus'; John Williamson, 'What Washington Means by Policy Reform', in John Williamson (eds) *Latin American Adjustment: How Much Has Happened?* (Institute Penguin: London, 2002); Narcis Serra, Shari Spiegel, and Joseph E. Stiglitz, 'Introduction: From the Washington Consensus Towards a New Global Governance', p. 2, also both chapters in Narcis Serra and Joseph E. Stiglitz (eds), *The Washington Consensus Reconsidered: Towards a New Global Governance* (Oxford University Press: Oxford, 2008); Jose Antonio Ocampo, Shari Spiegel, and Joseph E. Stiglitz, 'Capital Market Liberalization and Development', in Jose Antonio Ocampo and Joseph E. Stiglitz (eds), *Capital Market Liberalisation and Development* (Oxford University Press: Oxford, 2008), p. 5; Paul Moseley, Jane Harrigan, and John Toye, *Aid and Power: The World Bank and Policy-Based Lending*, vol. 1, Analysis and Policy Proposals (Routledge: London, 1995), p. 13. For counterarguments that the Washington Consensus failed see for example: Joseph Stiglitz, *Globalisation and Its Discontents*; Narcis Serra, Shari Spiegel, and Joseph E. Stiglitz, 'Introduction: From the Washington Consensus Towards a New Glo*The*bal Governance', p. 2, also both chapters in Narcis Serra and Joseph E. Stiglitz (eds), *Washington Consensus Reconsidered: Towards a New Global Governance* (Oxford University Press: Oxford, 2008), Jose Antonio Ocampo, Shari Spiegel, and Joseph E. Stiglitz, 'Capital Market Liberalization and Development', in Jose Antonio Ocampo and Joseph E. Stiglitz (eds), *Capital Market Liberalisation and Development* (Oxford University Press: Oxford, 2008), p. 5.

12. Paul Moseley, Jane Harrigan, and John Toye, *Aid and Power: The World Bank and Policy-Based Lending*, vol. 1, Analysis and Policy Proposals (Routledge: London, 1995), p. 13.
13. Moseley et al. *Aid and Power*, p. 15.
14. OECD, 'Glossary of Statistical Definitions', available http://stats.oecd.org/glossary/detail.asp?ID=6043, accessed 23 February 2012.
15. IATI, http://www.aidtransparency.net/, accessed 30 March 2017.
16. Hidemi Kimura, Yuko Mori and Yasuyki Sawada, 'Aid Proliferation and Economic Growth: A Cross-Country Analysis', *World Development* (2012), 40(1), pp. 1–10; for a different perspective with largely the same data set see, Raghuram G. Rajan and Arvind Subramaniam, 'Aid and Growth: What Does the Cross-Country Evidence Really Show?', *The Review of Economics and Statistics* (2008), 90(4), pp. 643–665.
17. A claim made by William Easterly, 'Can Foreign Aid Buy Growth?', *Journal of Economic Perspectives* (2003), 17(3), pp. 23–48, in response to the claims made, in Craig Burnside and David Dollar, 'Aid, Policies, and Growth', *The American Economic Review* (2000), 90(4), pp. 847–868.
18. Burnside and Dollar, 'Aid, Policies and Growth', pp. 847 and 864 (also: DFID, 'Eliminating World Poverty: Making Governance Work for the Poor', White Paper on International Development, July 2006, available http://www.official-documents.gov.uk/document/cm68/6876/6876.pdf, accessed 23 February 2012; CIDA, 'Canada Making a Difference in the World: A Policy Statement on Aid Effectiveness', September 2002, available http://www.acdi-cida.gc.ca/inet/images.nsf/vLUImages/pdf/$file/SAE-ENG.pdf, accessed 23 February 2012, p. 5; World Bank, 'Assessing Aid—What Works, What Doesn't and Why', available http://www-wds.worldbank.org/external/default/WDSContentServer/WDSP/IB/2000/02/23/000094946_99030406212262/Rendered/PDF/multi_page.pdf, accessed 23 February 2012; The Economist 'Help in the Right Places: Untangling the Aid Debate', *The Economist*, published 14 March 2002, available http://www.economist.com/node/1034563, accessed 23 February 2012; Easterly, 'Can Foreign Aid Buy Growth?', p. 24.
19. Burnside and Dollar, 'Aid, Polices and Growth', p. 847.
20. CPIA was developed by Paul Collier and David Dollar and is now used in the World Bank for the distribution of aid: Paul Collier and David Dollar, 'Can the World Cut Poverty in Half? How Policy Reform and Effective Aid Can Meet international Development Goals', *World Development* (2001), 29(11), pp. 1787–1802; Paul Collier and David Dollar, 'Aid Allocation and Poverty Reduction', *European Economic Review* (2002), 46, pp. 1475–1500; Carl-Johan Dalgaard,

Henrik Hansen and Finn Tarp, 'On the Empirics of Foreign Aid and Growth', *The Economic Journal* (2004), 114(496), pp. F191–F216 and F208–F209.
21. Carl-Johan Dalgaard, Henrik Hansen, and Finn Tarp, 'On the Empirics of Foreign Aid and Growth', *The Economic Journal* (2004), 114(496), pp. F208–F209.
22. Rajan and Subramanian, 'Aid and Growth', p. 655.
23. Comment by Arvind Subramanian of the IMF at The Council on Foreign Relations, 'Foreign Aid and Developing Economies' debate between William Easterly, Steven Radelet, Arvind Subramanian, Clay Lowery, and Nicholas D. Kristof, at the Council on Foreign Relations New York, 12 May 2006, video available online at http://www.cfr.org/foreign-aid/foreign-aid-developing-economies-video/p10698, transcript available http://www.cfr.org/economic-development/foreign-aid-developing-economies-rush-transcript-federal-news-service-inc/p10762, both accessed 28 February 2012.
24. Iftekhar Hasan, Paul Wachtel, and Mingming Zhouk, 'Institutional Development, Financial Deepening and Economic Growth: Evidence from China', *Journal of Banking and Finance* (2009), 33, pp. 157–170.
25. William Easterly and Claudia R. Williamson, 'Rhetoric *versus* Reality: The Best and Worst of Aid Agency Practices', *World Development* (2011), 39(11), pp. 1930–1949, p. 1934.
26. Kyriakos C. Neanidis and Dimitrios Varvarigos, 'The Allocation of Volatile Aid and Economic Growth: Theory and Evidence', *European Journal of Political Economy* (2009), 25, pp. 447–462.
27. "Well-managed countries force coordination on donors, but in the weak environments they often run amok. It is hard to explain this behavior, except that different donors like to "plant their flags" on something tangible. World Bank, 'Assessing Aid: What Works, What Doesn't and Why', p. 26; Kimura et al., 'Aid Proliferation and Economic Growth, p. 7.
28. Carmelia Minoiu and Sanjay G. Reddy, 'Development Aid and Economic Growth: A Positive Long-Run Relation', *The Quarterly Review of Economics and Finance* (2010), 50, pp. 27–39; For the importance of context see, Bräutigam, *Chinese Aid and African Development*, pp. 21–28.
29. The problem of fungibility is identified by many authors see for example: Burnside and Dollar, 'Aid, Policies and Growth', p. 848; William Easterly, 'Democratic Accountability in Development: The Double Standard', *Social Research* (2011), 77(4), pp. 1075–1104; Stephen Kosack, 'Effective Aid: How Democracy Allows Development Aid to

Improve the Quality of Life', *World Development* (2003), 31(1), pp. 1–22.
30. Halper, *The Beijing Consensus*, pp. 60–63.
31. Randall Peerenboom, *China Modernizes: Threat to the West or Model for the Rest?* (Oxford University Press: Oxford, 2007), p. 16.
32. For an in depth discussion see for example Sarah Raine and International Institute for Strategic Studies, *China's African Challenges* (Adelphi Papers; Routledge for International Institute for Strategic Studies: Abingdon, 2009).
33. Charles Gore, 'The Rise and Fall of the Washington Consensus as a Paradigm for Developing Countries', *World Development* (2000), 28(5), pp. 789–804, p. 799.
34. John Williamson, 'A Short History of the Washington Consensus', pp. 7–23; John Williamson, 'What Washington Means by Policy Reform', in John Williamson (eds), *Latin American Adjustment: How Much Has happened?* (Institute for International Economics: Washington, DC, 1990), pp. 7–33.
35. Moises Naim, 'Washington Consensus or Washington Confusion?', *Foreign Policy* (Spring, 2000), pp. 87–103, p. 90.
36. Ronald Inglehart and Christian Welzel, 'How Development Leads to Democracy: What We Know About Modernisation', *Foreign Affairs* (2009), 88(2), pp. 33–48, p. 37.
37. South Korea, Taiwan, Singapore and Hong Kong.
38. William Case, 'Comparing Politics in Southeast Asia', in *Politics in Southeast Asia: Democracy or Less* (Curzon: Richmond, Surrey, 2002).
39. Denny Roy, 'Singapore, China, and the 'Soft Authoritarian' Challenge', *Asian Survey* (1994), 34(3), pp. 231–242.
40. Williamson, 'A Short History of the Washington Consensus', pp. 7–23.
41. Halper, *The Beijing Consensus*, p. 36.
42. Joshua Cooper Ramo, *The Beijing Consensus* (Foreign Policy Centre: London 2004).
43. Peerenboom, *China Modernizes*.
44. For further discussion of the Beijing Consensus see: Shaun Breslin, 'The "China Model" and the Global Crisis: From Friedrich List to a Chinese Mode of Governance', *International Relations* (2011), 87(6), pp. 1323–1343; Stefan A. Halper, *The Beijing Consensus*; Scott Kennedy, 'The Myth of the Beijing Consensus', *Journal of Contemporary China* (2010), 19(65), pp. 461–77; Barry Naughton, 'China's Distinctive System Can It Be a Model for Others?', *Journal of Contemporary China* (2010), 19(65), pp. 437–60; Yang Yao, 'The End of the Beijing Consensus: Can China's Model of Authoritarian Growth Survive?', *Foreign Affairs*, January/February (2010) [online]; John Williamson,

'Is the "Beijing Consensus" Now Dominant?', Special Essay: *Asia Policy* (2012), 13, pp. 1–16; Suisheng Zhao, 'The China Model: Can It Replace the Western Model of Modernization?', *Journal of Contemporary China* (2010), 19(65), pp. 419–436.
45. See for example: Lai-Ha Chan and Pak K. Lee. 2017. 'Power, Ideas and Institutions: China's Emergent Footprints in Global Governance of Development Aid', *CSGR Working Paper No. 281/17*, Centre for the Study of Globalisation and Regionalisation, University of Warwick. Available at: www.warwick.ac.uk/csgr/papers/281-17.pdf; Shogo Suzuki, 'Will the AIIB Trigger Off a New Round of Rivalry in Economic Diplomacy Between China and Japan?', *CSGR Working Paper No. 279/15*, Centre for the Study of Globalisation and Regionalisation, University of Warwick (2015). Available at: www.warwick.ac.uk/csgr/papers/279-15.pdf.
46. Halper, *The Beijing Consensus*, p. 36.
47. See for example, Easterly, 'Democratic Accountability in Development', pp. 1082–1083; Dambisa Moyo, *Dead Aid: Why Aid Is Not Working and How There Is Another Way for Africa* (Penguin: London, 2010), pp. 23–24.
48. "The political climate must pressure the aid agencies ... to match the reality of aid practices to their rhetoric." Easterly and Williamson, 'Rhetoric *versus* Reality', p. 1946.
49. Ibid., p. 1946.
50. Carol Lancaster, 'The Chinese Aid System', *The Center for Global Development Essay*, June 2007, available http://www.cgdev.org, accessed 1 March 2012.
51. The tension between institutional change and economic development is also discussed in World Bank, 'World Development Report 2011: Conflict, Security and Development', available http://wdr2011.worldbank.org/sites/default/files/pdfs/WDR2011_Full_Text.pdf, accessed 9 July 2012, pp. 99–108.
52. The main theorist of this persuasion is Arturo Escobar see for example Arturo Escobar, *Encountering Development*, pp. 21–54; Michael Woolcock and Deepa Narayan, 'Social Capital; Implications for Development Theory, Research, and Policy', *The World Bank Research Observer* (2000), 15(2), pp. 225–249. For a counterpoint see Stuart Corbridge, 'Beneath the Pavement Only Soil: The Poverty of Post Development', pp. 138–148.
53. For an example see the debate The Council on Foreign Relations, 'Foreign Aid and Developing Economies'.
54. Barry Naughton, 'China's Distinctive System', pp. 437–460.

55. In the reports of speeches by the elites in China there is an emphasis in the reporting and the speeches that China is not a new model for development and that there remain many problems with exporting China's experience. See for example, Unknown, 'Kuai ping: Wen zongli weisheme bu ti "zhongguo moshi"?' [Fast Comment; Premier Wen Jiabao, "Why not speak of the 'China Model'"], The People. cn, published 14 March 2011, available http://opinion.people.com.cn/GB/14137435.html, accessed 5 July 2011 (author's translation); Xinhua, '"Zhongguo Moshi" zai bei re yi' ["'China Model' Hot again"], 20 September 2009, http://news.xinhuanet.com/world/2009-10/20/content_12269629.htm, accessed 4 August 2011; But, there are also activities by the PRC that suggest that China does believe that its model for development is exportable, see for example 2009 PRC National Day Parade, and the China Modernisation Report: China Modernization Report 2005—A study on the economic modernization, available http://www.modernization.com.cn/cmr2005%20overview.htm, accessed 12 December 2011; see also Elena Barbantseva, 'In Pursuit of an Alternative Model? The Modernisation Trap in China's Official Discourse', *East Asia: An International Quarterly*, September 2011 [online], pp. 1–17.
56. PRC State Council, 'China's Foreign Aid', White Paper (Information Office of the State Council: Beijing, April 2011), available http://english.gov.cn/official/2011-04/21/content_1849913_3.htm, accessed 2 March 2012.
57. Ibid.
58. MOFCOM, 'Main Mandate of the Ministry of Commerce', available http://english.mofcom.gov.cn/mission.shtml, accessed 1 March 2012.
59. PRC State Council, 'China's Foreign Aid'.
60. Deborah Bräutigam, 'Aid 'with Chinese Characteristics': Chinese Foreign Aid and Development Finance Meet the OECD-DAC Aid Regime', *Journal of International Development* (2011), 23(5), pp. 752–764, p. 754.
61. Ibid., p. 761.
62. Ibid., p. 205.
63. Sven Grimm, Rachel Rank, Matthew McDonald, and Elizabeth Schickerling, *Transparency of Chinese Aid: An Analysis of the Published Information on Chinese External Financial Flows* (Publish What you Fund and Centre for Chinese Studies Stellenbosch University, August 2011); also, Publish What you Fund, 'Chinese Aid More Transparent Than You Think', report available http://www.publishwhatyoufund.org/news/2011/09/new-report-chinese-aid-more-transparent-you-think/, accessed 2 March 2012.

64. Carol Lancaster notes that Aid from China takes the form of proposals for Chinese funding rather than aid being given and allocated by an external aid agency. Lancaster, 'The Chinese Aid System', p. 4.
65. Figure displaying Chinese aid spending can be found in the White Paper, PRC State Council, 'China's Foreign Aid'.
66. PRC State Council, 'China's Foreign Aid'; Bräutigam, *The Dragon's Gift*, pp. 168–174.
67. See PRC State Council, 'China's Foreign Aid'; also FOCAC, 'Forum on China–Africa Cooperation Beijing Action Plan (2007–2009), 16 November 2006, available http://www.focac.org/eng/ltda/dscbzjhy/DOC32009/t280369.htm, 14 May 2011 (Section 3).
68. Unknown, 'China Ahead of World Bank in Loans to Developing Nations', *The Guardian*, 18 January 2011, available http://www.guardian.co.uk/business/2011/jan/18/china-developing-country-loans, accessed 10 December 2011; Chris Hogg, 'China Banks Lend More Than World Bank', *BBC Online*, 18 January 2011, available online http://www.bbc.co.uk/news/world-asia-pacific-12212936, accessed 10 December 2011.
69. Bräutigam, 'Chinese Development Aid in Africa', p. 211; Deborah Bräutigam, *The Dragon's Gift*, pp. 168–172.
70. Deborah Bräutigam, *The Dragon's Gift*, p. 172.
71. Ibid., p. 211.
72. Global Humanitarian Assistance, available http://www.globalhumanitarianassistance.org/country-profiles, accessed 2 March 2012.
73. Interview with DFID Official London, 29 March 2012.
74. Deborah Bräutigam, 'Chapter 6: China, Africa and the International Aid Architecture', in Richard Schiere, Léonce Ndikumana and Peter Walkenhorst, *China and Africa: An Emerging Partnership for Development* (African Development Bank: Tunisia, 2011), pp. 103–126, p. 110.
75. May Tan-Mullins, Giles Mohan and Marcus Power, 'Redefining 'Aid' in the China–Africa Context', *Development and Change* (2010), 41(5), pp. 857–881, p. 863.
76. As noted earlier one of the key difficulties in looking at Chinese aid is that it is difficult to good data because of the merging of aid and investment.
77. Tan-Mullins et al., 'Redefining 'Aid'', pp. 872–874; Kirtian Kjøllesdal and Anne Welle-Strand, 'Foreign Aid Strategies: China Taking Over?', *Asian Social Science* (2010), 6(10), pp. 7–8.
78. See for example, Beijing Declaration of the Forum on China–Africa Cooperation, available http://www.focac.org/eng/ltda/dyjbzjhy/DOC12009/t606796.htm, accessed 14 May 2011.

79. PRC State Council, 'China's Foreign Aid'.
80. Bräutigam, *The Dragon's Gift*, p. 80.
81. Kjøllesdal and Welle-Strand, 'Foreign Aid Strategies', p. 8.
82. He Fan and Tang Yuehua, 'Determinants of Official Development Assistance in the Post-Cold War Period', *Chinese Journal of International Politics* (2008), 2, pp. 205–227, p. 227.
83. Beijing Declaration of the Forum on China–Africa Cooperation, available http://www.focac.org/eng/ltda/dyjbzjhy/DOC12009/t606796.htm, accessed 14 May 2011.
84. Ibid.
85. Ibid.
86. Ibid., p. 53.
87. MOFA (2006) 'China's Africa Policy', 12 January 2006, available http://www.fmprc.gov.cn/eng/zxxx/t230615.htm, accessed 30 November 2011.
88. Ian Taylor, 'The Forum on China–Africa Cooperation (FOCAC)' (Routledge: London, 2011), p. 94.
89. Ibid., p. 48.
90. It is important to note that media criticism of Chinese activities conflate the criticisms of Chinese companies and criticisms of the Chinese government (which is complicated by the presence of State Owned Enterprises (SOE's) in Africa). For criticisms of Chinese firms see for example: Simon Mundy, 'Chinese Accused of Zambian Labour Abuses', *Financial Times*, 20 January 2011, available https://www.ft.com/content/eaed6742-24b8-11e0-a919-00144feab49a, accessed 30 November 2011; The Economist, 'The Chinese into Africa: Trying to Pull Together', *The Economist*, 20 April 2011, available https://www.economist.com/briefing/2011/04/20/trying-to-pull-together, accessed 30 November 2011; Xan Rice, 'China's Economic Invasion of Africa', *The Guardian*, 6 February 2011, available https://www.theguardian.com/world/2011/feb/06/chinas-economic-invasion-of-africa, accessed 30 November 2011; David Blair, 'Why is China Trying to Colonise Africa?', *The Telegraph*, 31 August 2007, available https://www.telegraph.co.uk/comment/personal-view/3642345/Why-China-is-trying-to-colonise-Africa.html, accessed 30 November 2011.
91. For example, Jonathan Holslag, 'China's Diplomatic Victory in Darfur' BICCS Background Paper, Published 1 August 2007; Large, 'Beyond 'the Dragon in the Bush'', pp. 610–626.
92. Taylor, 'FOCAC', p. 48.
93. 'Beijing Declaration' of the Forum on China–Africa Cooperation, available http://www.focac.org/eng/ltda/dyjbzjhy/DOC12009/t606796.htm, accessed 14 May 2011 (point 9).

9 LIBERAL DEVELOPMENT: THE PRACTICE AND ASSUMPTIONS OF AID

94. Ibid. (point 5).
95. Ibid. (point 8).
96. For example: 'Beijing Declaration'; Hu Jintao, 'Programme for China–Africa Cooperation in Economic and Social Development', Speech at FOCAC Summit, available http://www.focac.org/eng/ltda/dyjbzjhy/DOC12009/t606797.htm, 14 May 2011 (point 5.3); Jiang Zemin, 'China and Africa—Usher in the New Century Together', Speech by President Jiang Zemin of the People's Republic of China at the Opening Ceremony of the Forum on China–Africa Cooperation Ministerial Conference, Beijing, 2000, available http://www.focac.org/eng/ltda/dyjbzjhy/SP12009/t606804.htm, 14 May 2011.
97. Ibid.
98. Taylor, *FOCAC*, p. 95.
99. Jiang Zemin, 'China and Africa—Usher in the New Century Together'.
100. Ibid.
101. "Only when the diversity of the world is respected can various ethnic groups and civilizations live in harmony, learn from each other and complement each other." Ibid.
102. Ibid.
103. Tang Jiaxuan, Speech by Foreign Minister Tang Jiaxuan at Forum on China–Africa Cooperation, 10 October 2000, available http://www.focac.org/eng/ltda/dyjbzjhy/SP12009/t606806.htm, accessed 6 December 2011.
104. Forum on China–Africa Cooperation, '*Addis Ababa Action Plan*' (2004–2006), available http://www.focac.org/eng/ltda/dyjbzjhy/SP12009/t606806.htm, accessed 14 May 2011.
105. Wen Jiabao, 'Let Us Build on Our Past Achievements and Promote China–Africa Friendly Cooperation on All Fronts', Address by H.E. Mr. Wen Jiabao, Premier of the State Council of the People's Republic of China at Opening Ceremony of the Second Ministerial Conference of the China–Africa Cooperation Forum, 15 December 2003, available http://www.focac.org/eng/ltda/dejbzjhy/SP22009/t606816.htm, accessed 14 May 2011.
106. Bräutigam, 'Chinese Aid in African Development', p. 8; Christopher M. Dent, 'Africa and China: A New Kind of Development Partnership', in Christopher M. Dent (ed), *China and African Development Relations* (Routledge, Contemporary China Series: London, 2011), pp. 3–20, p. 13; Lancaster, 'The Chinese Aid System', p. 5; Ali Zafar, 'The Growing Relationship Between China and Sub-Saharan Africa: Macroeconomic, Trade, Investment, and Aid Links', *World Bank Research Observer* (2007), 22(1), pp. 103–130, p. 126; Emma Mawdsley, 'China and

Africa: Emerging Challenges to the Geographies of Power', *Geography Compass* (2007), 1(3), pp. 405–21.
107. Grimm et al., 'Transparency of Chinese Aid', pp. 20–21.
108. Ibid., p. 7.
109. Barry Sautman and Yan Hairong, 'Friends and Interests: China's Distinctive Links with Africa', *African Studies Review* (2007), 50(3), pp. 75–114, pp. 86 and 90.
110. Zafar, 'The Growing Relationship', p. 126.
111. Sautman and Hairong, 'Friends and Interests', p. 88.
112. Interview with Owen Barder, Senior Fellow Center for Global Development, 8 March 2012.
113. Ibid.
114. Halper, *The Beijing Consensus*, p. 210.
115. Martyn Davies, Hannah Edinger, Natasya Tay, and Sanusha Naidu, *How China Delivers Development Assistance to Africa* (Centre for Chinese Studies, University of Stellenbosch, 2008), p. 11.
116. Taylor, FOCAC, p. 95.
117. For a chart of China's development assistance up to 2007 see Bräutigam, 'Chinese Development Aid in Africa', pp. 209–210; Bräutigam, 'China, Africa and the International Aid Architecture', *African Development Bank Group*, Working Paper No. 107 (2010), p. 17.
118. Sautman and Hairong, 'Friends and Interests', p. 88.
119. Ibid., p. 88.
120. Ibid.
121. Dent, 'Africa and China', p. 4.
122. President Zuma (South Africa), 'State of the Nation Address by His Excellency Jacob G. Zuma, President of the Republic of South Africa on the Occasion of the Joint Sitting of Parliament', *Cape Town*, 9 February 2012, available http://www.info.gov.za/speech/DynamicAction?pageid=461&sid=24980&tid=55960, accessed 1 March 2012.
123. Ibid.
124. Session Summary, 'Trade Winds: Chinese Investment in Africa', World Economic Forum 2006, available http://www.weforum.org/sessions/summary/trade-winds-chinese-investment-africa, accessed 2 March 2012; Sautman and Hairong, 'Friends and Interests', p. 80.

CHAPTER 10

Wider Implications of China's Rise as a Development Partner

According to Ian Taylor, '[t]he absolute emphasis China places on respect for state sovereignty and non-interference, as well as a willingness to deal with states ostracized by the West may appear promising to some African leaders. However, it profoundly challenges the self-proclaimed Western vision of a flourishing Africa governed by democracies that respect human rights and the rule of law and embrace free markets'.[1]

The remaining question for this chapter to tackle is what challenges the BC and/or China as a new aid donor present to existing practices of development and aid. This section looks at whether there is any evidence that China is challenging aid and development within the WB, OECD architecture and within the European Union (EU). Each subsequent element then seeks to tease out and isolate the challenge of China as opposed to changes taking place because of the wider 'emerging powers' grouping, or changes following internal criticisms or evaluation systems. Making the claim that in acting as a norm entrepreneur China uses the tool of populations in the High Level Forum at Busan; and it uses reinterpretation in the WB.

CHINA AND THE WORLD BANK

China's approach to development has had two discernible challenges to the approaches of the WB[2]: (1) China as a development partner has shaped WB policies and practices (entrepreneurship through reinterpretation); and (2) China has emerged as an alternative to the WB (essentially China is a 'new issue' for other states and groups to deal with).

According to the WB country profile for China, despite the fact that China is still a developing nation and is subject to assistance from the Bank in dealing with its own internal difficulties, the Bank characterises its relationship to China as follows:

> Given China's financial circumstances and its **appropriate development program**, the Bank Group aims to be a client-driven knowledge institution that uses lending and other operations to pilot reforms and support institutional development. This Country Partnership Strategy (CPS) focuses on five thematic areas of engagement that build on the Bank Group's international expertise while **maximizing the creation and dissemination of knowledge of China's development processes inside and outside China**.[3] (emphasis added)

Indeed, the Bank has promoted an ongoing relationship with China as a development partner not only to improve strategies for development within China but also to improve the Bank's effectiveness in how it approaches aid in other developing countries. In the report produced in 2007, the WB's approach towards engaging with China was two pronged, first to seek to utilise both China's knowledge from its own development pathway and success, second, to draw on China's emerging partnerships with the rest of the developing world.[4] Through these engagements, the WB sees the potential challenge of China in these institutions as internationalising China's experiences (as both an aid recipient and donor) making them fit with the experiences, practices and approaches of the WB.[5] Furthermore, the WB has increasingly been filling top positions with Chinese economists and bankers—directly importing their experience and knowledge.[6] Thus, the approach from the WB suggests that the BC, or the Chinese knowledge and approach to development, can be adapted and incorporated into the existing structures.

Whilst the WB is keen to integrate China into the existing development community, Chinese Banks (specifically the Chinese Development Bank and the Export–Import Bank of China) still continue to emerge as rival donors to the WB,[7] and in doing so are reshaping the terms under which China and developing countries engage with the WB.[8]

The nature of the relationship between China and the World Bank also contributes to the shaping of the architecture of development and aid. How aid partnerships develop and evolve over time and the nature of the relationship between donor and recipient is important in aid effectiveness. The characteristics of the donor may be as important as the characteristics of the recipient in making aid more effective.[9] Until the emergence of 'new donors', the relationship between donor and recipient was largely directed by the donor—the recipient as the weaker partner had a limited ability to voice preferences about how or in what form aid was delivered. However, in looking at China's relationship with the World Bank, a more discursive and responsive donor attitude has had a positive effect on the provision of aid.[10]

China's relationship with the World Bank preceded the emergence and institutionalisation of the Washington Consensus and the advent of conditionality of loans. Accordingly, China's relationship with the Bank is significantly different from the donor–client relationships that have emerged more recently. China knew what it wanted from the Bank and was able to use the advice of the Bank and other partner agencies such as the UNDP to pursue goals set by China rather than goals set through conditions prescribed by the Bank.[11] At the same time, the Bank's projects in China were country-specific and targeted towards achieving goals designated by China. Any conditions related to the projects or aid loans were based around the outcomes of the projects rather than around the creation of good policy environments.[12] There are elements of these experiences that can be seen in China's engagement with developing world partners, specifically in how China approaches aid donations and the role of the recipient government in the process. China's involvement with the World Bank also indicates that China's path to development—as shown in the overlap between the Washington and Beijing Consensuses—didn't reject all or accept all the prescriptions of Western aid agencies, but selectively learnt from them.[13] The issue then is whether this engagement with China has any specific and discernible challenge to the activities of the World Bank.

In 2007, China and the World Bank signed a Memorandum of Understanding on development in Africa. At the same time, China increased its donations to the numerous multilateral development agencies. A specific component of China's agreement with the Bank was on funding infrastructure projects.[14] The World Bank, which up to 2008 had side-lined infrastructure projects' role in development, highlighted both the importance of developing infrastructure and the role that China is playing in shaping the activities of other actors in this area in its 2008 report 'Building Bridges: China's Role as Infrastructure Financier in Sub-Saharan Africa'.[15] Despite the Bank's move away from infrastructure projects due to technical and practical problems with them, it is significant that the adoption of a programme in the Bank to move back towards funding infrastructure projects has happened in parallel with more 'learning from China' activities.

In terms of agricultural assistance, China's involvement in agricultural aid programmes and, importantly, the distinction between China's approach and OECD approaches to this topic are expertly set out by Deborah Bräutigam in *Chinese Aid and African Development*.[16] Agricultural aid has been off the OECD's radar for years. However, since the growth of China in this area and its provision of technical assistance for development of agriculture, there is a renewed interest in the role that agricultural developments can play in economic development within the WB. In the 2008 report on Agriculture for Development, the WB notes that agricultural development in China has been effective in reducing poverty, and that 'rapid agricultural growth in China, India, and Vietnam was the precursor to the rise of industry'.[17] Thus, there is a shift in what is discussed and what is included in 'development' as a result of the World Bank learning from experiences in China and other rapidly developing countries.[18]

To what extent can this trend be attributed to the challenge of China, rather than of other emerging powers? Although it is often reported that China along with India and Brazil is central in shaping any perceived international shifts in aid practices or approaches, China is the largest new aid donor, having the most independent path to its own development, and the practices and shifts that are being seen can be traced back to approaches of China to aid, which it has been pursuing for decades. In the cases of other emerging donors, these claims are much weaker. Thus although as a group, all emerging donors contribute to the shaping of the debate, this should not detract from the importance of China as a single entity in the debate. In an OECD report in 2011 on the emerging donors, it notes the singularity of the importance of China as compared to India and Brazil in this debate, and indeed, the challenge China is presenting to the approaches of India and Brazil.[19]

One specific outcome of China's engagement with the World Bank can be seen in the application of the Country Policy and Institution Assessment (CPIA). As noted earlier, the CPIA is one tangible link between the provisions of aid and good policy environments. Furthermore, the CPIA indicators are a reflection of the normative underpinnings of what is seen as a good policy environment.[20] However, the World Bank doesn't use only the CPIA to make decisions on aid donations (though it does inform decisions made). The decision that it should not only use the CPIA ratings as an element in aid distribution, China's influence over the decision was important. In the reform of the CPIA in 2011 and the rebalancing of the weighting of the Component 16 elements, the experience and success of China and other low performers in the CPIA contributed to changes made.[21]

In looking at more specific, small and incremental changes, numerous examples can be found of reinterpretation of rules away from 'whether practices count as aid' and in favour of 'whether practices promote development'. For example, in contracts between China and the Democratic Republic of Congo in 2007/8 the parties managed to persuade the IMF and WB to sign off on agreements as a part of debt sustainability even though the contracts—under the rules of the IMF and WB—would not normally qualify for this status.[22]

The issue of debt sustainability is another specific example of China's challenge to the practices of aid by traditional donors. In 2004, the WB and IMF produced a debt sustainability framework for assessing the manageability of a countries' debt situation (implemented in 2005).[23] In 2012, the framework was revisited and revised. In particular, there was a shift in the ways that various different types of debts were considered. In some countries, assessed as having debt problems (notably Angola and Sudan),[24] there has been a significant improvement in their debt ratio. They have taken on more commercial loans that support infrastructure development and then present a direct challenge to the economic growth—allowing for this change in the debt ratio. China has been a prominent donor to these types of projects through the commercial activities of the EXIM bank.[25] According to one EXIM bank official, there is an assessment at the start of projects and throughout their implementation on the viability of that project.[26] These loans, described by traditional donors as 'forbidden loans' because of their commercial basis in countries already heavily indebted, can be claimed to have had a positive effect on producing growth.[27]

This then reflects a difference between a Chinese understanding of debt and the understanding of debt in the World Bank.[28] It is too early to say if these loans and the subsequent ratio changes have a causal relationship. But in looking at the changes to the debt sustainability framework in 2012, there is recognition that debt sustainability needs to be situated within the broader economic dynamics of the specific country. It needs to be more targeted and more detailed.[29] As an official stated, 'all investments should have a financial return … it is important to take note of what non-concessional loans are used for' in order to determine if they are sustainable. These types of assessments are easier for China to make—China in these calculations is both a donor and a future customer. To illustrate, China provides aid to help the development of a nascent industry—an industry that China recognises it will need to purchase goods from in future—making that industry more effective and tied to commercial markets allows China to make long-term judgements. By contrast, the World Bank cannot make these judgements about the future needs or plans of states—as such it is less able to make dynamic judgements on debt sustainability.

Given this shift in the rhetoric of debt sustainability, how far is it possible to claim that any changes are in response to China's actions rather than just the continual assessment of current practices? Several people and places have suggested that it is indeed China that matters in the changes taking place in the debt sustainability framework.[30] There are three ways that China can be seen to challenge: firstly, in assessing existing practices, the international financial institutions take note of changes on the ground and feed them backup to head offices, and after assessments, changes are made.[31] Thus, as the environment in which debt relief and debt sustainability assessments are made changes, the tools for making assessments also need to change. China's actions in providing 'forbidden loans' and its presence on the ground change this environment, and therefore the structural presence of China in changing the environment has an effect. Secondly, China's different approach to aid and in particular the use of concessional and non-concessional loans gives other international institutions an alternative approach to emulate. Thirdly, China's EXIM bank objected to the framework as 'too static' on the grounds that it did not reflect the true ability of countries to repay some commercial loans.[32] Thus, China's effect can be seen as structural. It is both a passive alternative and as an active complainant.

Most significantly, the debt sustainability framework highlights the need for traditional donors to seek cooperation with China and other emerging donors in order to improve practices and knowledge.[33]

As a result, in looking at the specific effects of China's presence on the practices and policies of the World Bank (and IMF) a further challenge becomes evident: the need to incorporate China and other emerging powers into the aid architecture changes the composition of the institutions providing aid. The problem (as will be noted later in the section on Busan) of incorporating China and other emerging powers into existing structures is that it may produce more fragmented aid architecture. China is therefore changing the relationship of traditional donors to each other and to multilateral donors, as well as providing a variety of reasons for reassessment of practices and policies of aid and loans.

Thus, China can be seen to be acting as a norm entrepreneur within the WB. Through its engagement with the WB, it has used reinterpretation to alter the WB's approach to debt sustainability. In addition, China's approach to agricultural policies and infrastructure projects has also reinterpreted the WB's actions in developing countries. China's agency as an entrepreneur in this case can be distilled from the agency of other states (such as Brazil and India) because of the highlighted importance that the WB has itself given to China.

CHINA AND THE EUROPEAN UNION'S DEVELOPMENT STRATEGIES

At the national and regional levels, there is also evidence of a growing recognition that China is having an influence on aid and development discourses and practices.[34] In a recent European Union working paper, the conclusion stated that: 'the shifting balance of global economic and political power and the emergence of China and India as new actors in development cooperation and more generally, raise questions for EU strategy and policy, but also for the framing of development cooperation and its relationship to other policy areas'.[35] Hence, there is a need for the EU to respond and justify its own aid and development practices in a way that has not been done before. There are several places where Chinese influence can be seen within European practices and approaches in development.

According to Ian Taylor, in response to the Addis Ababa plan and FOCAC III, the German Chancellor was reported as saying 'We Europeans should not leave the commitment to Africa to the People's Republic of China ... European policy towards Africa should not be based on "charity arguments" as ... in the past but on our "stalwart interests"'.[36] This suggests that China has prompted two shifts in Western approaches to aid: (1) there is a need to show a greater commitment and responsiveness to the needs of developing states (particularly those in Africa); and (2) these commitments need to have a longevity to them that can only be guaranteed if they stem from ongoing state interests. The significant element is not that the EU has changed its practices but that it felt it necessary to make its interests—in supporting a particular development approach—clear and its increasing need to produce results (that reinforce a liberal vision of development) from its practices.

Thus, China's approach to aid—that it needs to serve both the recipient and the donor—also has the potential to spill over into the practices of Western donors. However, in many ways this has always been the case, the marriage of development to a liberal interpretation of good governance was in the interests of the traditional aid agencies of developed countries.[37] The most interesting part of this statement then is that there has become a need for developed countries to defend their development practices. There is now an external impetus for changes to take place in the aid arena. What changes then is this impetus having?

First, in dealing with African states with greater commitment and responsiveness, there has been a subtle shift in how EU aid applies conditions and how it treats African leaders. As *The Economist* reported in 2007, the EU went to great lengths to ensure that they maintain their links with Africa and that African leaders were treated with respect, including the regimes that the EU is highly critical of on the basis of their disregard for human rights. The reporter clearly attributed this change to the rise of China's popularity in Africa and its perceived different approach from that of the West.[38] This changing relationship is also seen in the Lisbon declaration where the language of the declaration is focused on a more balanced relationship between EU and Africa.[39] Comparing the Lisbon declaration of 2007[40] to the Cairo declaration in 2000,[41] there is recognition in the Lisbon document that the EU needed 'to move away from a traditional relationship and forge a real partnership characterised by equality and the pursuit of common objectives'.[42] Further, through these documents there is greater emphasis on issues such as agriculture, food and infrastructure support and a reduction in the amount of space given over to discussion of democratic developments.[43] To what extent is this shift attributable to China, and to what extent is it a reflection of the pressures from the African Union, internal EU reflection or just an evolution of ideas and practices over time? If one looks at the formulation of the FOCAC documents and the summit meetings, including the management of the 'event' and of FOCAC summits, there are clear parallels to be drawn between the EU summits and FOCAC. This falls short of seeing China as the driver of any changes within the EU. However, it is possible to suggest that China has provided an alternative approach to the pattern of engagement that had previously existed between the EU and Africa. In providing an alternative, African countries have the ability to choose between different patterns of engagement that could not previously be vocalised by those African countries. Indeed, the different approaches between China and Africa, and the EU and Africa, are noted in a House of Lords Report that suggests Chinese activities in Africa are more appealing than operating with the OECD countries.[44] However, how the EU formulates a 'new' approach to Africa will remain to be seen.

The report also notes that there are many potential problems with China's engagement in Africa, and these require oversight; but also that there are many areas in which the EU, China and Africa could form useful strategic partnerships.[45] One of the unique elements of China's engagement with Africa has been its principle of equality and non-interference.[46] Furthermore, the report notes that Chinese engagement with Africa through a mixture of trade and aid was proving economically beneficial to many African states.[47] According to Wissenbach, 'debates in Europe about a more comprehensive view of development co-operation overcoming the strict separation of ODA and economic co-operation such as investment, trade and remittances seems to indicate that Western countries seek to emulate China's successful strategy of engagement with Africa'.[48] Thus, there is also recognition of some successes in how China delivers its aid packages—nestled within much broader trade and investment packages—proving successful in Africa; as a result, there are some changes taking place in the EU. The EU needs to be more responsive to the demands of African states when discussing issues of development. In part, these demands are shaped by the alternative experience of dealing with China.

In the case of China's entrepreneurship and the EU, it may be seen that China's involvement in aid delivery presents a 'new issue' for the EU. As such, China's approach to aid and its entrepreneurship of its approach present itself as a challenge to the EU because it is a 'new issue' to be responded to in order that EU aid continues to be effective and sought after.[49]

High Level Forum on Aid Effectiveness

There has also been a process of adjustment in the policies of the traditional donor countries in response to the rise of China. There is a palpable sense that new aid donor countries need to be incorporated into the existing aid practices[50]; in order to prevent the emergence of an alternative set of practices that challenge the agreements and processes that have been emerging in the dominantly Western aid community.[51] During the lead up to, and throughout, the Fourth Summit on Aid Effectiveness in Busan in December 2011, China's threat to pull out of talks, as it was not ready to enter into such a partnership under the specified conditions, prompted a series of talks to ensure continued involvement and commitment from China.[52] However, the strenuous measures to incorporate China have met with a reaction from the traditional donors who are less happy with the lowering of the standards for the provision of aid.[53]

Like the High Level Forums (HLFs) in Paris (2006) and Accra (2008),[54] Busan was a summit meeting on improving aid effectiveness. However, unlike Paris and Accra, a key focus of Busan was to bring in 'new' development partners, notably China, India, Brazil and South Africa. A major outcome of the summit was the creation of a new multilateral grouping: The Global Partnership for Effective Development Cooperation. In particular, it helped shape a new population in looking at aid in future; pivotal in the creation of this grouping was the role of China.[55] Significantly, these new actors are not held to the same standards as those signed up to the Paris and Accra agreements. As a result of these new actors and in particular China, there will be a need in future to apply a broader range of criteria and change the indicators for aid effectiveness.[56]

The agreement over this new grouping and the outcome document was the process of discussion and debates both at the HLF and in the months preceding it. According to the Chair of the DAC, the outcome of Busan 'represents hours of push and pull, with developing countries and civil society doing much of the pushing'.[57] Busan then is seen as a signal of the changing geopolitical realities and the rise of new development partners. It is also a reflection of the success of these new partners in their own development.[58]

Another more subtle outcome may be seen in the changing question. It has shifted from 'how to incorporate emerging donors into the existing architecture' to 'how committed are the traditional donors to having a single international approach on development'.[59] Furthermore, the answer to the second question varies across the different aid participants: for developing nations, the ability to use a split in the development community may be seen as a good thing; traditional donors may reappraise the benefits in a unitary aid architecture. Emerging donors may find it politically beneficial to have a number of approaches or they may find it helpful to be able to act in concert.

There is also a shift in the type of commitments made. In contrast to the technical commitments made in both Paris and Accra,[60] the outcome document of Busan is far more flexible; it avoids technical commitments of the same type as Accra and Paris[61]; instead, the focus of the document is the development of 'shared principles' and recognising the differences between South–South and North–South approaches to development.[62] Significantly, the commitments made by the developing partners remain voluntary.[63]

Another key outcome is a change in the development rhetoric. Whilst prior to Busan, there was a concerted effort to deal with aid effectiveness; in the post-Busan world, there is a focus on 'development effectiveness'.[64] Thus not only has there been a shift in the architecture of development, there has been a shift in the rhetoric of development. The tone of the document may be different because of a desire for the emerging donors to be happy not only to have a caveat in their favour but also to shape the tone of the document in a way acceptable to them.[65] Whilst it remains unclear which parties wanted particular changes, it is clear that the presence of new donors has shaped the outcome.

In the discussion of Busan above, there is an emphasis on the role of *all* the new development partners in shaping the outcome of the HLF, rather than a focus on the role that China played in the process.[66] There are two reasons for thinking of China as the driving force for these changes. First, the changes made at Busan bore a number of hallmarks of a particularly Chinese approach at play. The movement away from aid and towards economic development pursued through a range of policies (not just aid) links in with the Chinese practices discussed above.

Second, China and other developing countries, through other forums prior to Busan, have arrived at similar approaches to the architecture of development. For example, in the framing of the African approach at Busan, there is also evidence of the influence of the FOCAC approach in shaping African views on how to change development. In their consensus paper, they state 'New forms of South-South Cooperation are evolving as the most promising partnership approach to support African-owned and led processes of building and managing a knowledge economy for development, as well as, solidarity amongst developing countries'.[67] Later in the same document, they go on to state: 'Principally, Africa is seeking a new consensus frame for a global development partnership which is essentially driven by localized systems. The changes in the global development environment demand that we critically review existing structures for managing aid and jointly develop *new international development cooperation architecture* to adequately and promptly address the unfinished Aid agenda, within the development effectiveness framework'.[68]

Similarly, the framing of Indian, Brazilian and South African approaches to the Busan forum shows the potential for having been previously shaped by China through the BRICS gathering earlier in 2011. What is the alternative to this explanation? In making the case of China shaping the attitudes and approaches of other states, there is a link back into China's path to development, whereas this is less clear in the cases of India, Brazil or South Africa. However, China has been active in developing and extending the multilateral forums that bring these developing countries together in order to create a unified approach at forums such as Busan.[69] As a result, it may be that rather than shaping the future of aid and development, Busan comes to be seen as a reflection of decisions taken elsewhere and thus the shifting political geographies.[70] Importantly, reflecting back to Chapter 4, China can be seen to amplify its own entrepreneurship by coordinating its actions with the BRICS as a population rather than acting alone. In this sense, its actions in challenging the aid architecture have been similar to its actions with the BRICS in R2P—the notable difference is that its use of the tool in development is to be an agent of entrepreneurship rather than as an objector.

A further element suggesting that China was the driving force behind these changes is in the press coverage of Busan. A great deal of attention was focused on China's specific role in shaping the final document and the need to ensure China's partnership. China's threat to pull out prompted a series of talks to ensure China's continued involvement and commitment.[71] Indeed, even though these extraneous measures have met with a less positive reaction from the traditional donors unhappy with the lowering of the standards, China's engagement was seen as so important that this outcome was tolerated.[72] In the reports on Busan, China is singled out for special consideration, whereas the other BRICS countries are only reported on as a collective.[73] Thus, there is an indication that China was the country most responsible for the changes. For China, then there is a 'value-added' to its ability to create change by being able to coordinate its actions with a broad group of developing countries, and certainly the rest of the BRICS played an important role in the commitments made in Busan. Thus, a picture emerges that China is a cause of a challenge, and that it can be seen to be using the tool of populations—the BRICS—in amplifying its entrepreneurship. Nonetheless, it is difficult to identify how much agency is China's. This is where it is important to have already set out China's stance and position on aid, as the outcome of Busan and, in particular, the language of the document relate back the modalities of Chinese aid, and the approach to aid set out above. So whilst it is true that it is methodologically difficult to claim China is solely the agent of these changes in the document—and this is not the claim here—it is possible to see China as instrumental in presenting a challenge when Busan is coupled with the discussion of Chinese aid above.

However, another element to advancing this view of the challenge of China is that China has been *blamed* for changes and is actually being used as a scapegoat so that the OECD-DAC countries avoid fulfilling their obligations from Paris and Accra, as well as enabling them to avoid making any further specific commitments.[74] In supporting this claim, Owen Barder (a delegate at Busan) makes several points. Firstly, he argues that the real objections that China had to signing the outcome document were dealt with by insertion of assurances that the commitments of non-DAC donors were on a 'voluntary basis'. Any subsequent changes or disagreements were not to satisfy China as is claimed by some reports, but because China presented an opportunity for others to make changes that they could claim were to encourage China to sign. Thus, there is an argument that China was important in Busan because of its presence rather than any real commitment or specific changes China wanted to implement in the aid structure. However, this view was not supported by DFID officials who highlighted the importance of the tone of the whole document to ensure a commitment from China.[75]

Finally, Busan highlights the existing recognition among the OECD-DAC donors that there is a problem in implementing the commitments made at Paris and Accra as a result of their 'learning on the ground'.[76] As noted throughout this chapter, there is a growing recognition of a problem with the political economy equilibrium that is in play between aid and development.[77] This recognition then acts as a facilitating condition for any changes. But crucially in the past, there was little political interest in bringing about change, and little guidance as to what change should look like, other than to abandon aid entirely—China changes this. It provides a *need* to make aid more effective, it provides a *need* to provide a better argument for the link between economic and political development, and it provides an *alternative* of what aid may be and its modality. Whether these alternatives are good or not is a discussion for another place.

Notes

1. Ian Taylor, *The Forum on China–Africa Cooperation (FOCAC)* (Routledge: London, 2011), p. 91.
2. Lin Yifu is set to have an impact on the policies of the World Bank—despite getting his PhD from Chicago—he defected to mainland China from Taiwan and was educated in Marxist Political Economy at Peking University, on completion of his PhD he returned and became a Professor at Peking University before becoming the World Bank Chief Economist. See Martin Jacques, 'Chinese in Top Job at World Bank', *China Daily*, 3 June 2008, online http://www.chinadaily.com.cn/business/2008-06/03/content_6731511.htm, accessed 10 December 2010.
3. World Bank, 'Country Partnership Strategy: China', available http://web.worldbank.org/WBSITE/EXTERNAL/COUNTRIES/EASTASIAPACIFICEXT/CHINAEXTN/0,,contentMDK:20583507~pagePK:141137~piPK:141127~theSitePK:318950,00.html, accessed 1 July 2011.
4. 'As China's global role and integration grow, and its direct engagement with developing countries continues to expand, the Bank is well positioned both to facilitate increased South-South cooperation and to work with Chinese agencies that provide assistance directly to developing countries'. World Bank, *China and the World Bank: A Partnership for Innovation* (World Bank: Washington, DC, 2007), p. 76, available http://siteresources.worldbank.org/INTCHINA/Resources/318862-1121421293578/cn_bank_partnershp_innovation.pdf, accessed 10 December 2011.
5. 'By bringing an international perspective to Chinese experiences, helping to adapt these experiences to the context of African developing countries, and disseminating current international understanding of critical factors for aid effectiveness, the Bank can help to improve the quality and challenge of China's overseas cooperation and capacity building programs'. World Bank, *China and the World Bank: A Partnership for Innovation* (World

Bank: Washington, DC, 2007), p. 77, available http://siteresources.worldbank.org/INTCHINA/Resources/318862-1121421293578/cn_bank_partnershp_innovation.pdf, accessed 10 December 2011.
6. Martin Jacques, 'Chinese in Top Job at the World Bank', *The China Daily*, 3 June 2008, available http://www.chinadaily.com.cn/business/2008-06/03/content_6731511.htm, 10 December 2010.
7. The Guardian, 'China Ahead of World Bank in Loans to Developing Nations', *The Guardian*, 18 January 2011; Hogg, 'China Banks Lend More than World Bank', *BBC Online*, 18 January 2011.
8. 'In a world weary of the limited effectiveness of most development programs in curtailing endemic poverty, China's growing role in countries around the world provides ample opportunity to reconstruct the landscape of economic aid and financing'. Teresita Cruz-del Rosario and Phillie Wang Runfei, 'Is China the New World Bank?' *Project Syndicate*, 21 February 2011, available http://www.project-syndicate.org/commentary/rosario1/English, accessed 10 December 2011.
9. Carmelia Minoiu and Sanjay G. Reddy, 'Development Aid and Economic Growth: A Positive Long-Run Relation', *The Quarterly Review of Economics and Finance* (2010), 50, pp. 27–39, p. 37.
10. This is slightly more nuanced across some OECD donors; Japan and South Korea have long had recipient-led practices; and however, they have not been successful in changing the actions of other OECD members.
11. Pieter Bottelier, 'China and the World Bank: How a Partnership was Built', *Journal of Contemporary China* (2007), 16(51), pp. 239–258, p. 245.
12. Ibid., pp. 239–258, p. 251.
13. Suisheng Zhao, 'The China Model: Can It Replace the Western Model of Modernization?', *Journal of Contemporary China* (2010), 19(65), pp. 419–436, p. 424.
14. Wenping He, 'China's Aid to Africa: Policy Evolution, Characteristics and Its Role', in Jens Stilhoff Sörensen (ed.), *Challenging the Aid Paradigm: Western Currents and Asian Alternatives* (Palgrave Macmillan: Basingstoke, 2010), pp. 138–165, p. 153.
15. Vivien Foster, William Butterfield, Chuan Chen, and Nataliya Pushak, *Building Bridges: China's Role as Infrastructure Financier in Sub-Saharan Africa* (World Bank: Washington, DC, 2008), available http://siteresources.worldbank.org/INTAFRICA/Resources/Building_Bridges_Master_Version_wo-Embg_with_cover.pdf, accessed 12 March 2012.

16. Deborah Bräutigam, *Chinese Aid and African Development* (Macmillan Press: Basingstoke, 1998).
17. World Bank, *World Development Report 2008: Agriculture for Development—Overview* (World Bank: Washington, DC, 2007), p. 7, available http://siteresources.worldbank.org/INTWDRS/Resources/477365-1327599046334/8394679-1327614067045/WDROver2008-ENG.pdf, accessed 12 March 2007; see also World Bank, *World Development Report: Agriculture For Development* (World Bank, Washington, DC, 2008), available http://siteresources.worldbank.org/INTWDRS/Resources/477365-1327599046334/8394679-1327606607122/WDR_00_book.pdf, accessed 12 March 2012.
18. Yahia Mohamed Mahmoud, 'Chinese Foreign Aid: The Tale of Foreign Enterprise', in Jens Stilhoff Sörensen (ed.), *Challenging the Aid Paradigm: Western Currents and Asian Alternatives* (Palgrave Macmillan: Basingstoke, 2010), pp. 186–213, p. 203.
19. Myriam Dahman Saidi and Christina Wolf, Recalibrating Development Cooperation: How Can African Countries Benefit From Emerging Partners? Working Paper No. 302 (OECD Development Centre: Paris, France, 2011), pp. 13–22.
20. Christine Arndt and Charles Oman, 'The Politics of Governance Ratings', *Maastricht Graduate School of Governance Working Paper MGSoG/2008/WP003*, April 2008.
21. Nancy Alexander, 'The Country Policy and Institutional Assessment (CPIA) and Allocation of IDA Resources: Suggestions for Improvements to Benefit African Countries', Henrich Boll Steifing, Commissioned by Development Finance International, 16 August 2010.
22. Deborah Bräutigam, 'Chapter 6: China, Africa and the International Aid Architecture', in Richard Schiere, Léonce Ndikumana, and Peter Walkenhorst (eds), *China and Africa: An Emerging Partnership for Development* (African Development Bank: Tunisia, 2011), pp. 103–126 and 22–23.
23. IMF and International Development Association, *Debt Sustainability in Low-Income Countries: Further Considerations on an Operational Framework and Policy Implications*, approved by Gobind Nankani and Mark Allen, 10 September 2004, available http://siteresources.worldbank.org/INTDEBTDEPT/PolicyPapers/20279458/DSfullpapersept.pdf, accessed 2 April 2012.
24. Helmut Reisen and Sokhna Ndoye, *Prudent Versus Imprudent Lending to Africa: From Debt Relief to Emerging Lenders* (OECD Development Centre Working Paper No. 268, February 2008), p. 37.
25. Ibid, pp. 32–33.

26. Changhui Zhao, China Export Import Bank, OUCAN Conference Oxford, 14 March 2012.
27. Helmut Reisen and Sokhna Ndoye, *Prudent Versus Imprudent Lending to Africa: From Debt Relief to Emerging Lenders* (OECD Development Centre Working Paper No. 268, February 2008), p. 33.
28. Martine Dahle Huse and Stephen L. Muyakwa, *China in Africa: Lending, Policy Space and Governance* (Norwegian Campaign for Debt Cancellation: Council for Africa, 2008), p. 22.
29. In particular, there has been a reassessment of the stress tests the relationship of debt to the broader economic landscape in the country. World Bank and the IMF, *Revisiting the Debt Sustainability Framework for Low-Income Countries*, approved by Otaviano Canuto and Siddhardth Tiwari, 11 January 2012, available http://web.worldbank.org/WBSITE/EXTERNAL/TOPICS/EXTDEBTDEPT/0,,contentMDK:23125643~menuPK:4876135~pagePK:64166689~piPK:64166646~theSitePK:469043~isCURL:Y,00.html, accessed 2 April 2012.
30. Helmut Reisen and Sokhna Ndoye, *Prudent Versus Imprudent Lending to Africa: From Debt Relief to Emerging Lenders* (OECD Development Centre Working Paper No. 268, February 2008), p. 34.
31. Interview with Owen Barder, Senior Fellow Center for Global Development, 8 March 2012 (Busan Delegate).
32. Deborah Bräutigam, 'Chapter 6: China, Africa and the International Aid Architecture', in Richard Schiere, Léonce Ndikumana, and Peter Walkenhorst (eds), *China and Africa: An Emerging Partnership for Development* (African Development Bank: Tunisia, 2011), pp. 103–126, p. 120.
33. Helmut Reisen and Sokhna Ndoye, *Prudent Versus Imprudent Lending to Africa: From Debt Relief to Emerging Lenders* (OECD Development Centre Working Paper No. 268, February 2008), p. 42.
34. Most recent example of this can be seen in this Oxfam comment on the effect of China and Brazilian aid transactions, Henry Tugendhat, 'What Can DFID Learn from Chinese and Brazilian Aid Programmes?', posted 27 March 2013 From *Poverty to Power*, blog of Duncan Green, available http://www.oxfamblogs.org/fp2p/?p=14090, last accessed 5 April 2013.
35. John Humphrey, 'European Development Cooperation in Changing World: Rising Powers and Challenging After the Financial Crisis', EDC Working Paper, available http://www.edc2020.eu/fileadmin/publications/EDC_2020_Working_Paper_No_8_-_November_2010.pdf, accessed 7 December 2011.
36. Ian Taylor, *The Forum on China–Africa Cooperation (FOCAC)* (Routledge: London, 2011), p. 74.

37. Indeed, according to Simon Reich it is because their policies are so closely related to these interests that they are now struggling to extend their legitimacy. Simon Reich, *Global Norms, American Sponsorship and the Emerging Patterns of World Politics* (Palgrave Macmillan: Basingstoke, 2010), pp. 49–50.
38. The Economist, 'A Desperate Suitor: After China and America, It's Europe's Turn to Woo Africa', *The Economist*, 6 December 2006; Kirtian Kjøllesdal and Anne Welle-Strand, 'Foreign Aid Strategies: China Taking over?', *Asian Social Science* (2010), 6(10), p. 9
39. Council of the EU, 'Lisbon Declaration—EU Africa Summit', Press Release 9 December 2007, available http://register.consilium.europa.eu/pdf/en/07/st16/st16343.en07.pdf, accessed 12 March 2012.
40. Council of the European Union, 'The Africa-EU Strategic Partnership: A Joint Africa-EU Strategy', 9 December 2007, http://www.consilium.europa.eu/uedocs/cms_data/docs/pressdata/en/er/97496.pdf, accessed 12 March 2012.
41. Council of the European Union, 'Africa–Europe Summit Under the Egis of the OAU and the EU' Cario 3–4 April 2000, available http://unpan1.un.org/intradoc/groups/public/documents/cafrad/unpan002865.pdf, accessed 12 March 2012.
42. Council of the EU, 'Lisbon Declaration—EU Africa Summit', Press Release 9 December 2007, available http://register.consilium.europa.eu/pdf/en/07/st16/st16343.en07.pdf, accessed 12 March 2012, point 9(a).
43. There is still a long section on democracy building in the Lisbon document but in comparison with the large sections on specific 'hard' support it is less of the whole document.
44. House of Lords European Union Committee, 7th Report of Session 2009–2010, 'Stars and Dragons: The EU and China', Vol. 1—Report, published 23 March 2010, available http://www.publications.parliament.uk/pa/ld200910/ldselect/ldeucom/76/76i.pdf, accessed 12 March 2012, para. 298.
45. Ibid., para. 275–305.
46. Ibid., para. 286.
47. Ibid., para. 288.
48. Uwe Wissenbach, 'China–Africa Relations and the European Union: Ideology, Conditionality, *Realpolitick* and What is New in South-South Co-operation', in Christopher M. Dent (ed.), *China and Africa Development Relations* (Routledge Contemporary China Series, Routledge: Abingdon, 2011), pp. 21–41, p. 29.
49. 'The European Union feels the pressure of Chinese Aid. Africa is looking more and more to the South and the European private sector has to

deal with competition on the African ground'. Veronika Tywuschik, 'EU, China and Africa: A Trilateral Partnership in Theory, a Bilateral One in Practice?' The EU Centre for Development Policy Management, available http://www.ecdpm.org/Web_ECDPM/Web/Content/Download.nsf/0/013A7866FA668EA8C125798F004FA24A/$FILE/Editorial%20-%20EU-Africa%20e-alert_%20No%209_2007.pdf, accessed 19 February 2013.
50. Interviews with DFID Officials 29 March 2012; 7 May 2012; and 16 May 2012.
51. Position Paper: Partner Countries' Vision and Priority Issues for HLF4, available http://www.aideffectiveness.org/busanhlf4/images/stories/hlf4/Partner_Country_Position_Paper_-_Final.pdf, accessed 7 December 2011; see also Jonathan Glennie, 'Has the World Met its Paris Aid Commitments?' *The Guardian—Poverty Matters Blog*, 3 January 2011, available http://www.nsi-ins.ca/english/pdf/China%20at.%20Doha.pdf, accessed 7 December 2011.
52. Interview with DFID official 16 May 2012; Mark Tran, 'China Pulls Out of Aid Partnerships', *The Guardian*, 29 November 2011, available http://www.nsi-ins.ca/english/pdf/China%20at.%20Doha.pdf, accessed on 7 December 2011; Mark Tran, 'China and India to Join Aid Partnership on New Terms', *The Guardian*, 1 December 2011, available http://www.guardian.co.uk/global-development/2011/dec/01/china-india-aid-partnership, accessed 7 December 2011.
53. Comment from Mexico in Mark Tran, 'China and India to Join Aid Partnership on New Terms', *The Guardian*, 1 December 2011, available http://www.guardian.co.uk/global-development/2011/dec/01/china-india-aid-partnership, accessed 7 December 2011.
54. 'Paris Declaration on Aid Effectiveness' (2005), 'The Accra Agenda for Action' (2008), both available http://www.oecd.org/dataoecd/11/41/34428351.pdf, accessed 6 December 2011.
55. Interview with DFID official 16 May 2012.
56. Ibid.
57. Brian Atwood, 'Brian Atwood OECD-DAC Chair: Reflects on Busan Progress', 8 December 2011, available online at posted by Owen Barder on website for the Centre For Global Development, available http://blogs.cgdev.org/globaldevelopment/2011/12/brian-atwood-oecd-dac-chair-reflects-on-busan-progress.php, accessed 5 March 2012.
58. Interview with DFID official, 7 May 2012.
59. Interview with DFID official, 29 March 2012.
60. 'Paris Declaration on Aid Effectiveness' (2005), 'The Accra Agenda for Action' (2008), both available online at http://www.oecd.org/dataoecd/11/41/34428351.pdf, accessed 6 December 2011.

61. Significantly, Accra and Paris both produced standards for accountability and effectiveness of aid.
62. Fourth High Level Forum on Aid Effectiveness, 'Busan Partnership for Effective Development Cooperation', Busan, Republic of Korea, 29 November–1 December 2011, published on 1 December 2011, available http://www.aideffectiveness.org/busanhlf4/images/stories/hlf4/OUTCOME_DOCUMENT_-_FINAL_EN.pdf, accessed 5 March 2012.
63. Ibid., p. 1.
64. Noted in the document of the Fourth High Level Forum on Aid Effectiveness, 'Busan Partnership for Effective Development Cooperation', Busan, Republic of Korea, 29 November–1 December 2011, published on 1 December 2011, available http://www.aideffectiveness.org/busanhlf4/images/stories/hlf4/OUTCOME_DOCUMENT_-_FINAL_EN.pdf, accessed 5 March 2012, p. 9.
65. According to Owen Barder because of the opt-out clause in the start of the Busan outcome document, it is not clear whether the change is attributable to the emerging donors preferences or the preferences of the traditional donors. Interview with Owen Barder, Senior Fellow Center for Global Development, 8 March 2012 (Busan Delegate), however, a DFID official suggests that the nature of international negotiations may mean that the overall tone of the document could have been the result of a need for the tone to reflect emerging donor preferences as well as including an opt-out clause. Interview with DFID official 29 March 2012.
66. Han Fraeter, 'Three-Way-Learning South-South Agenda in Busan' blog published at the meetings centre published on 1 December 2011, available http://blogs.worldbank.org/meetings/three-way-learning-the-south-south-agenda-in-busan, accessed 5 March 2012.
67. NEPAD, 'Final Draft African Consensus and Position on Development Effectiveness: Aid Reform for Africa's Development', Fourth High Level Forum on aid effectiveness, Busan, September 2011, available http://www.africa-platform.org/sites/default/files/events/FINAL%20DRAFT%20-%20AFRICAN%20CONSENSUS%20POSITION%20ON%20DEVELOPMENT%20EFFECTIVENESS%20Sept%202011v3_1.pdf, accessed 7 December 2011 (point 21(d)).
68. Ibid., (point 50) (Original emphasis).
69. For example, China has been an important architect of the BRICS grouping. In particular—outside of the aid architecture—at the Copenhagen climate accords, China was seen to be central among the BRICS East Asia Forum 'South Africa Joins BRICS', *East Asia Forum*, published 1 April 2011, available http://www.eastasiaforum.org/2011/04/01/south-africa-joins-bric-with-china-s-support, accessed 18 July 2011;

Jon Herskovitz, 'Debutante S. Africa Adds Political Cement to BRICS', *Reuters* (US edition), published on 13 Apr 2011, available http://www.reuters.com/article/2011/04/13/brics-safrica-idU-SL3E7FD16Z20110413, accessed 18 July 2011.
70. This would then link with the impression of one of the delegates at Busan that: 'I expect that we will look back on the Busan agreement as a reflection of changing realities, including the growing range of different kinds of donors and shifting geopolitical power. I think it less likely that we will look back on Busan as having done much to shape those realities'. Owen Barder, 'What Happened at Busan' Owen Abroad: Thoughts on Development and Beyond, blog posted on 11 December 2011, available http://www.owen.org/blog/5131, accessed 5 March 2012.
71. Mark Tran, 'China Pulls Out of Aid Partnerships', *The Guardian*, 29 November 2011, available http://www.nsi-ins.ca/english/pdf/China%20at.%20Doha.pdf, accessed 7 December 2011; Mark Tran, 'China and India to Join Aid Partnership on New Terms', *The Guardian*, 1 December 2011, available http://www.guardian.co.uk/global-development/2011/dec/01/china-india-aid-partnership, accessed 7 December 2011.
72. Mark Tran, 'China and India to Join Aid Partnership on New Terms', *The Guardian*, 1 December 2011, available http://www.guardian.co.uk/global-development/2011/dec/01/china-india-aid-partnership, accessed 7 December 2011.
73. Indeed, one interviewee noted that China was the subject of special attention before Busan and that it was seen as a being instrumental at Busan they were keen that China was no board but not 'at all costs' Author Interviews with DFID officials, [phone] 16 May 2012 and 7 May 2012.
74. Interview with Owen Barder, Senior Fellow Center for Global Development, 8 March 2012.
75. Interviews with DFID official, 29 March 2012.
76. Ibid.
77. Ibid.

CHAPTER 11

Conclusion: China and the Norms of Development

The aim of this part was to answer three crucial questions: Is China's approach to development discernibly different from the West? Is China 'exporting' its model for development? Is this evidence of its shift to trying to create normative challenges? These three questions then relate to whether China is able to be a norm entrepreneur (whether it has the capacity) and whether it is challenging the existing liberal norms of development.

This chapter concludes that China is challenging particular liberal norms of development. China effectively presents a challenge to norms regarding how development should be pursued, as well as challenging the assumptions of what a developed state 'should' look like. This discussion presents the argument that China does this by acting as a norm entrepreneur, using the tools of populations within the OECD, the creation of new institutions and reframing debates on development. This conclusion sets out how the conceptual framework from the conceptual apparatus (Part 1) aids the understanding of China's international challenge. Following this, it sets out China's challenge to liberal interpretations of development.

CHINA AS A NORM ENTREPRENEUR IN DEVELOPMENT

The analysis provided in this part indicates that in development, China is acting as a norm entrepreneur. Thus, in terms of development, China's agential challenge is different to the predominantly ad hoc objection to liberal norms of sovereignty demonstrated in Part II. Nonetheless, it may use some of the same tools in amplifying its agency.

As noted in Chapter 4, norm entrepreneurship requires a capacity to develop, propose and propel international norms to acceptance by the requisite 1/3 of all states. In the previous Part on sovereignty, it was argued that in the case of R2P China lacked sufficient capacity to achieve this. In contrast, here it has been demonstrated that in the area of development China fulfils these criteria—although this is partly obscured when facilitating conditions are not clearly separated out from China's agency.

One of the biggest critiques of the Beijing Consensus (BC) and of China's ability to be seen as producing challenges in international order is that in China's actions there is an absence of a 'grand strategy'. Barry Buzan argues that 'China does not yet seem to have a coherent view of either what kind of state it wants to be, or what kind of international society it would like to be part of'.[1] Compounding this situation are questions over whether the 'China model' or the Chinese approach is exportable—as we have seen in these chapters, debate is raging between economists, development experts and political scientists as to whether China's development can be seen as a model for others or even whether it is sustainable for itself. In responding to these problems, it is identified that in order to 'see' China's actions it is essential to separate the facilitating conditions. It also demonstrates the need for the approach of thick description and a use of the tools for identifying how China expresses its challenge to liberal norms.

This chapter has demonstrated that China's approach to development practices may have some significant overlap with Korea and Japan, thus creating a methodological problem in isolating China's agency. However, in looking at development within the OECD framework, Korea and Japan are signed up to the approaches of the OECD (although they may not follow all the guidelines), and as a result their ability to challenge these practices is limited.[2] Indeed, if the challenge based around shared Chinese, Japanese and Korean approaches to development was arising because of Japan or Korea, it would be expected that these challenges would have been seen when Japan and Korea ratified the OECD convention, in 1964 and 1996, respectively.[3] In terms of the presentation of a challenge, the timing and relationship of China to the OECD are different and therefore can have an effect on the attribution of a challenge. By contrast to Japan and Korea, China is a big power that is outside the set of global structures[4]; it wants to have its voice heard but it also sees benefits in being seen to be different.

In terms of separating out other emerging donors, it is problematic, but possible, to do this through the use of a thick narrative. This chapter deliberately and painstakingly set out China's approach to aid, situating it within China's experiences and exiting practices and therefore setting out which challenges to aid practices can be linked to China's role. This approach enhanced the ability to isolate China as the root of a challenge on a particular range of issues, for example debt sustainability, or involvement in turn-key projects.

In looking at India, it can be seen that it has experienced its own path to development that is different to both the Washington Consensus (WC) and the Beijing Consensus (BC) approaches. India is not as dependant on FDI as China and has adopted an approach to development that fosters home-grown Multi-National Corporations (MNCs) and the development of local knowledge. As a result, challenges to aid that seem to be so closely related to the BC experiences are less likely to be the result of India's actions. Brazil again has adopted a different path to development that is perhaps closer to the WC than the BC.

It is therefore clear that the key changes which are taking place in the development community are as a response to 'China plus others' rather than just 'emerging powers' as an organised collective. New powers are all pursuing similar strategies, but the outcomes emerging suggest that China is *primus inter pares* in this group. In terms of liberalism, it is perhaps fairest to state that China has increased political plurality in the development arena rather than increasing individual freedoms beyond the level of the state.

In terms of the agency of China as an entrepreneur, by recalling the discussions of power in Chapter 3, and of legitimacy and tools for challenge in Chapter 2, it was noted that power is more than just the ability to compel another (through coercion) to do your will; rather, in the international order power has begun to be used in more subtle and implicit ways. For a state to be powerful, and to produce mimicking behaviour, it is not necessary for them to extol the virtues of their system, merely existing as a functioning entity is enough. Moreover, through that functionality, it is possible to shape actors' understandings of world order. 'The language of "international order" or "global governance" is never politically neutral. Indeed, a capacity to produce and project proposals, conceptions and theories of order is a central part of the practice of power'.[5]

As we can see from the discussion of what China is doing in development, its power goes beyond merely providing a different approach (although this contributes to it being an entrepreneur), it is also providing developing states the 'tools', to actualise the model. Furthermore, those methods are not only being taken up by single states, but elements are being subsumed into international institutional practice, and despite China's 'developing state' status, it is being brought on board in strategic partnerships with these institutions to further develop its model and form part of the 'mopping-up process'.

Tools for Normative Change

In looking at China's engagement with the development agenda, architecture and underlying framework, it is possible to see the application of a number of the different tools.

In terms of reframing the debate, if one looks at Busan, the debt sustainability framework and practices on aid effectiveness, China's presence is clearly helping to shape the debate. Structurally, China's presence on the ground is changing the environment in which other actors operate which challenges how those other actors 'do' aid. This is revealed not only in the structural presence of China—reflected in the development of new institutions and changing memberships—but it is also seen in the agential integration of China into the existing frameworks. The importance of China as a development partner for the OECD at Busan was central in this—despite the focus on engaging all rising powers, the centrality of China was noted.[6]

In looking at the shaping of the development world, this is vital: China can have an influence in the debates within the OECD, but also exclude OECD members from its new institutions and forums—such as FOCAC. China's actions require a structural response, and this response is then a precondition for a normative challenge within the OECD— China has a voice in future framing of debates. In addition, China's normative challenge arises from outside the OECD.

Looking at the framing of the criticisms of aid effectiveness, China is a catalyst for challenges that were already recognised within the OECD. On the one hand, this suggests that China is rising at a moment conducive to normative change—the failure of the WC, seen as an event, facilitates normative change. On the other hand—as noted by interviewees in Chapters 9 and 10—challenges to aid practices are often as a response to experiences on the ground of what works and what doesn't, rather than academic debate and criticisms. China entered the debate at a moment most conducive to change, but its ability to present a practical and logical challenge and alternative has altered the nature of, and the direction of, challenges.

In looking specifically at other institutions, China's presence is focusing the rhetoric and sharpening the need for aid donations from the EU to 'work'—in both achieving development but also in terms of achieving EU interests. In the World Bank, China's contributions are not only in terms of the incorporation of the World Bank's achievements within China but also in learning from China as a donor—for example, its challenge to debt sustainability.

In looking at the tools of new institutions, China can also be seen to be effective in amplifying its challenge. China and other development donors are creating new 'parallel' institutions (outside the scope of this book, but a relevant note here is that this is also evident in the creation of the New Development Bank and the Asian Investment Infrastructure bank). Even though there are attempts to incorporate them and their experiences into the existing architecture, there are also new institutions being created that fulfil broadly similar functions.[7] These new institutions can be seen as shaping international order in two ways. First, they increase the political pluralism within order. They increase the competition between different actors and force traditional donors to make their institutions more responsive and efficient. Traditional donors have been trying to make aid 'work better' for the past decade, but as noted above there is a need for an external 'shock' to make this a reality. The presence of an organised and effective alternative is acting as this shock.

Second, China, despite not wanting to explicitly promote its approach, has created new institutions and country groupings that allow these ideas to gain legitimacy and open up the possibility that these groups, having already formed a consensus over development issues, will caucus together in broader international institutions—as they did in Busan—in order to change 'what development is'. However, as in the case of the AIIB there is a notable weakness in the normative power of China in creating these institutions. In particular, in considering the discussion of power, China as a creative agent of the AIIB lacked the credibility and legitimacy to bring other states on board—indeed, it was not until the UK joined the bank that other states came on board. As a result, although it is possible that the presence of China has the potential to 'break the cartel' or fracture the fragile coalition between existing development partners, China's challenge to development can best be contextualised in a wider framework in which it is a further element that giving weight to the argument that the WC—or even the post-WC—needs further reconsideration. Its presence is a challenge to the ideology that underpins the practices of the traditional donors. But, it still has insufficient power to 'create' a new normative structure.

In addition, there is also a case that China is seen by other actors as a 'new issue', in development. In the case of the EU and also the WB, there is also an argument advanced in this chapter that China is a new issue for other actors to respond to. China is acting as a norm entrepreneur in the environments and institutions that it is within. However, its actions in promoting aid and trade also present a challenge by becoming a new issue to which other actors must respond. For example, the EU and WB have sought to engage with China, adapting and learning from some of China's approaches, as in the case of the WB's approach to debt sustainability. At the same time, the EU has become more vocal in stating its interests in aid projects (it may always have acted according to its own interests but it is now more vocal about this). Further, there has been more intensity in the EU's external affairs relations with China over aid-related issues.[8] As a result, China's entrepreneurship in this area is amplified by other actors responding to China as a new issue. Hence, this is a tool of China's actions in the aid arena.

In looking back to Busan, China also uses populations within institutions in order to amplify its position. As noted in the section on Busan, China may actually be primus inter pares within a population that strives for a 'differently liberal' interpretation and application of development norms.

Liberal International Order

In terms of the liberal international order, China's challenge is vague. The lack of specificity and the absence of a clear end, mean that many of the changes that China is a part of creating may not be incompatible with a liberal international order. The methods to achieving them may not promote democracy, or the respect for human rights, but they do to an extent promote the rule of law and the gradual liberalisation of trade. In the long run, it may actually be that the BC does result in liberal democracies flourishing—similarly, it may produce a number of economically liberal authoritarian states. China's challenge in not presenting an 'end'—the absence of specification of what the state should look like, how reforms should happen or when they happen, and the lack of what modernisation should be—means that China's approach may be compatible with a liberal international order.

The mechanisms and the processes that China utilises do in some significant ways challenge a liberal pursuit of development, for example, the absence of transparency in aid donations or the lack of desire to reform institutions and hold elections. But, crucially these challenges are suggested from liberals as well as by China—the significance is that China is making them a reality—its challenge is seemingly practical rather than ideological.

Notes

1. Barry Buzan, 'The Inaugural Kenneth N. Waltz Annual Lecture A World Order Without Superpowers: Decentred Globalism', *International Relations* (2011), 25(3), pp. 1–12.
2. Interview with DFID official, 29 March 2012.
3. See Ratification details from OECD, 'List of OECD member countries: Ratification of OECD Convention', available http://www.oecd.org/general/listofoecdmembercountries-ratificationoftheconventionontheoecd.htm, accessed 22 February 2013.
4. Martine Dahle Huse and Stephen L. Muyakwa, *China in Africa: Lending, Policy Space and Governance* (Norwegian Campaign for Debt Cancellation: Council for Africa, 2008), p. 8.
5. Andrew Hurrell, 'One World? Many Worlds? The place of Regions in the Theory of International Society', *International Affairs* (2007), 83(1), pp. 127–146, p. 140.
6. Interview DFID officials, 7 May 2012; 16 May 2012.
7. Noting the emergence of the BRIC bank and the Latin American Development bank as well as FOCAC.
8. See, for example, Veronika Tywuschik, 'EU, China and Africa: A Trilateral Partnership in Theory, a Bilateral One in Practice?' The EU Centre for Development Policy Management, available http://www.ecdpm.org/Web_ECDPM/Web/Content/Download.nsf/0/013A-7866FA668EA8C125798F004FA24A/$FILE/Editorial%20-%20EU-Africa%20e-alert_%20No%209_2007.pdf, accessed 19 February 2013.

CHAPTER 12

Conclusion: China's Challenges to Liberal Norms

This book addressed the question of whether China's rise is challenging the liberal norms of international order focusing on the period to 2012. Particularly, it sought to respond to a particular puzzle presented by the literature: that rising powers—as traditionally understood—have two options in their relation to international order, to challenge it or to support it. Yet, in looking at China's engagement it can be seen as both a challenger and a supporter.

In responding to this puzzle, it was necessary to explore the mechanisms and processes through which China may challenge international norms. The theoretically possible tools and forms of agency available to China were set out in Chapter 4. The empirical chapters then adopted a thick descriptive methodology, in conjunction with an Aristotelian approach to causation (set out in Chapter 1), in order to distil China's international agency from other possible causes. Consequently, this book addressed a gap in the literature on China's rise and international order.

This conclusion responds to these aims. First, it sets out how this book contributes to understanding the puzzle of China's rise. It states the benefits of looking at mechanisms and processes through which rising powers may challenge international order, and assessing the utility of the mechanisms used in the project. Second, it sets out how China challenges the liberal interpretations of some international norms, demonstrating that China's agency in these challenges is different from previous rising powers, and thus how China uses different tools to present its challenge. Finally, this conclusion sets out whether China is challenging international order through its interaction with the liberal norms examined.

Responding to the Puzzle

The existing literature that explores rising powers and international orders centres on discussions of whether a rising power is satisfied or dissatisfied,[1] that is, whether the rising power has a motive to challenge international order. In the case of China, this is clearly set out in the literature in Chapter 1. On the one hand, China has a clear motive to want to challenge and change the existing order—because of the liberal focus and because the distribution of benefits still favours the western architects of order. On the other hand, China's rise is contingent on this order and it therefore has no motive to present a challenge to it. As a result, scholars looking at China's rise closely and its interactions with international order highlight that China's rise does not easily fit the classic patterns of rising powers, making predictions or possibilities rich and diverse.[2] In order to understand China's unique position, it is necessary to develop more nuanced and focused tools to explore the nature of China's interaction, that take account of the social nature of international order, the particular facets of its liberal character and the unique opportunities for a rising power to challenge from within international institutions.

This book has sought to develop a clear theoretical and conceptual framework that takes into account all of these factors and then to apply this framework to China. Viewing China's actions through this framework made it possible to identify that China challenges the specific elements of international order (the norms), but does not challenge the stability of the structures of that order (the institutions). The framework adopted also allows for the separation of China's agency from other agents presenting a challenge and for the identification of facilitating factors in the presentation of a challenge.

According to this framework, China's agency can be divided along the dimensions of norm entrepreneurship, persistent objection and ad hoc objection. This is important in understanding the challenge China presents and is especially important in being able to understand why competing pictures of China's behaviour within international order have emerged.

In the case of ad hoc objection, China's behaviour may be seen as engagement with the debates and processes that contribute to the liberal international order (e.g. in the case of UNPKOs and R2P). However, as demonstrated in the analysis above, ad hoc objection presents the opportunity for China to challenge how these norms are accepted over time, thus allowing China to challenge the continuation of a particular liberal interpretation of the norm. In the case of entrepreneurship, China's challenge is clearer and contributes to the narrative that China is challenging international order through the creation of new institutions (such as Forum on China–Africa Cooperation (FOCAC)). This framework, therefore, allows for an appreciation of the *type* of challenge China presents and *how* it challenges as these types of analyses are not possible within the current literature.[3]

The tools available to states in presenting a challenge to international order are also useful in understanding China's challenge. As noted in Chapter 3, China is rising into a socially constructed international order. In order for the challenge to, or acceptance of, norms to alter the character of international order, it is necessary to cooperate with other states. These tools allow for an understanding of how China positions its challenge to fit with the understandings and the preferences of other states so that China's challenge is amplified and is (in the long run) more likely to be considered. In this it is not claimed that China actively seeks to modify the views of other states, but in China's interactions with other states (through the creation of new institutions and populations) its own preferences have a greater potential effect.

There is also utility in the separation, or the identification of, conditions that facilitate a challenge to international order. Firstly, this is necessary because it is methodologically important in seeking to identify China's agency and separate its role in a challenge from other factors; secondly, it is useful as it may make it easier for China to challenge norms and therefore alter the standard of evidence for the expected data. Consequently, what may be seen is how China guides and nudges an existing challenge towards China's preferences rather than being the source of the challenge originally. As a result, the expected data would need to reflect a multiplicity of challenges, but an outcome tending towards China's preferences.

In the analysis provided, it is clear that the separation of facilitating factors is important in the cases of both R2P and international aid. In the case of R2P, without taking care to separate and clarify the role that the Libyan action had in frustrating the norm, a misleading and inaccurate presentation of China's agency may have resulted. In the case of international aid, it is vital to separate out the importance of the challenges already facing the existing practices. This discussion, in addition to that of the heritage of China's approach to aid, enables a clear presentation of China's agency.

The theoretical and conceptual model contributes to the ability to identify China's agency in challenging international norms as well as contributing to understanding why we see an apparent paradox in China's behaviour. Viewed from the perspective of this model, China is a challenger to international norms. However, this challenge is not always presented as China acting as a norm-maker, rather than a norm-taker.[4] This dichotomy in the literature is misleading, although it is understandable given the limits of the tools available to analyse China's behaviour. The framework used allows for China's challenge to take a number of different forms; it can vary in the types of agency (entrepreneurship and objection—persistent and ad hoc) and it can vary in the tools a rising power may use. As a result, the theoretical framework is necessary for overcoming the problems of the existing literature.

How Does China Challenge International Norms?

This section sets out whether China can be seen to have used any of the forms of agency or the tools of normative change in challenging international norms. In Chapter 4, the theoretically possible combinations of these tools and forms of agency were set out. In the empirical chapters, not all forms of agency or all tools were seen to have been used equally. This section sets out the instances and examples of the use and utility of this approach.

Reframing

China has been effective in seeking a reinterpretation of the norms of sovereignty. In part, this is aided by the practical problems of implementing the 'liberal' approach to sovereignty. However, there are some distinctive features of China's agency. In peacekeeping missions, China has advocated for the restraint of the use of force (e.g. in Bosnia). In addition, China has used ad hoc objection regarding some peacekeeping missions, such as Cambodia and East Timor. In these cases, China made it clear that its acquiescence was born from a recognition of a need for something to be done about unfolding humanitarian disasters, and in these cases, the requirements of the specific situation required action. However, by abstaining it made it clear that it did not recognise an emerging principle of humanitarian intervention. China has also tried (and not succeeded) in its entrepreneurship to reinterpret R2P in the enunciation of 'Responsible Protection' (RP).

China has also prompted a reconsideration of the norms of development. The case of Busan indicates that the rise of China has given the opportunity for other development partners to reconsider what they can actually achieve, and by what means they are most likely to be successful in achieving these ends. As a result, China's rise has already had a structural effect on development, which is a necessary precursor to a normative challenge within the High Level forums. China's ability to provide an alternative to the Washington Consensus is important in seeing China's approach as different to the Organisation for Economic Cooperation and Development (OECD) donors. Thus, China can be seen as a more successful entrepreneur in the case of development, using the tool of reframing. The presence of China, with its normative alternative to the WC, presents the opportunity to reframe the debate, towards a differently liberal approach.

New Institutions

China has been busy creating new institutions such as FOCAC. These institutions are relatively young, and still evolving. However, their challenge to the architecture and norms of the liberal international order is becoming increasingly evident. FOCAC, in particular, is presenting a challenge to the shaping of the EU-African dialogues and Summits. Indeed within some African states, the experiences of FOCAC are then shaping how those states approach relations with other development agencies and actors. Furthermore, the FOCAC is shaping how African states respond and deal with each other, as well as how they respond to other actors.

New institutions can be seen in two forms: institutions that China creates and institutions that are recreated because of China. In exploring the normative rather than the institutional challenges that China presents, it is important to focus on the normative rather than structural dimension of new institutions. Thus, the main area of focus is on the institutions that China creates. However, because China's rise also appears to challenge the structure of the OECD high level meetings it is necessary to note this challenge here.

Indeed, as this hasn't been a focus here, the extent to which China can be seen as shaping the dialogues at Busan and within the OECD is hard to judge. In some sense, China is the catalyst but not the architect for these changes. However, it is the rise and success of China, as a developing country, which has prompted its incorporation into existing dialogues such as in Busan. This structural change was not a result of China's agency. Nonetheless, the resulting normative challenge—reflected in the outcome document from Busan—clearly reflected China's presence (and agency as an entrepreneur) in the negotiations. Thus, it is important to separate out China's norm entrepreneurship from the structural changes inspired by the response of others to China's rise.

In looking at China's own agency in the creation of new institutions, there is greater uncertainty regarding the effects these institutions have on international order. All new institutions create uncertainty and their challenge is not predictable; how they fit with existing institutions or how they are accommodated by other institutions is likely to have the most important effect in understanding China's challenge to a liberal international order. At present, this process of accommodation—although it has begun as can be seen in the case of the EU's response to FOCAC—is incomplete. Moreover, how other states respond to these changes increases uncertainty. As China attempts to push for changes through norm entrepreneurship, the West may engage in persistent objection, ad hocism or even counter-entrepreneurship. The dynamics of how this part of China's rise unfolds will be interesting and may never be complete.

By contrast, bringing China inside an existing institution or dialogue situates China's actions within existing patterns or negotiations. Whilst there is space for China to push for normative change, the choices available are significantly reduced because of the need to reconcile new actions with existing rules, the slow and gradual process of adjustment, and the readjustment of the expectations of all actors.[5]

As noted in the discussion of China and aid, particularly since Xi Jinping came to power in 2012, the creation of the New Development Bank and the AIIB both suggest that China is clearly seeking to institutionalise an alternative aid approach. However, this approach is neither radically different to the 'West', partly because it still lacks an alternative central 'idea', but also because the staff employed have a track-record working practices developed in the World Bank, IMF and Asian Development bank.

The approach also faces significant problems in the absence or weakness of the legitimacy of China as a development actor; hence, in returning to look at the necessary elements of power to enable China to become a normative power, it is lacking in both legitimacy and credibility, but it is also still an ideas importer rather than an exporter in this area.

Whilst the implications of these interactions are difficult to interpret they do suggest something about the liberal international order: ideas and the mechanisms for challenging ideas matter. The 'need' to act legitimately within institutions, and use mechanisms that are recognised as legitimate by other actors, then acts as both a constraint and an enabling condition for normative change. One the one hand, this is a facilitating condition because institutions provide the social forums in which discussion and debate can take place; on the other hand, the need for norms to 'fit' within an existing meta-normative structure and its specific institutional expression only enables a constrained form of normative change.

Populations

In terms of populations, the strongest evidence for the importance of populations in challenging international norms is within the discussion of R2P. In this case, new or existing populations such as the G77, NAM or BRICS all benefit from the changing balance of power in UN. Yet, they also utilise the fracturing or exposure of limitations of some norms. Within these groupings, states—like China—can find it beneficial to gather support from like-minded states. In the case of R2P, these states amplify China's challenge to the norm.

Populations can be seen as being most effective in the case of entrepreneurship (such as the BRICS at Busan). In this case, the ability for China to amplify its preferences was enabled by its ability to link its position to other BRICS states. However, in the case of R2P, they can also be seen to be important for objection.

New Issues

The final tool for discussion here is new issues: that is, an issue of international note that is not clearly related to existing 'meta' or interstitial norms. New issues present an opportunity to reshape how existing norms fit together and alter the normative hierarchy. New issues then challenge the existing relationships between norms—which norm should be higher in the normative hierarchy and which is actually more internalised.

Crucially, rising powers can use all the other tools to frame new issues and gain legitimacy for their interpretation of them (through regions or new institutions), and because of the absence of dedicated norms governing these issues they have greater latitude framing the debate on these issues.[6] However, there is also great competition for leadership and authority over the debate. There is a need to have legitimacy and credibility as an international actor in order to make the most of the opportunities to be a leader over these issues.

In terms of the tools used by China, new issues have rarely been seen to be used. In part, this is expected in the conceptual framework because an individual state cannot just 'create' a new issue. In the analysis provided, the best possible example of a new issue is R2P; however, reframing and populations are more obviously the tools used to express China's position.

CHINA AND THE LIBERAL INTERNATIONAL ORDER

On the one hand, China's increasing engagement with liberal instruments of order—international institutions—in an increasingly constructive manner reaffirms international order as being guided by engagement through dialogue and debate. In doing this, China demonstrates the importance and centrality of a particular use for the rule of law. In creating new institutions and using populations, international order increases in plurality—more states and institutions have a role in dialogue and debate. Indeed, through its engagement with the institutions and practices of international order, China voluntarily binds both the extent of change that is possible and the speed at which changes may occur.

On the other hand, in this engagement around issues of sovereignty, China adopts an ad hoc and case-by-case approach in dealing with international situations. This engagement results in the prevention of the emergence of particular liberal interpretations of international norms, by preventing the consistent application of these norms. Thus, China challenges some elements of liberalism from becoming fully fledged international norms with consistent practices.

China's rise also challenges the interpretation of what is liberal. China uses liberal methods of change within institutions and the role of

12 CONCLUSION: CHINA'S CHALLENGES TO LIBERAL NORMS

freedom of speech to present a persuasive argument. In the case of sovereignty, China uses arguments to present an alternative context in which norms are interpreted—framing its abstentions or vetoes to the use of force in the need for humanitarian responses (e.g. its statement on RP). This enables a shift away from a particular liberal interpretation.

China's approach to challenging the norms of development is liberal in approach, but through this liberal challenge China changes how norms may be interpreted in future by effectively highlighting the failure of a particular 'liberal' interpretation. As a result, China is not challenging highly internalised meta-norms, but rather the less internalised liberal interpretations and implementations of these norms—the interstitial norms. In addition, by shaping the development architecture, China is altering who is a part of the process of normative evolution, moving the centre of gravity of the membership away from liberal states, towards other types of regime. Consequently, China also shapes how norms may evolve in future. For example, development is moving towards a form of guided market liberalism—this then is still in some sense liberal but prioritises different elements of liberalism. Thus, in some important ways China's rise makes the world more liberal—but simultaneously limits the scope of that liberalism. This indicates that China is challenging the specific content of international order but not the 'frame of mind' of that order.

The most interesting outcome of this project is not that it tells us something about China or China's Grand Strategy or China's mindset, but that it tells us about the durability and the weaknesses in liberalism. It can be expressed in many different ways, and its methods of change or reconstruction can be used by both liberal and non-liberal actors alike. This understanding of liberalism is not new; it can be seen in the comparison of Hobbes and Locke, or Burke and Paine. However, as noted in the literature review (in Chapter 1), the weakness in the current literature on China's rise is that it focuses on China rather than the context that China is rising into; even the research on China's socialisation focuses on how China is changed rather than how China affects changes. In particular, China's engagement with the liberal international order highlights and refocuses attention on the tensions within liberalism.

A central element in the development of the Cold War, and the clash between great powers, was the ideological challenge presented by the USSR. As noted in that chapter it is unclear whether China presents a similar ideological challenge. According to a number of authors discussed in the literature (including Aaron Friedberg), China does indeed present an ideological challenge, which contributes to his argument that China is a growing threat. This is not a claim supported by the evidence presented here. Rather, the evidence suggests that, through objection and entrepreneurship, China is nudging international order towards a more conservative form of liberalism—but the character of international order will remain liberal.

Rather than presenting an ideological challenge, China's challenge is pragmatic and instrumental. Whilst, this practical approach does not exclude the possibility that incremental pragmatic and practical changes may result in an ideological challenge over time; there is no clear evidence of an ideological alternative emerging that is not liberal—the alternative that is emerging is differently liberal. More significantly, because of the incrementalism of this approach there is also no indication that the challenges China presents are the result of a *mens rea* by Beijing, but rather are the result of the presence of China acting as a catalyst at a time and moment of disruption and evaluation of the liberal international order.

The idea of the dominance of a liberal schema and the absence of genuine alternatives that avoid being polluted by the liberal international order is fascinating and is a task being taken up by an increasing number of academics.[7] Applying these conclusions to a range of works from other scholars supports the idea of the dominance of a liberal schema and the absence of alternatives[8]—whether that is in policy or theory.

In the final assessment, China is presenting a structural and quasi-normative challenge to the liberal interpretation of international norms. However, this challenge is limited by the need for China to continue to be recognised by other actors as a responsible and legitimate actor and increase its legitimacy and authority. As a result, China—through the mechanisms set out above—is making incremental changes to norms within international institutions, which further constrain the extent to which China can express a revisionist stance as well as the means through which it can express its challenge. In the final analysis, the liberal international order is being challenged by a rising China, but this challenge doesn't affect the dominance of the liberal ideology (the liberal 'frame of mind') but rather the particular expression and dominance of a specific interpretation of liberalism.

In considering China's power in this context, it may be a growing structural power, but it doesn't have the authority to present an alternative order. In terms of the consideration of China as a 'cause' of change, this book has sought to indicate that China is one among many factors, at a particular moment of wavering global polarity, that contributes to changes that are being witnessed. It may be most appropriate to consider China as *primus inter pares* of factors affecting the type and form of liberalism in international order.

NOTES

1. A.F.K. Organski, *World Politics* (Alfred A. Knopf: New York, 1968), pp. 363–375.
2. For example: Michael Beckley, 'China's Century? Why America's Edge Will Endure', *International Security* (Winter 2011/2012), 36(3), pp. 41–78; Buzan, 'China in International Society: Is 'Peaceful Rise' Possible?'; Rosemary Foot and Andrew Walter, *China, The United States and Global Order* (Cambridge University Press: New York, 2011); Alistair Iain Johnston, *Social States: China in International Institutions, 1980–2000* (Princeton University Press: Princeton, 2007); Ann E. Kent, *Beyond Compliance: China, International Organizations, and Global Security* (Stanford University Press: Stanford, 2009); Pak K. Lee, Gerald Chan and Lai-Ha Chan, 'China in Darfur: Rule-Makers or Rule-Taker', *Review of International Studies* (2011), 38(2), pp. 423–444.
3. Although it is noted that the literature on specific cases does allow for this analysis, however, this perpetuates the problem of how China as a rising power should be conceptualised.
4. This dichotomy is presented in James Reilly, 'A Norm-Maker or Norm-Taker? Chinese Aid in Southeast Asia', *Journal of Contemporary China*, 21(73), pp. 71–91; also Pak K. Lee, Gerald Chan and Lai-Ha Chan, 'China in Darfur: Rule-Makers or Rule-Taker', *Review of International Studies* (2011), 38(2), pp. 423–444.
5. This links to the logic of Appropriateness, J.G. March and J.P. Olsen, 'The Logic of Appropriateness', http://www.arena.uio.no/publications/papers/wp04_9.pdf, Working Paper WP 04/09, last accessed 23 April 2013; also Jan E. Stets and Peter J. Burke 'Identity Theory and Social Identity Theory', *Social Psychology Quarterly* (2000), 63(3), pp. 224–237 and 226–227.
6. The need to reconcile actions within international order with actions that have already happened is important for both legitimacy and credibility of individual states but also to maintain institutions and the identities of other actors. Peter J. Burke, 'Identity Theory and Social Identity Theory', *Social Psychology Quarterly* (2000), 63(3), pp. 224–237 and 226–227.

7. For example, Lindsay Cunningham-Cross, 'Narrating a Discipline: The Search for Innovation in Chinese International Relations' in Nicola Horsburgh, Astrid Nordin, and Shaun Breslin (eds.), *Chinese Politics and International Relations: Innovation and Invention* (Routledge: London, 2014); Peter Marcus Kristensen, '"You need to do something that the Westerners cannot understand"—The Innovation of a Chinese School of IR' paper presented at China Postgraduate Network Edinburgh June 2012; Peter Marcus Kristensen and Ras Tind Nielsen, 'Constructing a Chinese School of International Relations: A Sociological Approach to Intellectual Innovation', *International Political Sociology* (2013), 7(1).
8. Clark, *Hegemony in International Society*, (Oxford University Press: Oxford, 2011) p. 239.

Bibliography

Authored and Edited Books

Aksu, Eşref, *The United Nations, Intra-State Peacekeeping and Normative Change* (Manchester University Press: Manchester, 2003).
Annan, Kofi, *We the People's: The Role of the United Nations in the 21st Century* (United Nations: New York, 2000).
Aristotle, *Metaphysics* Books 4–6 (Clarendon Press: Oxford, 1993).
Armstrong, David, *Revolution and World Order: The Revolutionary State in International Society* (Clarendon Press: Oxford, 1993).
Armstrong, David, Lorna Lloyd, and John Redmond, *International Organisation in World Politics* (Palgrave: Houndmills, 2004).
Barry, Buzan, and Amitav Acharya (eds), *Non-Western International Relations Theory: Perspectives on and Beyond Asia* (Oxford: Routledge, 2010).
Beetham, David, *The Legitimation of Power* (Palgrave Macmillan: London, 1991).
Bell, Daniel A., *China's New Confucianism: Politics and Everyday Life in a Changing Society* (Princeton University Press: Princeton, 2010).
Bergsten, C. Fred, Charles Freedman, Nicholas Lardy, and Derek J. Mitchell, *China's Rise: Challenges and Opportunities* (Peterson Institute for International Economics: Washington, DC, 2008).
Bräutigam, Deborah, *Chinese Aid and African Development* (Macmillan Press: Basingstoke, 1998).
Bräutigam, Deborah, *The Dragon's Gift: The Real Story of China in Africa* (Oxford University Press: Oxford, 2011).

Bull, Hedley, *The Anarchical Society: A Study of Order in World Politics* (Columbia University Press: New York, 2002).
Buzan, Barry, *The United States and the Great Powers: World Politics in the Twenty-First Century* (Polity: Cambridge, 2004).
Carlson, Allen, 'Protecting Sovereignty, Accepting Intervention: The Dilemma of Chinese Foreign Relations in the 1990's'. *China Policy Series* (New York: National Committee on US-China Relations, 2002).
Carlson, Allen, *Unifying China, Integrating With the World: Securing Chinese Sovereignty in the Reform Era* (Stanford University Press: Stanford, CA, 2005).
Case, William, 'Comparing Politics in Southeast Asia'. *Poltics in Southeast Asia: Democracy or Less* (Richmond, Surrey: Curzon, 2002).
Clark, Ian, *The Post-Cold War Order: The Spoils of Peace* (Oxford University Press: Oxford, 2001).
Clark, Ian, *Hegemonny in International Society* (Oxford Unversity Press: Oxford, 2011).
Davison, Ian, *Values, Ends and Society* (University of Queensland Press: St Lucia, 1977).
De Bary, William Theodore, *Asian Values and Human Rights: A Confucian Communitarian Perspective* (Harvard University Press: Cambridge, MA; London, 1998).
Deng, Francis M., Sovereignty as Responsibility: Conflict Management in Africa (R.R. Donnelley and Sons Co: Virginia, 1996).
Deng, Yong, *China's Struggle for Status: The Realignment of International Relations* (Cambridge University Press: Cambridge, 2008).
Donnelly, Jack, *International Human Rights* (Westview Press: Boulder, 2007).
Dworkin, Ronald M., *Law's Empire* (Hart, 2004).
Elliott, Jane, *Using Narrative in Social Research: Qualitative and Quantitative Approaches* (Sage: London, 2005).
Falk, Richard A., *A Study of Future Worlds* (The Free Press: New York, 1975).
Finnemore, Martha, *National Interests in International Society* (Cornell University Press: Ithaca, 1996).
Fish, Stanley Eugene, *Doing What Comes Naturally: Change Rhetoric and the Practice of Theory in Literary and Legal Studies* (Clarendon: Oxford, 1989).
Foot, Rosemary, *The Practice of Power: US Relations with China Since 1949* (Clarendon: Oxford, 1995).
Foot, Rosemary, and Andrew Walter, *China, the United States and Global Order* (Cambridge University Press: New York, 2011), pp. 298–300.
Forsythe, D.P., T.G Weiss, and R.A Coate, *The UN and Changing World Politics* (Westview Press: Colorado, 1997).
Fukuyama, Francis, *The End of History and the Last Man* (Hamish Hamilton: London, 1992).

Fravel, M. Taylor, 'China's Attitude Toward UN Peacekeeping Operations Since 1989,' *Asian Survey* (1996), 36(11), pp. 1102–1122.
Friedberg, Aaron L., *A Contest for Supremacy: China, America, and the Struggle for Mastery in Asia* (W.W. Norton and Company: New York, 2011).
Gaddis, John Lewis, *The United States and the Origins of the Cold War, 1941–1947* (Columbia University Press: New York, 2000).
Gallagher, Mary E., *Contagious Capitalism: Globalisation and the Politics of Labor in China* (Princeton University Press: Princeton, 2005).
Germain, Randall, *Global Politics and Financial Governance* (Palgrave Macmillan: Basingstoke, 2010).
Gilpin, Robert, *War and Change in World Politics* (Cambridge University Press: Cambridge, 1982).
Gray, Colin S., *Another Bloody Century* (Weindenfeld and Nicolson: London, 2005).
Gray, John, *Liberalism* (Concepts in the Social Sciences; Buckingham: Open University Press, 1995).
Gray, John, *Two Faces of Liberalism* (Polity Press: Cambridge, 2000).
Haas, Ernst B., *When Knowledge Is Power: Three Models of Change in International Organizations* (University of California Press: Berkeley, 1990).
Halper, Stefan A., *The Beijing Consensus: How China's Authoritarian Model Will Dominate the Twenty-First Century* (New York: Basic Books, 2010).
Halperin, Sandra, and Oliver Heath, *Political Research: Methods and Practical Skills* (Oxford University Press: Oxford, 2012).
Hamann, Eduarda P., and Robert Muggah, *Implementing the Responsibility to Protest: New Directions for International Peace and Security?* (IGARAPE Institute: Brasilia, Brazil, 2013).
Hegel, G.W.F., *Hegel's Philosophy of Right*, trans. T.M Knox (Oxford University Press: London, 1952).
Held, David, *Democracy and Global Order: From Modern State to Cosmopolitan Governance* (Polity Press: Cambridge, 1995).
Heritier, Adrienne, 'Theories of Institutional Change', in Adrienne Heritier (eds), *Explaining Institutional Change in Europe* (Oxford University Press: Oxford, 2007).
Hobbes, Thomas, *Leviathan* (C.B. Macpherson, eds) (Penguin Books: London, 1968).
Hoffmann, Stanley, *Janus and Minerva: Essays in the Theory and Practice of International Politics* (Westview Press: Boulder, 1987).
Hollis, Martin, *The Philosophy of Social Science: An Introduction* (Cambridge University Press: Cambridge, 2008).
Huntington, Samuel P., 'Political Development and Political Decay' *World Politics* (1965), 17(3), pp. 386–430;

Hurrell, Andrew, *On Global Order: Power, Values, and the Constitution of International Society* (Oxford University Press: Oxford, 2007).
Huse, Martine Dahle, and Stephen L. Muyakwa, *China in Africa: Lending, Policy Space and Governance* (Norwegian Campaign for Debt Cancellation: Council for Africa, 2008).
Ikenberry, G. John, *After Victory: Institutions, Strategic Restraint, and the Rebuilding of Order after Major Wars* (Princeton University Press: Princeton, 2001).
———, *Liberal Leviathan: The Origins, Crisis, and Transformation of the American World Order: The Rise, Decline and Renewal* (Princeton University Press: Princeton, 2011).
Jackson, Robert H., *Quasi-States: Sovereignty, International Relations, and the Third World* (Cambridge University Press: Cambridge, 1990).
Jacques, Martin, *When China Rules the World* (Penguin: London, 2012).
Johnston, Alistair Iain, *Social States: China in International Institutions, 1980–2000* (Princeton University Press: Princeton, 2007).
Johnson, Janet B., and H.T. Reynolds, *Political Science Research Methods*, 4th ed. (CQ Press, 2004).
Judt, Tony, *Postwar: A History of Europe Since 1945* (Pimlico: London, 2007).
Kang David C., *China Rising: Peace, Power and Order in East Asia* (Columbia University Press: New York, 2007).
Kagan, Robert, *The Return of History and the End of Dreams* (Atlantic Books: London, 2009).
Kennedy, Paul M., *The Rise and Fall of the Great Powers: Economic Change and Military Conflict from 1500 to 2000* (Fontana: London, 1989).
Kent, Ann E., *Beyond Compliance: China, International Organizations, and Global Security* (Stanford University Press: Stanford, 2009).
Keohane, Robert O., *After Hegemony: Cooperation and Discord in the World Political Economy* (Princeton University Press: Oxford, 2005).
Knutsen, Torbjørn L. *The Rise and Fall of World Orders* (Manchester University Press: Manchester, 1999).
Krasner, Stephen D., *Sovereignty: Organized Hypocrisy* (Princeton, NJ: Princeton University Press, 1999).
Kurki, Milja, *Causation in International Relations: Reclaiming Causal Analysis* (Cambridge University Press: Cambridge, 2008).
Lampton, David M., *The Three Faces of Chinese Power: Might, Money, and Minds* (University of California Press: Berkeley, 2008).
Leonard, Mark, *What Does China Think?* (Fourth Estate: London, 2008).
Leys, Colin, *The Rise and Fall of Development Theory* (James Curry: Oxford, 1996), pp. 3–44.
Locke, John, *Two Treatise of Government*, ed. Peter Lassetts (Cambridge University Press: Cambridge, 2004).

Luttwak, Edward N., *The Rise of China Vs. The Logic of Strategy* (Belknap, Harvard University Press: Cambridge, MA, 2012).
Mahoney, James, and Kathleen Thelen (eds), *Explaining Institutional Change: Ambiguity, Agency and Power* (Cambridge University Press: Cambridge, 2009).
Mearsheimer, John J., *The Tragedy of Great Power Politics* (W.W. Norton New York, 2001).
Mill, John Stuart, *Utilitarianism, On Liberty, On Considerations for Representative Government* (Everyman: London, 1993).
Moseley, Paul, Jane Harrigan, and John Toye, *Aid and Power*, (Routledge: London, 1991).
Moseley, Paul, Jane Harrigan, and John Toye, *Aid and Power: The World Bank and Policy-Based Lending* (Vol. 1 Analysis and Policy Proposals; London: Routledge, 1995).
Moyo, Dambisa, *Dead Aid: Why Aid Is Not Working and How There Is Another Way for Africa* (Penguin: London, 2010).
North, Douglass C., 'The New Institutional Economics and Third World Development', in John Harriss, Janet Hunter, and Colin M. Lewis (eds), *The New Institutional Economics and Third World Development* (London: Routledge, 1995), pp. 17–26
Nye, Joseph S., *Soft Power: The Means to Success in World Politics* (Public Affairs: New York, 2004).
Organski, A.F.K., *World Politics* (Alfred A. Knopf: New York, 1968).
Parsons, Talcott, *Structure and Process in Modern Societies* (Free Press of Glencoe: Illinois, 1960).
Peerenboom, Randall, *China Modernizes: Threat to the West or Model for the Rest?* (Oxford: Oxford University Press, 2007).
Philpott, Daniel, *Revolutions in Sovereignty: How Ideas Shaped Modern International Relations* (Princeton University Press: Princeton and Oxford, 2001).
Prantl, Jochen, *The UN Security Council and Informal Groups of States: Complementing or Competing for Governance?* (Oxford University Press: Oxford, 2006).
Ramo, Joshua Cooper, *The Beijing Consensus* (Foreign Policy Centre: London 2004).
Reich, Simon, *Global Norms, American Sponsorship and the Emerging Patterns of World Politics* (Palgrave Macmillan: Basingstoke, 2010).
Ropp, Paul S., *China Is World History* (The New Oxford World History; New York: Oxford University Press, 2010), pp. 135–155.
Rousseau, John Jacques, *The Social Contract and Discourses* (G.D.H. Cole trans) (Everyman Classics: Vermont, 1993).
Ruggie, John Gerard, *Constructing the World Polity: Essays on International Institutionalization* (Routledge: London, 1998).

Saich, Tony, *Governance and Politics of China* (London: Palgrave, 2001).
Sen, Amartya, *Development as Freedom* (Oxford University Press: Oxford, 2001).
Shambaugh, David, *The Modern Chinese State* (Cambridge University Press: Cambridge, 2000).
Shirk, Susan, *China: Fragile Superpower* (Oxford University Press: Oxford, 2007).
Smith, A.D., *The Concept of Social Change: A Critique of the Functionalist Theory of Social Change* (London and Boston: Routledge and Kegan Paul, 1973).
Smith, David, *The Dragon and the Elephant: China, India and the New World Order* (Profile Books: London, 2008).
Smith, Martin A., *Power in the Changing Global Order* (Polity: Cambridge, 2012).
Stake, Richard E., *The Art of Case Study Research* (Sage: Thousand Oaks, California, 1995).
Steiner, Zara, *The Lights that Failed: European International History 1919–1933* (Oxford University Press: Oxford, 2005).
Stiglitz, Joseph, *Globalisation and Its Discontents* (Penguin: London, 2002).
Storey, Ian, *Southeast Asia and the Rise of China: The Search for Security* (Routledge: Abingdon, 2011).
Tansey, Oisin, *Regime Building: Democratization and International Administrations* (Oxford University Press: Oxford, 2009).
Taylor, Ian, *The Forum on China–Africa Cooperation (FOCAC)* (Routledge: London, 2011).
Toye, John, 'The New Institutional Economics and Its Implications for Development Theory, in John Harriss, Janet Hunter, and Colin M. Lewis (eds), *The New Institutional Economics and Third World Development* (London: Routledge, 1995), pp. 49–68.
Trachtenberg, Marc, *A Constructed Peace: The Making of the European Settlement* (Princeton University Press: Princeton, 1999).
Waltz, Kenneth N., *Theory of International Politics* (Addison-Wesley: Reading, MA., 1979).
Ward, Thomas, *The Ethics of Destruction: Norms and Force in International Relations* (Ithaca; London: Cornell University Press, 2001).
Wendt, Alexander, *A Social Theory of International Politics* (Cambridge: Cambridge University Press, 1999).
Williamson, John, 'A Short History of the Washington Consensus', *Law and Business Review of the Americas* (2009), 15(1), pp. 7–23
White, Hugh, *The China Choice: Why America Should Share Power* (Black Inc. Publishers: Collingwood, Vic. 2012).
Wuthnow, Joel, *Chinese Diplomacy at the UN Security Council* (Routledge: Abingdon, 2013).
Yang, Dali L., *Holding China Together and National Integration in the Post-Deng Era* (Cambridge University Press: Cambridge, 2004).

Yang, Mayfair Mei-Hui, *Gifts Favors and Banquets: The Art of Social Relationships in China* (Cornell University Press: Ithaca, 1994).
Zaum, Dominik, *The Sovereignty Paradox* (Oxford University Press: Oxford, 2007).

Journal Articles, Book Chapters, Conference Papers and Working Papers

Abbott, Kenneth W., and Duncan Snidal, 'Hard and Soft Law in International Governance', *International Organization* (2000), 54(3), pp. 421–456.

Abbott, Kenneth W., Robert O. Keohane, Andrew Moravcsik, Anne-Marie Slaughter, and Duncan Snidal, 'The Concept of Legalisation', *International Organization* (2000), 54(3), pp. 17–35.

Acharya, Amitav, 'How Ideas Spread: Whose Norms Matter? Norm Localization and Institutional Change in Asian Regionalism', *International Organisation* (2004), 58(2), pp. 239–275.

———, 'State Sovereignty After 9/11: Disorganised Hypocrisy', *Political Studies* (2007), 55, pp. 274–296.

Aggarwal, Vinod K., 'Reconciling Multiple Institutions: Bargaining, Linkages, and Nesting', in Vinod K. Aggarwal (ed.), *Institutional Designs for a Complex World: Bargaining, Linkages, and Nesting* (Cornell University Press: Ithaca, 1998), pp. 1–29.

Aintree, Larry, *China and Conflict Affected States: Between Principle and Pragmatism*, January 2012, http://www.saferworld.org.uk/downloads/pubdocs/FAB%20Sudan%20and%20South%20Sudan.pdf, accessed 14 February 2013.

Arndt, Christine, and Charles Oman, 'The Politics of Governance Ratings', *Maastricht Graduate School of Governance Working Paper MGSoG/2008/WP003*, April 2008.

Axelrod, Robert, 'An Evolutionary Approach to Norms', *The American Political Science Review* (1986), 80(4), pp. 1095–1111.

Axworthy, Lloyd, and Allan Rock, 'R2P: a New and Unfinished Agenda', *Global Responsibility to Protect* (2009), 1, pp. 54–69.

Baker, J.A., 'America in Asia: Emerging Architecture for a Pacific Community', *Foreign Affairs* (1991), 70(5), pp. 1–18.

Baldwin, David A., 'Power Analysis and World Politics: New Trends Versus Old Tendencies', *World Politics* (1979), 31(2), pp. 161–194.

Banda, Maria, *The Responsibility to Protect: Moving the Agenda Forward*, Canadian UN Association, March 2007.

Barbantseva, Elena, 'In Pursuit of an Alternative Model? The Modernisation Trap in China's Official Discourse', *East Asia: An International Quarterly*, September 2011 [online], pp. 1–17.

Barkin, J. Samuel, and Bruce Cronin, 'The State and the Nation: Changing Norms and the Rules of Sovereignty in International Relations', *International Organization* (1994), 48(1), pp. 107–130.

Barma, Naazneen Giacomo Chiozza, Ely Ratner, and Steven Weber, 'A World Without the West? Empirical Patterns and Theoretical Implications', *Chinese Journal of International Politics* (2009), 2(4), pp. 525–544.

Barnett, Michael, and Raymond Duvall, 'Power in International Relations', *International Organization* (2005), 59(1), pp. 39–75.

Beckley, Michael, 'China's Century? Why America's Edge Will Endure', *International Security* (Winter 2011/2012), 36(3), pp. 41–78.

Bellamy, Alex J., 'Responsibility to Protect or Trojan Horse? The Crisis in Darfur and Humanitarian Intervention After Iraq', *Ethics & International Affairs* (2005), 19(2), pp. 31–54.

Bellamy, Alex J., 'The Responsibility to Protect and the Problem of Military Intervention', *International Affairs* (2008), 84(4), pp. 615–639.

Bellamy, Alex, and Sara E. Davies, 'The Responsibility to Protect in Southeast Asia: Progress and Problems', *Security Dialogue* (2009), 40(6), pp. 547–574.

Bellamy, Alex J., and Catherine Drummond, 'The Responsibility to Protect in Southeast Asia: Between Non-interference and Sovereignty as Responsibility', *The Pacific Review* (2011), 24(2), pp. 179–200.

Berman, Sheri, 'Ideas, Norms, and Culture in Political Analysis', *Comparative Politics* (2001), 33(2), pp. 231–250.

Berry, Jeffrey M., 'Validity and Reliability Issues in Elite Interviewing', *PS: Political Science and Politics* (2002), 35(4), pp. 679–682.

Bianchi, Andrea, 'Ad-Hocism and the Rule of Law', *European Journal of International Law* (2002), 13(1), pp. 263–272.

Bourdieu, Pierre (author) Jack Goody (ed.), Richard Nice (trans.) *Outline of a Theory of Practice* (Cambridge University Press: Cambridge, 1997).

Bräutigam, Deborah, 'China, Africa and the International Aid Architecture', *African Development Bank Group*, Working Paper (2010) No. 107.

Bräutigam, Deborah, 'Aid 'with Chinese Characteristics': Chinese Foreign Aid and Development Finance Meet the OECD-DAC Aid Regime', *Journal of International Development* (2011a), 23(5), pp. 752–764.

Bräutigam, Deborah, 'Chapter 6: China, Africa and the International Aid Architecture', in Richard Schiere, Léonce Ndikumana, and Peter Walkenhorst (eds), *China and Africa: An Emerging Partnership for Development* (African Development Bank: Tunisia, 2011b), pp. 103–126.

Breau, Susan C., 'The Impact of the Responsibility to Protect on Peacekeeping', *Journal of Conflict and Security Law* (2006), 11(3), pp. 429–464.

Breslin, Shaun, 'The "China Model" and the Global Crisis: From Friedrich List to a Chinese Mode of Governance', *International Relations* (2011), 87(6), pp. 1323–1343.

Brown, Chris, 'History Ends, Worlds Collide', *Review of International Studies* (1999), 25/05, pp. 41–57.
Brown, Chris, 'Do Great Powers have Great Responsibilities? Great Powers and Moral Agency', *Global Society* (2004), 18(1), pp. 5–19.
Brunnee, Jutta, and Toope Stephen, 'Norms, Institutions and Un Reform: The Responsibility to Protect', *Journal of International Law and International Relations* (2006), 2(1), pp. 121–137.
Buckley, Peter J., Chengqi Wang, and Jermey Clegg, 'The Impact of Foreign Ownership, Local Ownership and Industry Characteristics on Spillover Benefits from Foreign Direct Investment in China', *International Business Review* (2007), 16, pp. 142–158.
Bull, Hedley, 'Grotian Conception of International Society', in Herbert Butterfield and Martin Wight (eds), *Diplomatic Investigations: Essays in the Theory of International Politics* (London: George Allen & Unwin, 1966), pp. 51–73.
Burnside, Craig, and David Dollar, 'Aid, Policies, and Growth', *The American Economic Review* (2000), 90(4), pp. 847–868.
Buzan, Barry, 'Conclusion: How and to Whom Does China Matter?', in Barry Buzan and Rosemary Foot (eds), *Does China Matter? A Reassessment: Essays in Memory of Gerald Segal* (Routledge: Abingdon, 2004), pp. 143–164, p. 145.
———, 'China in International Society: Is 'Peaceful Rise' Possible?' *Chinese Journal of International Politics* (2010), 3(1), pp. 5–36.
———, 'The Inaugural Kenneth Waltz Lecture A World Order Without Superpowers: Decentred Globalism', in *International Relations* (2011), 25(3), pp. 3–25.
Byman, Daniel L., and Matthew C. Waxman, 'Kosovo and the Great Air Power Debate', *International Security* (2000), 24(4), pp. 5–38.
Callahan, William, 'China's Dreams of the Future', *China Seminar Series* (Oxford: St Anthony's College: University of Oxford, 2011).
Campbell, Ivan, Thomas Wheeler, Larry Attree, Dell Marie Butler, and Bernardo Mariani, '*China and Conflict-Affected States: Between Principle and Pragmatism*' (Saferworld Report, 2012).
Carlson, Allen, 'More Than Just Saying No: China's Evolving Approach to Sovereignty and Intervention Since Tiananmen', in Johnston and Ross (eds), *New Directions in the Study of China's Foreign Policy*, pp. 217–241.
Cerulo, Karen, Identity Construction: New Issues, New Directions *American Review of Sociology* (1997), 23, pp. 385–409.
Charney, Jonathan I. 'Universal International Law', *The American Journal of International Law* (1993), 87(4), pp. 529–551.
Checkel, Jeffrey T. 'Why Comply? Social Learning and European Identity Change', *International Organization* (2001), 55(3), pp. 553–588.

Chin, Gregory, and Ramesh Thakur, 'Will China Change the Rules of Global Order', *The Washington Quarterly* (October 2010), 33(4), pp. 119–138.

Chinkin, C.M., 'The Challenge of Soft Law; Development and Change in International Law', *International and Comparative Law Quarterly* (1989), 38, pp. 850–866.

Clark, Ian, and Christian Reus-Smit, 'Liberal Internationalism, the Practice of Special Responsibilities, and the Evolving Politics of the Security Council', *International Politics* (2013), 50, pp. 38–56.

Clemens, Elisabeth S., and James M. Cook, 'Politics and Institutionalism: Explaining Durability and Change', *Annual Review of Sociology* (1999), 25, pp. 441–466.

Cockayne, James, and David M. Malone, 'The Security Council and the 1991 and 2003 Wars in Iraq', In Vaughan Lowe, Adam Roberts, Jennifer Welsh, and Dominik Zaum, *The United Nations Security Council and War: The Evolution of Thought and Practice Since 1945* (Oxford University Press: Oxford, 2008).

Collier, Paul, and David Dollar, 'Can the World Cut Poverty in Half? How Policy Reform and Effective Aid Can Meet International Development Goals', *World Development* (2001), 29(11), pp. 1787–1802.

Collier, Paul, and David Dollar, 'Aid Allocation and Poverty Reduction', *European Economic Review* (2002), 46, pp. 1475–1500.

Cohen, Roberta, 'The Burma Cyclone and the Responsibility to Protect', *Global Responsibility to Protect* (2009), 1, pp. 253–257.

Cook, Alistair D.B., and Lina Gong, 'The Cambodian Legacy and the Responsibility to Protect in Asia', *Peace Review* (2011), 23(4).

Cooper, Andrew F., and Thomas Fues, 'Do the Asian Drivers Pull Their Diplomatic Weight China, India, and the United Nations', *World Development* (2008), 36(2), pp. 293–307.

Cooper, Robert, 'World Economy Past and Future 1950–2030', *HPAIR 2010—Asian Ascendants* (Harvard University, 2010).

Corbridge, Stuart, 'Beneath the Pavement Only Soil: The Poverty of Post Development', *Journal of Development Studies* (1998), 34(6), pp. 138–148.

Cortell, Andrew P., and James W. Davis, Jr., 'How Do International Institutions Matter? The Domestic Impact of International Rules and Norms', *International Studies Quarterly* (1996), 40(4), pp. 451–478.

Cotton, James, 'Against the Grain: East Timor Intervention', *Survival* (2001), 43(1), pp. 127–143.

Creswell, John W., and Dana L. Miller, 'Determining Validity in Qualitative Inquiry', Theory into Practice (2000), 39(3), pp. 124–130.

Culpepper, Pepper D., 'The Politics of Common Knowledge: Ideas and Institutional Change in Wage Bargaining', *International Organization* (2008), 62(1), pp. 1–33.

Cunningham-Cross, Lindsay, 'Narrating a Discipline: The Search for Innovation in Chinese International Relations' in Nicola Horsburgh, Astrid Nordin, and Shaun Breslin (eds), *Chinese Politics and International Relations: Innovation and Invention* (Routledge: London, 2014).

Dahl, Robert A., 'The Concept of Power', *Behavioral Science* (1957), 2(3), pp. 201–215.

Dalgaard, Carl-Johan, and Henrik Hansen, Finn Tarp, 'On the Empirics of Foreign Aid and Growth', *The Economic Journal* (2004), 114 (496), pp. F191–F216 and F208–F209.

Davies, Martyn, Hannah Edinger, Natasya Tay, and Sanusha Naidu, *How China Delivers Development Assistance to Africa* (Centre for Chinese Studies, University of Stellenbosch, 2008).

Davies, Howard, 'How and When? China's Entry into the Global Financial System', *China Development Forum: China's Global Integration* (London School of Economics, 2011).

Demchak, Chris, 'Organizational and Societal Resilience as a Cybersecurity Strategy', *University of Reading Research Seminar Series* (2010).

Dent, Christopher M., 'Africa and China: A New Kind of Development Partnership' in Christopher M. Dent (ed.), *China and African Development Relations* (Routledge, Contemporary China Series: London, 2011), pp. 3–20.

Deudney, Daniel, and G. John Ikenberry, 'The Nature and Sources of Liberal International Order', *Review of International Studies* (1999), 25(2), pp. 179–196.

Donnelly, Jack, 'Sovereign Inequalities and Hierarchy in Anarchy: American Power and International Society', *European Journal of International Relations* (2006), 12(2), pp. 139–170.

Donnelly, Thomas, 'Rising Powers and the Agents of Change', *National Security Outlook* (American Enterprise Institute for Public Policy: Washington, DC, 2006), pp. 1–6.

Dorussen, Han, Hartmut Lenz, and Spyros Blavoukos, 'Assessing the Reliability and Validity of Expert Interviews', *European Union Politics* (2005), 6(3), pp. 315–337.

Dosi, Giovanni, Luigi Marengo, Andrea Bassanini, and Marco Valente, 'Norms as Emergent Properties of Adaptive Learning: The Case of Economic Routines', *Journal of Evolutionary Economics* (1999), 9, pp. 5–26.

Dowling, John, and Jeffrey Pfeffer, 'Organizational Legitimacy: Social Values and Organizational Behavior', *The Pacific Sociological Review* (1975), 18(1), pp. 122–136.

Easterly, William, 'Can Foreign Aid Buy Growth?', *Journal of Economic Perspectives* (2003), 17(3), pp. 23–48.

Easterly, William, 'Democratic Accountability in Development: The Double Standard', *Social Research* (2011), 77(4), pp. 1075–1104.

Easterly, William, and Claudia R. Williamson, 'Rhetoric versus Reality: The Best and Worst of Aid Agency Practices', *World Development* (2011), 39(11), pp. 1930–1949.

Eckstein, Harry, 'Case Study and Theory in Political Science' in Fred I. Greenstein and Nelson W. Polsby (eds), *Handbook of Political Science Volume 7: Strategies of Inquiry* (Addison-Wesley: Reading, MA, 1975), pp. 79–137.

Economy, Elizabeth C., and A. Segal, 'The G-2 Mirage: Why the US and China Are Not Ready to Upgrade Ties', *Foreign Affairs* (2009), 14, pp. 14–23.

Escobar, Arturo, *Encountering Development: The Making and Unmaking of the Third World* (Princeton University Press: Princeton, 1994), pp. 21–54.

Evans, Gareth, 'The Achievements and Shortcomings of the United Nations', in Ramesh Thakur (ed.), *Past Imperfect, Future Uncertain: The United Nations at Fifty* (Palgrave Macmillan: Basingstoke, 1998).

Finnemore, Martha, 'Norms, Culture, and World Politics: Insights from Sociology's Institutionalism', *International Organization* (1996), 50(2), pp. 325–347.

———, 'Fights About Rules: The Role of Efficacy and Power in Changing Multilateralism', *Review of International Studies* (2005), 31(Supplement S1), pp. 187–206.

Finnemore, Martha, and Kathryn Sikkink, 'International Norm Dynamics and Political Change', *International Organization* (1998), 52(4), pp. 887–917.

Florini, Ann, 'The Evolution of International Norms', *International Studies Quarterly* (1996), 40(3), pp. 363–389.

Fullilove, Micheal, 'China and the United Nations: The Stakeholder Spectrum', *Washington Quarterly* (Summer 2011), pp. 63–85.

Franck, Thomas M., 'The Power of Legitimacy and the Legitimacy of Power: International Law in an Age of Power Disequilibrium', *The American Journal of International Law* (2006), 100(1), pp. 88–106.

Friedberg, Aaron L., 'The Future of U.S–China Relations: Is Conflict Inevitable?' *International Security* (2005), 30(2), pp. 7–45.

Focarelli, Carlo, 'The Responsibility to Protect Doctrine and Humanitarian Intervention: Too Many Ambiguities For a Working Doctrine', *Journal of Conflict and Security Law* (2008), 13(2), pp. 191–213.

Foot, Rosemary, 'Introduction', in Rosemary Foot, John Lewis Gaddis, and Andrew Hurrell (eds), *Order and Justice in International Relations* (Oxford University Press: Oxford, 2003).

———, 'The Responsibility to Protect (R2P) and Its Evolution: Beijing's Influence on Norm Creation in Humanitarian Areas', *St Anthony's International Review* (2011), 6(2), pp. 47–66.

Gat, Azar, 'The Return of Authoritarian Great Powers', *Foreign Affairs* (2007), 86, pp. 59–70.

Gray, Colin S., 'The 21st Century Security Environment and the Future of War', *Parameters*, (Winter 2008–2009), pp. 14–26.

———, 'Why Worry? Sino-American Relations and World Order' FCO Update, available http://ukinchina.fco.gov.uk/en/about-us/working-with-china/Foreign_and_Security_Policy/News_Updates/Why_Worry, Updated 13 March 2012, accessed 2 May 2012.

Geddes, Barbara, 'How the Cases You Choose Affect the Answers You Get: Selection Bias in Comparative Politics', *Political Analysis* (1990), 2(1), pp. 131–150.

Geertz, Clifford, *The Interpretation of Cultures: Selected Essays* (Basic Books: New York, 1973), pp. 3–30.

Goertz, Gary, and Paul F. Diehl, Toward a Theory of International Norms: Some Conceptual and Measurement Issues, *The Journal of Conflict Resolution* (1992), 36(4), pp. 634–664.

Gerring, John, 'Case Selection for Case-Study Analysis: Qualitative and Quantitative Techniques', in Janet M. Box-Steffensmeier, Henry E. Brady, and David Collier (eds), *The Oxford Handbook of Political Methodology* (Oxford University Press: Oxford, 2010), pp. 645–684.

Gilboy, George J., 'The Myth Behind China's Miracle', *Foreign Affairs* (2004), 83, pp. 33–48.

Gilpin, Robert, 'The Theory of Hegemonic War', *Journal of Interdisciplinary History* (1998), 18(4), pp. 591–613.

Glanville, Luke, 'Retaining the Mandate of Heaven: Sovereign Accountability in Ancient China', *Millennium—Journal of International Studies* (2010a), 39(2), pp. 323–343.

Glanville, Luke, 'The Antecedents of 'Sovereignty as Responsibility'', *European Journal of International Relations* (2010b), 17(2), pp. 233–255.

Goldman, Merle, 'Politically-Engaged Intellectuals in the Deng-Jiang Era: A Changing Relationship with the Party-State', *The China Quarterly* (1996), 145, pp. 35–52.

Gore, Charles, 'The Rise and Fall of the Washington Consensus as a Paradigm for Developing Countries', *World Development* (2000), 28(5), pp. 789–804.

Grieco, Joseph M., 'Anarchy and the Limits of Cooperation: A Realist Critique of the Newest Liberal Institutionalism', *International Organization* (1988), 42(3), pp. 485–507.

Grimm, Sven, Rachel Rank, Matthew McDonald, and Elizabeth Schickerling, *Transparency of Chinese Aid: An Analysis of the Published Information on Chinese External Financial Flows* (Publish What you Fund and Centre for Chinese Studies Stellenbosch University, August 2011).

Hall, Ian, 'China Crisis? Indian Strategy, Political Realism, and the Chinese Challenge', *Asian Security* (2012), 8(1), pp. 84–92.

Hamilton, Rebecca, 'The Responsibility to Protect: From Document to Doctrine—But What of implementation?' *Harvard Human Rights Journal* (2006), 19, pp. 289–296.

He, Baogang, 'Chinese Sovereignty: Challenges and Adaptation', *EAI Working Paper*, No. 104, published 23 September 2003.

He, Fan, and Tang Yuehua, 'Determinants of Official Development Assistance in the Post-Cold War Period', *Chinese Journal of International Politics* (2008), 2, pp. 205–227.

Harris, Stuart, 'China's Regional Policies: How Much Hegemony?', *Australian Journal of International Affairs* (2005), 59(4), pp. 482–492.

Hart, Andrew F., and Bruce D. Jones, 'How Do Rising Powers Rise?', *Survival: Global Politics and Strategy* (2010), 52(6), pp. 63–88.

Harvey, William S., 'Strategies for Conducting Elite Interviews', *Qualitative Research* (2011), 11, pp. 432–441.

Harwit E., and D. Clark, 'Shaping the Internet in China: Evolution of Political Control over Network Infrastructure and Content', *Asian Survey* (2001), 43(3), pp. 377–408 and 392–400.

Hasan, Iftekhar, Paul Wachtel, and Mingming Zhouk, 'Institutional Development, Financial Deepening and Economic Growth: Evidence from China', *Journal of Banking and Finance* (2009), 33, pp. 157–170.

He, Yin, China's Changing Policy on UN Peacekeeping, Asia Paper, July 2007.

He, Yin, 'China's Doctrine on UN Peacekeeping', in Cedric De Coning, Chiyuki Aoi, and John Karl Srud (eds), *UN Peacekeeping Doctrine in a New Era: Adapting to Stabilisation, Protection and New Threats* (Routledge: London, 2017).

Heathershaw, John, 'Unpacking the Liberal Peace: The Dividing and Merging of Peacebuilding Discourses', *Millennium—Journal of International Studies* (2008) 36(3), pp. 597–621.

Heinbecker, Paul, 'Kosovo', in David M. Malone (ed.), *The UN Security Council: From the Cold War to the 21st Century* (Lynne Rienner: Boulder, London, 2004), pp. 537–550.

Hirono, Miwa, 'China's Charm Offensive and Peacekeeping: The Lessons of Cambodia—What Now for Sudan?' *International Peacekeeping* (2011), 18(3), pp. 328–343.

Hodgson, Geoffrey M., 'Institutions and Individuals: Interaction and Evolution', *Organisational Studies* (2007), 28(1), pp. 95–116.

Hogg, Michael A., 'A Social Identity Theory of Leadership', *Personality and Social Psychology Review* (2001), 5(3), pp. 184–200.

Holslag, Jonathan, 'Trapped Giant: China's Military Rise', *Adelphi Papers* (2010), 416.

Holslag, Jonathan, 'China's Diplomatic Victory in Darfur' BICCS Background Paper Published 1 August 2007.

Holsti, K.J., 'The Concept of Power in the Study of International Relations', *Background* (1964), 7(4), pp. 179–194.

Huang, Yasheng, 'Why China Will Not Collapse', *Foreign Policy* (1995), 99, pp. 54–68.

Hughes, Christopher, 'Controlling the Internet Architecture Within Greater China', in F. Mengin (ed.), *Cyber China: Reshaping National Identies in the Age of Information* (Palgrave Macmillan: New York, 2004).

Humphrey, John, 'European Development Cooperation in Changing World: Rising Powers and Challenging After the Financial Crisis', EDC Working Paper, available http://www.edc2020.eu/fileadmin/publications/EDC_2020_Working_Paper_No_8_-_November_2010.pdf, accessed 7 December 2011.

Hurd, Ian, 'Legitimacy and Authority in International Politics', *International Organization* (1999), 53(2), pp. 379–408.

Hurrell, Andrew, 'Order and Justice in International Relations: What Is at Stake?' in Rosemary Foot, John Lewis Gaddis, and Andrew Hurrell (eds), *Order and Justice in International Relations* (Oxford University Press: Oxford, 2003).

Hurrell, Andrew, 'Power, Institutions, and the Production of Inequality', in M. Barnett and R. Duvall (eds), *Power in Global Governance* (Cambridge University Press: Cambridge, 2004).

———, 'Hegemony, Liberalism and Global Order: What Space for Would-Be Great Powers?' *International Affairs* (2006), 82(1), pp. 1–19.

Ikenberry, G. John, 'The Rise of China and the Future of the West: Can the Liberal System Survive?' *Foreign Affairs* (2008), 87(1), pp. 23–37.

———, 'Liberal Internationalism 3.0: America and the Dilemmas of the Liberal World Order', *Perspectives on Politics* (2009), 7(1), pp. 71–87.

Ikenberry, G. John, and Daniel Deudney, 'The Myth of the Autocratic Revival: Why Liberal Democracy Will Prevail', *Foreign Affairs* (2009), 88, pp. 77–93.

Inglehart, Ronald, and Christian Welzel, 'How Development Leads to Democracy: What We Know About Modernisation', *Foreign Affairs* (2009), 88(2), pp. 33–48.

International Crisis Group, 'China's Growing Role in UN Peacekeeping' (Beijing, New York, Brussels, 2009).

James, Alan, 'Law and Order in International Society', in Alan James (ed.), *The Bases of International Order* (Oxford University Press: London, 1973).

Johnston, Alastair Iain, 'Chapter 3: International Structures and Chinese Foreign Policy', in Samuel S. Kim (ed.), *China and the World: Chinese Foreign Policy Faces the New Millennium* (Westview Press: Boulder, 1998).

———, 'Treating International Institutions as Social Environments', *International Studies Quarterly* (2001), 45(4), pp. 487–515.

———, 'Is China a Status Quo Power?' *International Security* (2003) 27(4), pp. 5–56.

Johnstone, Ian, 'Security Council Deliberations: The Power of the Better Argument', *European Journal of International Law* (2003), 14 (3), pp. 437–480.

Jones, Catherine, 'Understanding Multiple and Competing Roles: China's Roles in International Order', Unpublished Paper, Presented at ACPS Kings College London, June 2011.

Jones Catherine, 'The Party's over for the Use of Sanctions', Unpublished Conference Paper PSA Conference, March 2013.

Jones, David Martin, and Michael L.R. Smith, 'Making Process, Not Progress: ASEAN and the Evolving East Asian Regional Order', *International Security* (2007), 32(1), pp. 148–184.

Jorgensen, Dale, 'China's Economy', *HPAIR Harvard Conference 2010* (Harvard: Cambridge, MA, 2010).

Kahn, Paul W., 'American Hegemony and the International Law: Speaking Law to Power: Popular Sovereignty, Human Rights and the New International Order', *Chicago Journal of International Law* (Spring 2000), 1, pp. 1–18.

Kaplan, Robert D., 'The Geography of Chinese Power', *Foreign Affairs* (2010), 89(3).

Katasumata, Hiro, 'Establishment of the Asean Regional Forum: Constructing a 'Talking Shop' or a 'Norm Brewery'?' *Pacific Review* (2006), 19(2), pp. 181–198.

———, 'Mimetic Adoption and Norm Diffusion: 'Western' Security Cooperation in Southeast Asia?' *Review of International Studies* (2011), 37, pp. 557–576.

Kennedy, Paul M. *The Rise and Fall of the Great Powers: Economic Change and Military Conflict from 1500 to 2000* (Fontana: London, 1989).

Kennedy, Scott, 'The Myth of the Beijing Consensus', *Journal of Conetmporary China* (2010), 19(65), pp. 461–477.

Kim, Woosang, 'Power Transitions and Great Power War from Westphalia to Waterloo', *World Politics* (1992), 45(1), pp. 153–172.

Kimura, Hidemi, Yuko Mori, and Yasuyki Sawada, 'Aid Proliferation and Economic Growth: A Cross-Country Analysis', *World Development* (2012), 40(1), pp. 1–10.

Kjøllesdal, Kirtian, and Anne Welle-Strand, 'Foreign Aid Strategies: China Taking Over?' *Asian Social Science* (2010), 6(10), pp. 7–8.

Kleine-Ahlbrandt, Stephanie, and Andrew Small, 'China's New Dictatorship Diplomacy: Is Beijing Parting with Pariahs?' *Foreign Affairs* (2008), 87(1), pp. 38–56.

Koh, Harold Hongju, 'Why Do States Comply with International Law?', *Yale Law Journal* (1997), 106(8), pp. 2599–2659.

Kolb, Andreas S., 'The Responsibility to Protect (R2P) and the Responsibility While Protecting (RwP): Friends or Foes?' Global Governance Institute CGI Analysis Paper 6 (2012).

Kosack, Stephen, 'Effective Aid: How Democracy Allows Development Aid to Improve the Quality of Life', *World Development* (2003), 31(1), pp. 1–22.

Kratochwil, Friedrich, and John Gerard Ruggie, 'International Organization: A State of the Art on an Art of the State', *International Organization* (1986), 40(4), pp. 753–775.

Krisch, Nico, 'International Law in Times of Hegemony: Unequal Power and the Shaping of the International Legal Order', *European Journal of International Law* (2005), 16(3), pp. 369–408.

Kristensen, Peter Marcus, '"You Need to Do Something That the Westerners Cannot Understand"—The Innovation of a Chinese School of IR', Paper Presented at China Postgraduate Network Edinburgh, June 2012.

Kristensen, Peter Marcus, and Ras Tind Nielsen, 'Constructing a Chinese School of International Relations: A Sociological Approach to Intellectual Innovation', *International Political Sociology* (2013), 7(1), pp.19–40.

Lanteigne, Marc, 'A Change in Perspective: China's Engagement in East Timor UN Peacekeeping Operations', *International Peacekeeping* (2011), 18(3), pp. 313–327.

Lancaster, Carol, 'The Chinese Aid System', *The Center for Global Development Essay*, June 2007, available http://www.cgdev.org, accessed 1 March 2012.

Large, Daniel, 'China's Sudan Engagement: Changing Northern and Southern Political Trajectories in Peace and War', *China Quarterly* (2009), 199, pp. 610–626.

Lau, H., 'Rethinking the Persistent Objector Doctrine in International Human Rights Law', *Chicago Journal of International Law* (2005–2006), 6(1), pp. 495–510.

Layne, Christopher, 'The Waning of U.S. Hegemony—Myth or Reality? A Review Essay', *International Security* (2009), 34(1), pp. 147–172.

Lee, Pak K., Gerald Chan, and Lai-Ha Chan, 'China in Darfur: Rule-Makers or Rule-Taker', *Review of International Studies* (2011), 38(2), pp. 423–444.

Legro, Jeffrey W., 'What China Will Want: The Future Intentions of a Rising Power', *Perspectives on Politics* (2007), 5(3), pp. 515–534.

Lei, Zhao, 'Two Pillars of China's Global Peace Engagement Strategy: UN Peacekeeping and International Peacebuilding', *International Peacekeeping* (2011), 18(3), pp. 344–363.

Levy, Jack S., 'Presidential Address: Case Studies: Types, Designs and Logics of Inference', *Conflict Management and Peace Research* (2008), 25, pp. 1–18.

Li, Cheng, 'China's Team of Rivals', *Foreign Policy* (2009), 171, pp. 88–89.

Lindner, Johannes, 'Institutional Stability and Change: Two Sides of the Same Coin', *Journal of European Public Policy* (2003), 10(6), pp. 912–935.

Liu, Tiewa, 'China and the Responsibility to Protect: Maintenance and Change of Its Policy for Intervention', *The Pacific Review* (2012), 25(1), pp. 153–173.

Liu, Tiewa, and Haibin Zhang, 'Debates in China about the Responsibility to Protect as a Developing International Norms: A General Assessment', *Conflict Security and Development* (2014), 14(4), pp. 403–427.

Lowe, Vaughan, 'Chapter 10: The Politics of Law-Making: Are the Method and Character of Norm Creation Changing?' in Michael Byers (ed.), *The Role of Law in International Politics: Essays in International Relations and International Law* (Oxford University Press: Oxford, 2000), pp. 207–227.

Mamdani, Mahmood, 'Responsibility to Protect or Right to Punish', *Journal of Intervention and Statebuilding* (2010), 4(1), pp. 53–67.

Mahmoud, Yahia Mohamed, 'Chinese Foreign Aid: The Tale of Foreign Enterprise' in Jens Stilhoff Sörensen (ed.), *Challenging the Aid Paradigm: Western Currents and Asian Alternatives* (Palgrave Macmillan: Basingstoke, 2010), pp. 186–213.

Malone, David, 'The UN Security Council and the Post-Cold War World: 1987–1997', *Security Dialogue* (1997), 28(4), pp. 393–408.

March, J.G., and J.P. Olsen, 'The Logic of Appropriateness', http://www.arena.uio.no/publications/papers/wp04_9.pdf, Working Paper WP 04/09, last accessed 23 April 2013.

Mawdsley, Emma, 'China and Africa: Emerging Challenges to the Geographies of Power', *Geography Compass* (2007), 1(3), pp. 405–421.

Mearsheimer, John J., 'China's Unpeaceful Rise', *Current History* (2006) 105(690), pp. 160–162.

Mearsheimer, John, and Stephen Walt, 'The Israeli Lobby', *Journal of Palestine Studies* (2006), 35(3), pp. 83–105.

Medeiros, Evan S., 'Strategic Hedging and the Future of Asia-Pacific Stability', *The Washington Quarterly* (2005), 29(1), pp. 145–167.

Miller, K 'Coping with China's Financial Power', *Foreign Affairs* (2010), 89, pp. 96–109.

Minoiu, Carmelia, and Sanjay G. Reddy, 'Development Aid and Economic Growth: A Positive Long-Run Relation', *The Quarterly Review of Economics and Finance* (2010), 50, pp. 27–39.

Monteiro, Nuno P. 'Unrest Assured: Why Unipolarity Is Not Peaceful' *International Security* (Winter 2011/2012), 36(3), pp. 9–40.

Morada, Noel M. 'The ASEAN Charter and the Promotion of R2P and Southeast Asia: Challenges and Constraints', *Global Responsibility to Protect*, 1 (2009), pp. 185–207.

Mosher, Steven, 'Does the PRC Have a Grand Strategy of Hegemony?' http://www.au.af.mil/au/awc/awcgate/congress/mos021406.pdf, accessed 1 March 2010.

Murphy, Jr., Cornelius F. 'The Grotian Vision of World Order', *The American Journal of International Law* (1982), 76(3), pp. 477–498.

Naim, Moises, 'Washington Consensus or Washington Confusion?', *Foreign Policy*, (Spring 2000), pp. 87–103.

Nau, Henry R., 'Why 'the Rise and Fall of Great Powers' Was Wrong', *Review of International Studies* (2001), 27(4), pp. 579–592.

Naughton, Barry, 'China's Distinctive System Can It Be a Model for Others?' *Journal of Contemporary China* (2010), 19(65), pp. 437–460.
Neanidis, Kyriakos C., and Varvarigos Dimitrios, 'The Allocation of Volatile Aid and Economic Growth: Theory and Evidence', *European Journal of Political Economy*, (2009), 25, pp. 447–462.
Northedge, F.S., 'Order and Change in International Society', in Alan James (ed.), *The Bases of International Order* (Oxford University Press: London, 1973), pp. 1–23.
Ocampo, Jose Antonio, Shari Spiegel, and Joseph E. Stiglitz, 'Capital Market Liberalization and Development', in Jose Antonio Ocampo, and Joseph E. Stiglitz (eds), *Capital Market Liberalisation and Development* (Oxford University Press: Oxford, 2008).
O'Hanlon, Michael, 'Why China Cannot Conquer Taiwan', *International Security* (2000), 25(2), pp. 51–86.
O'Neill, Kate, Jörg Balsiger, and Stacy D. Van Deveer, 'Actors, Norms, and Impact: Recent International Influence of the Agent-Structure Debate' *Annual Review of Political Science* (2004), 7, pp. 149–175.
Pape, Robert A., 'The True Worth of Air Power',*Foreign Affairs* (2004), 83(2), pp. 116–130.
Peerenboom, Randall, 'The Fire-Breathing Dragon and the Cute, Cuddly Panda: The Implication of China's Rise for Developing Countries, Human Rights, and Geopolitical Stability', *Chicago Journal of International Law* (2006), 7(1), pp. 17–50.
Prantl, Jochen, 'Informal Groups of States and the UN Security Council, *International Organization* (2005), 59, pp. 559–592.
Publish What You Fund, 'Chinese Aid More Transparent than You Think', Report Available http://www.publishwhatyoufund.org/news/2011/09/new-report-chinese-aid-more-transparent-you-think/, accessed 2 March 2012.
Putnam, Robert D., 'Diplomacy and Domestic Politics: The Logic of Two-Level Games', *International Organization* (1988), 42(3), pp. 427–460.
Raine, Sarah, and International Institute for Strategic Studies, *China's African Challenges* (Adelphi Papers; Abingdon: Routledge for International Institute for Strategic Studies, 2009).
Rajan, Raghuram G., and Arvind Subramanian, 'Aid and Growth: Cross-Country Evidence Really ShowCross-Country Evidence Really Showtry Evidence Really Show?' *The Review of Economics and Statistics* (2008), 90(4), pp. 643–665.
Reilly, James, 'A Norm-Maker or Norm-Taker? Chinese Aid in Southeast Asia', *Journal of Contemporary China*, 21(73), pp. 71–91.
Reilly, James, and Bates Gill, 'Sovereignty, Intervention and Peacekeeping: The View from Beijing', *Survival* (2000), 42(3), pp. 41–60.

Reisen, Helmut, and Sokhna Ndoye, *Prudent Versus Imprudent Lending to Africa: From Debt Relief to Emerging Lenders* (OECD Development Centre Working Paper No. 268, February 2008).

Reus-Smit, C., 'Human Rights and the Social Construction of Sovereignty', *Review of International Studies* (2001), 27(4), pp. 519–538.

Rice, Condolezza, 'Campaign 2000: Promoting the National Interest', *Foreign Affairs* (2000), 79(1), pp. 45–63.

Richardson, Courtney, 'A Responsible Power? China and the UN Peacekeeping Regime', *International Peacekeeping* (2011), 18(3), pp. 286–297.

Reilly, James, and Bates Gill, 'Sovereignty, Intervention and Peacekeeping: The View from Beijing', *Survival* (2000), 42(3), pp. 41–60.

Ringmar, Erik, 'The Recongnition Game: Soviet Russia Against the West', *Cooperation and Conflict* (2002), 37(2), pp. 115–136.

Risse, Thomas, '"Let's Argue!": Communicative Action in World Politics', *International Organization* (2000), 54(1), pp. 1–39.

Rogers, Phillippe D., 'China and United Nations Peacekeeping Operations', *Naval War College Review* (2007), 60(2), pp. 72–93.

Rothman, Kenneth J., and Sander Greenland, 'Causation and Casual Inference' in Lippincott (ed.), *Epidemiology Studies: In Modern Epidemiology*, pp. 7–28 and 8–9.

Rosegrance, Richard, 'Power and International Relations: The Rise of China and Its Effects', *International Studies Perspectives* (2006), 7, pp. 31–35.

Ross, Robert S., 'Beijing as a Conservative Power', *Foreign Affairs* (1997), 76(2).

———, 'Comparative Deterrence: The Taiwan Strait and the Korean Penninsula', in Johnston Alastair Iain and R.S. Ross (eds), *New Directions in the Study of China's Foreign Policy* (Stanford University Press: Stanford, 2006), pp. 13–49.

Roy, Denny, 'Singapore, China, and the 'Soft Authoritarian' Challenge', *Asian Survey* (1994), 34(3), pp. 231–242.

Roy, Denny. 'The "China Threat" Issue: Major Arguments', *Asian Survey* (1996), 36(8), pp. 758–771.

RSIS Conference on 'Regional Consultation on the Responsibility to Protect, report published by NTS RSIS, Singapore 2010, available http://www.rsis.edu.sg/publications/conference_reports/RtoP_240810.pdf, last accessed 24 April 2013.

Ruggie, John Gerard, 'International Regimes, Transactions, and Change: Embedded Liberalism in the Postwar Economic Order', *International Organization* (1982), 36(2), pp. 379–415.

Saferworld, 'Sovereignty and Non-interference', *Saferworld, Seminar Report: China and South Sudan: New Perspectives on Development and Conflict Prevention*, 30 May 2012, available, http://www.saferworld.org.uk/

downloads/pubdocs/China%20and%20South%20Sudan%20Seminar%20 Report%20.pdf, accessed 14 February 2013.
Saferworld, *Saferworld Briefing: China and South Sudan*, August 2012, available http://www.saferworld.org.uk/downloads/pubdocs/China-South%20 Sudan%20briefing%20English.pdf, accessed 14 February 2013.
Saidi, Myriam Dahman, and Christina Wolf, Recalibrating Development Cooperation: How Can African Countries Benefit from Emerging Partners? Working Paper No. 302 (OECD Development Centre: Paris, France, 2011), pp. 13–22.
Sautman, Barry, and Yan Hairong, 'Friends and Interests: China's Distinctive Links with Africa', *African Studies Review* (2007), 50(3), pp. 75–114.
Scents, Sonya, and Shaun Breslin, *China and the International Human Rights System* (Royal Institute of International Affairs, Chatham House: London, 2012).
Schroeder, Paul W., 'The 19th-Century International System: Changes in the Structure', *World Politics* (1986), 39(1), pp. 1–26.
Schroeder, Paul W., 'The New World Order: A Historical Perspective', *ACDIS Occasional Paper* (1994).
Segal, Gerald, 'Does China Matter?' *Foreign Affairs* (1999), 78, pp. 24–36.
Sending, Ole Jacob, 'Constitution, Choice and Change: Problems with the 'Logic of Appropriateness' and Its Use in Constructivist Theory', *European Journal of International Relations* (2002), 8(4), pp. 443–470.
Serra, Narcis, Shari Spiegel, and Joseph E. Stiglitz, 'Introduction: From the Washington Consensus Towards a New Global Governance', in Narcis Serra, and Joseph E. Stiglitz (eds), *The Washington Consensus Reconsidered: Towards a New Global Governance* (Oxford University Press: Oxford, 2008).
Monica, Serrano, 'Implementing the Responsibility to Protect: The Power of R2P Talk', *Global Responsibility to Protect* (2010), 2, pp. 167–177.
Shafaeddin, S.M., 'Is China's Accession to the WTO Threatening the Exports of Developing Countries?' *China Economic Review* (2004), 15, pp. 109–144.
Shih, Chih-Yu, 'Breeding a Reluctant Dragon: Can China Rise into Partnership and Away from Antagonism?' *Review of International Studies* (2005), 31(4), pp. 755–774.
Shannon, Vaughan P., 'Norms Are What States Make of Them: The Political Psychology of Norm Violation', *International Studies Quarterly* (2000), 44(2), pp. 293–316.
Shapcott, Richard, 'Solidarism and After: Global Governance, International Society and the Normative 'Turn' in International Relations', *Pacific Review* (2000) 12(2), pp. 147–165.
Slaughter, Anne-Marie, 'The Real New World Order', *Foreign Affairs* (1997), 76(3), pp. 183–197.

Simpson, Gerry, 'Two Liberalisms', *European Journal of International Law,* 12/3 (June 1, 2001), 537–572.

Smith, Steve, 'Is the Truth out There? Eight Questions about International Order', in John A. Hall and T. V. Paul (eds), *International Order and the Future of World Politics* (Cambridge University Press: Cambridge, 1999).

Stähle, Stefan, 'China's Shifting Attitutde to UN Peacekeeping Operations', *China Quarterly* (2008), 195, pp. 631–655.

Stahn, Carsten, 'Responsibility to Protect: Political Rhetoric or Emerging Legal Norm?' *The American Journal of International Law* (2007), 101(1), pp. 99–120.

Stets, Jan E., and Peter J. Burke, 'Identity Theory and Social Identity Theory', *Social Psychology Quarterly* (2000), 63(3), pp. 224–237 and 226–227.

Shi, Yinhong, Statement at RCUNIO Conference on R2P at Beijing University, March 2012, Conference Report.

Sutter, Robert G., 'China's Rise in Asia—Promises, Prospects and Implications for the United States' (Occasional Paper Series: Asian Centre for Security Studies, 2005).

Suzuki, Shogo, 'Why Does China Participate in Intrusive Peacekeeping? Understanding Paternalistic Chinese Discourses on Development and Intervention', *International Peacekeeping* (2011), 18(3), pp. 271–285.

Stein, Arthur A., 'The Politics of Linkage', *World Politics* (1980), 33(1), pp. 62–81.

Stein, T.L., 'The Approach of the Different Drummer: The Principle of the Persistent Objector in International Law', *Harvard International Law Journal* (1985), 26(2), pp. 457–482.

Steidlmeier, P., 'Gift Giving, Bribery and Corruption: Ethical Management of Business Relationships in China', *Journal of Business Ethics* (1999), 20, pp. 121–132.

Synder, Quddus Z., Integrating Rising Powers: Liberal Systemic Theory and the Mechanism of Competition', *Review of International Studies*, published online 30 November 2011, pp. 1–23.

Tammen, Ronald L., and Jacek Kugler, 'Power Transition and China–US Conflicts', *Chinese Journal of International Politics* (2006), 1, pp. 35–55.

Tan-Mullins, May, and Giles Mohan, Marcus Power, 'Redefining 'Aid' in the China–Africa Context', *Development and Change* (2010), 41(5), pp. 857–881.

Tansey, Oisín, 'Process Tracing and Elite Interviewing: A Case for Non-Probability Sampling', *PS: Political Science and Politics* (2007), 40(4), pp. 765–772 and 766–768.

Teitt, Sarah, 'China and the Responsibility to Protect', *Asia-Pacific Center on R2P*, 19 December 2008, http://responsibilitytoprotect.org/files/China_and_R2P%5B1%5D.pdf, accessed 22 April 2013.

Teitt, Sarah, 'The Responsibility to Protect and China's Peacekeeping Policy', *International Peacekeeping* (2011), 18(3), pp. 298–312.

Tesón, Fernando R., 'The Liberal Case for Humanitarian Intervention', in J.L. Holzgrefe and Robert O. Keohane (eds), *Humanitarian Intervention: Ethical, Legal, and Political Dilemmas* (Cambridge University Press: Cambridge, 2003), pp. 93–129.

Thakur, Ramesh (2011), The United Nations in Global Governance: Rebalancing Multilateralism for Current and Future Challenges', Paper Presented at UN General Assembly 65th Session Thematic Debate on the United Nations and Global Governance, available http://www.un.org/en/ga/president/65/initiatives/GlobalGovernance/Thakur_GA_Thematic_Debate_on_UN_in_GG.pdf, accessed 19 July 2012.

Thakur, Ramesh, and Thomas G. Weiss, 'R2P: From Idea to Norm—and Action?' *Global Responsibility to Protect* (2009), 1, pp. 22–53.

Tuinstra, F., 'Puzzling Contradictions of China's Internet Journalism', *Neiman Reports* (Harvard University Press: Cambridge, 2006).

Van Evera Stephen, *Guide to Methods for Students of Political Science*, (Cornell University Press: Ithaca and London), pp. 48–88.

Ward, Adam, 'Closing Argument: Beijing Calling',*Survival* (2009), 51(6), pp. 249–252.

Wei, Chen, and Liu Jinju (2005), 'Future Population Trends in China: 2005–2050', Working Paper 191, COPS, Monash University, September 2009, available http://www.monash.edu.au/policy/ftp/workpapr/g-191.pdf, accessed 17 July 2012.

Weiner, Antje, 'Contested Compliance: Interventions on the Normative Structure of World Politics', *European Journal of International Relations* (2004), 10(2), pp. 189–234.

Weiss, Thomas G., Ramesh Thakur, Mary Ellen O'Connell, Aidan Hehir, Alex J. Bellamy, David Chandler, Rodger Shanahan, Rachel Gerber, Abiodun Williams, and Gareth Evans, The Responsibility to Protect: Challenges and opportunities in the light of the Libyan Intervention, e-International Relations, November 2011, available http://www.e-ir.info/wp-content/uploads/R2P.pdf, accessed 8 February 2013.

Weiss, Thomas, 'R2P after 9/11 and the World Summit' *Wisconsin International Law Journal*, 24(3), available http://hosted.law.wisc.edu/wordpress/wilj/files/2012/02/weiss.pdf, accessed 8 February 2013.

Welsh, Jennifer, Carolin Thielking, and S. Neil Macfarlane, 'The Responsibility to Protect: Assessing the Report of the International Commission on Intervention Amd State Sovereignty', *International Journal* (2002), 57, pp. 489–512.

Welsh, Jennifer M., 'From Right to Responsibility: Humanitarian Intervention and International Society', *Global Governance* (2002), 8, pp. 503–521.

———, 'Turning Words into Deeds: But, What of Implementation?' *Global Responsibility to Protect* (2010), 2(1–2), pp. 149–154.
Wendt, Alexander, 'Constructing International Politics', *International Security* (1995), 20(1), pp. 71–81.
———, 'Why the World State Is Inevitable', *European Journal of International Relations* (2003), 9(3), pp. 491–542.
White, Hugh, 'The Limits to Optimism: Australia and the Rise of China', *Australian Journal of International Affairs* (2005), 59(4), pp. 469–481.
Williamson, John, 'What Washington Means by Policy Reform', in John Williamson (eds), *Latin American Adjustment: How Much Has Happened?* (Institute Penguin: London, 2002).
Williamson, John, 'What Washington Means by Policy Reform' in John Williamson (eds), *Latin American Adjustment: How Much Has Happened?* (Institute for International Economics: Washington, DC, 1990), pp. 7–33.
Williamson, John, 'Is the "Beijing Consensus" Now Dominant?' *Special Essay: Asia Policy* (2012), 13, pp. 1–16.
Wissenbach, Uwe, 'China–Africa Relations and the European Union: Ideology, Conditionality, *Realpolitick* and What Is New in South-South Co-operation', in Christopher M. Dent, (ed.), China and Africa Development Relations (Routledge Contemporary China Series, Routledge: Abingdon, 2011), pp. 21–41.
Wuthnow, Joel, 'China and the Processes of Cooperation in Un Security Council Deliberations', *Chinese Journal of International Politics* (2010), 3(1), pp. 55–77.
Yan, Xuetong, 'The Rise of China and Its Power Status', *Chinese Journal of International Politics* (2006), 1(1), pp. 5–33.
———, 'International Leadership and Norm Evolution', Journal of Chinese International Relations (2011), 4(3), pp. 233–264.
Yang, Dali L., 'China in 2002: Leadership Transition and the Political Economy of Governance', *Asian Survey* (2003), 43(1), pp. 25–40.
Yaqing, Qin, 'Why Is There No Chinese International Relations Theory?' in Buzan, and Acharya (eds), *Non-Western International Relations Theory: Perspectives on and Beyond Asia.*
Yao, Yang (2010), 'The End of the Beijing Consensus: Can China's Model of Authoritarian Growth Survive?' *Foreign Affairs*, Jan/Feb (2010)[online].
Zafar, Ali, 'The Growing Relationship Between China and Sub-Saharan Africa: Macroeconomic, Trade, Investment, and Aid Links', *World Bank Research Observer* (2007), 22(1), pp. 103–130.
Zha, Daojiong, 'Comment: Can China Rise?' *Review of International Studies* (2005), 31(4), pp. 775–785.

Zhao, Suisheng, 'The China Model: Can It Replace the Western Model of Modernization?' *Journal of Contemporary China* (2010), 19(65), pp. 419–436.
Zheng, Bijian, 'China's "Peaceful Rise" To Great-Power Status', available http://www.irchina.org/en/news/view.asp?id=397, accessed 25 November 2009.
Zhang, Feng, 'The Rise of Chinese Exceptionalism in International Relations', *European Journal of International Relations* (Online, October 2011).
———, 'Rethinking China's Grand Strategy: Beijing's Evolving National Interests and Strategic Ideas in the Reform Era', *International Politics* (2012), 49, pp. 318–345.
Zhenxi, Jiang, Statement at RCUNIO Conference on R2P at Beijing University, March 2012, Conference Report.

INDEX

A
Africa, 18, 137, 153, 164, 171, 192, 198, 200, 202–205, 207, 208, 210–213, 217, 219–223, 225, 229–232, 234, 236–243, 251
  China-African relations, 233
  FOCAC, 201–205, 229–231, 233
Agency, 2, 4–7, 15–18, 45, 46, 52, 54, 58, 60, 66, 70, 72, 74, 77, 78, 80, 87–89, 116, 123, 128–130, 137, 139, 148, 152, 162, 177, 190, 200, 203, 210, 215, 219, 229, 235, 246, 247, 253–256, 258
  ad-hoc objection, 16, 69, 72, 116, 177, 245, 254, 256
  norm entrepreneur, 18, 70, 76, 203, 229, 245
  persistent objection, 16, 69, 72, 177, 254, 258
Aid, 18, 34, 72, 100, 127, 137, 142, 145, 157, 186–215, 217–243, 247–251, 255, 256, 258, 263
  definitions, 189, 190, 196, 198, 200; Chinese, 200; OECD-DAC, 197, 199, 207, 208, 210
  effectiveness, 18, 34, 189–193, 207, 208, 224, 225, 232–234, 248
  interpretations, 100, 101, 118, 203, 245
  transparency, 36, 190, 207, 251
Aristotle, 16, 24
  causation (Aristotlean), 57, 253
  four causes, 16
Asian Investment Infrastructure Bank (AIIB), 194, 217, 249, 258

B
Beijing Consensus/China Model, 185, 186, 194–196, 198, 212, 216–218, 222, 237, 246

C
Catalyst, 186, 193, 195, 210, 248, 258, 262

INDEX

Challenge, 1–4, 6–8, 11–18, 20, 32–34, 45, 47–49, 52, 56–59, 61, 64–66, 68, 70–73, 75, 77–80, 83–88, 102, 112, 115, 116, 124, 126, 128, 139, 140, 142–146, 149, 151, 152, 154, 155, 157, 159, 160, 162, 177, 180, 181, 186–188, 190, 192, 194, 196, 199, 200, 210–212, 216, 223–228, 231, 232, 235, 236, 245–251, 253–262

China, 1–24, 27, 28, 31, 33–43, 45, 52, 54–59, 66, 72, 77, 78, 83–88, 94, 95, 100, 104, 108, 111–139, 143–163, 167–174, 177–182, 185–190, 192–212, 215–243, 245–251, 253–264

D

Development, 2, 3, 7, 8, 12, 18, 20, 24, 29, 30, 32, 34, 36, 37, 46, 47, 51, 56, 59, 65, 76, 78, 84, 99, 106, 110, 114, 117, 119, 120, 125, 131, 136, 137, 148, 149, 151, 163, 164, 179, 182, 185–199, 201–234, 236–243, 245–251, 257–259, 261
- definition, 189, 198–201
- fragmentation of donors, 191, 208
- liberal, 2, 3, 7, 8, 83, 102, 106, 131, 178, 179, 185–187, 189, 193, 203, 211, 230, 245, 246, 250, 251, 257, 261, 262
- OECD-DAC, 197, 199, 207–211

F

Forum on China-Africa Cooperation (FOCAC), 187, 201–206, 219, 229–231, 233, 248, 255, 257, 258

G

Global, 1–3, 7, 12, 19, 22–24, 27, 31, 33, 34, 37–40, 43, 53, 54, 56, 78, 89, 92, 109, 110, 128, 131, 132, 135, 137, 148, 163–167, 169–172, 182, 186, 200, 210, 213, 216, 217, 219, 222, 229, 232, 234, 236, 239–243, 246, 247, 263

H

Hume
- causation, 16
- Humean, 16, 57

I

Interference, 116, 118, 128–130, 136, 160, 161, 172, 178, 181, 194, 195, 201, 204, 206, 223, 231

Intervention, 2, 3, 17, 39, 66, 74, 102, 105, 108, 109, 111, 112, 115, 116, 119, 121, 123–126, 128–130, 133–136, 138, 140, 143, 146–149, 153, 154, 156, 159–165, 167–170, 177–179, 182, 204, 257

L

Legitimacy, 17, 29, 31, 32, 35, 38, 46–49, 52, 60, 61, 67, 73, 74, 77–82, 85, 86, 91–94, 100, 104, 109, 115, 118, 126, 137, 139, 145, 151, 162, 192, 199, 204, 210, 240, 247, 249, 259, 260, 262, 263

Liberal, 1, 3–5, 7, 8, 10, 18, 46, 62, 74, 99, 100, 103, 105, 106, 130, 178, 180, 181, 187, 188, 250, 253, 255, 260–262

Liberalism, 4, 8, 9, 15, 18, 23, 24, 39, 40, 43, 53, 56, 62, 68, 101, 103, 131, 180, 187, 188, 247, 260–263
Logic of appropriateness, 48, 55, 84, 95, 263
Logic of consequences, 4, 48, 85, 99, 117, 121, 126, 180, 188

N

Norms/normative, 1–5, 7, 9, 14, 15, 18, 44, 46, 48, 49, 58–65, 67, 70, 73, 74, 77, 79, 80, 82, 85–87, 101, 106, 147, 177, 179, 185, 193, 246, 253, 256, 259–262
  challenge, 3, 4, 6, 17, 57–59, 64, 65, 71, 88, 255
  change, 4, 12, 27, 59–61, 66–68, 100, 256, 258, 259
  interstitial, 60, 62, 65, 87, 146, 259, 261
  intersubjective, 61
  liberal, 2, 3, 6, 8, 9, 17, 86, 88, 146, 246, 253
  life cycle, 63, 64, 66, 67, 70, 84, 179
  meta, 60, 62, 64, 87, 106, 146, 259, 261
  primary, 62, 65

O

Order, 1–24, 27, 29–35, 37–40, 43–60, 62–65, 68, 70–77, 79–88, 91, 94, 99–102, 104, 106–108, 110–112, 116, 127, 129, 135, 137, 140, 141, 143, 144, 146, 150, 151, 156, 161, 169, 170, 177, 178, 180–182, 185–189, 191, 199, 202–207, 210, 211, 228, 231, 232, 234, 246, 247, 249–251, 253–255, 257–263
  concept, 27, 31, 32, 44, 104, 140, 141, 143, 161, 186, 187
  construction, 14, 43, 46, 48, 52, 53, 62, 66, 82, 84, 86
  frame of mind, 44, 59, 156, 261, 262
  ideas, 12, 14, 15, 18, 46, 47, 49–51, 53, 186, 249, 259
  inter-subjective, 43, 46, 60, 65, 82, 107
  normative/norms, 11, 13, 14, 34, 45–47, 58, 81, 85, 146
  regional, 12, 34, 127–129, 156, 161
  social, 8, 14, 16, 28, 31–34, 37, 45, 46, 48, 50–53, 57, 59, 60, 62, 65, 66, 71–73, 81, 82, 102, 254, 259
  structure, 43, 44, 50, 58, 59, 67, 71, 87, 205, 250, 259
  teleology, 9, 43, 45, 210

P

Peace enforcement. *See* Peacekeeping
Peacekeeping, 17, 74, 88, 102, 111, 112, 114–121, 124–138, 144, 154, 158, 160, 161, 165, 167, 168, 170, 174, 182, 205, 256
Power, 1, 2, 5, 7–14, 16–24, 27–40, 43, 45–48, 51–56, 61, 64, 71, 72, 77, 78, 80–87, 89, 91–95, 104, 111, 128, 129, 134, 135, 139, 158, 162, 163, 166, 180, 182, 195, 213, 214, 217, 219, 222, 229, 239, 243, 246, 247, 249, 250, 254, 256, 258, 259, 263
  authority, 28, 29, 31–33, 47, 51, 52, 64, 72, 204, 260, 263

coercion, 30, 64, 159, 247
context, 17, 27–29, 31, 32, 45, 47, 52, 61, 76, 77, 80, 82, 83, 104, 263
definition, 14, 27, 28, 31
dimensions of, 13, 28, 34, 45, 46, 64, 111
elements of, 16, 28, 30, 33, 43, 47, 63, 72, 80, 83, 159, 163, 180, 248, 259
legitimate use, 29, 61, 64, 71, 72, 81, 115
material, 7, 11, 14, 16, 28–33, 46–48, 61
normative, 5, 11, 13–15, 17, 27–34, 45–48, 52, 59, 61, 80, 82, 84, 85, 87, 111, 205, 249, 250, 259
relational, 2, 27, 28, 30, 31
social, 8, 11, 14, 28, 29, 31–34, 37, 46, 48, 71, 72, 84, 195, 254

R

Recognition, 31–36, 39, 79, 81, 89, 99, 101–106, 111, 112, 146, 147, 156, 160, 188, 228–231, 235, 236, 256

as a great power, 31–36, 111
as a leader, 48
as a legitimate actor, 262
Responsibility to Protect (R2P), 14, 17, 22, 64, 78, 88, 102, 109, 110, 112, 114, 126, 127, 131, 136, 139–142, 147–150, 161, 163–172, 174, 181
responsibility while protecting, 121, 142
Responsible Protection (RP), 139

U

United Nations (UN), 3, 5, 89, 107, 117, 122, 125, 132–135, 157, 163, 167, 168, 170, 174, 186
General Assembly, 141, 148, 149
Secretary General, 120, 140–142, 151
Security Council, 5, 32, 34, 122, 125

W

Washington Consensus (WC), 185, 187–193, 195, 196, 212, 213, 216, 255, 257

CPSIA information can be obtained
at www.ICGtesting.com
Printed in the USA
LVHW08*1914060918
589361LV00013B/160/P